The
Sewing Circle

Other Books by the Author

NONFICTION

Stanwyck: The Life and Times of Barbara Stanwyck
Chanel: A Woman of Her Own
Sonia Delaunay: The Painter of the Lost Generation
Silk Roads: The Asian Adventures of Clara and André Malraux
Gloria and Joe: The Star-Crossed Love Affair of Gloria Swanson and Joe Kennedy
Cousteau: A Biography
60 Minutes
Open Road
Private Power
Living for Design: The Yves Saint Laurent Story
John Huston: A Biography
Hearts and Minds: The Common Journey of Jean-Paul Sartre and Simone de Beauvoir
Malraux: A Biography
New Hollywood: American Movies in the 1970s
William Wyler
Billy Wilder

FICTION

Unisave
Borderlines

The
Sewing Circle

Sappho's Leading Ladies

Axel Madsen

KENSINGTON BOOKS
http://www.kensingtonbooks.com

To Dana Henninger

KENSINGTON BOOKS are published by

Kensington Publishing Corp.
850 Third Avenue
New York, NY 10022

All Kensington titles, imprints and distributed lines are available at special quantity discounts for bulk purchases for sales promotion, premiums, fund raising, educational or institutional use.

Special book excerpts or customized printings can also be created to fit specific needs. For details, write or phone the office of the Kensington Special Sales Manager: Kensington Publishing Corp., 850 Third Avenue, New York, NY, 10022. Attn. Special Sales Department. Phone: 1-800-221-2647.

Kensington and the K logo Reg. U.S. Pat. & TM Off.

ISBN 0-7582-0101-X

First Kensington Trade Paperback Printing: February, 2002
10 9 8 7 6 5 4 3 2 1

Printed in the United States of America

Membership in the closed society of the motion picture industry is almost never revoked for moral failings.
—John Gregory Dunne, *Playland*

Contents

Contents

1

Mystery and Allure

This is a book about appearances, about denied attachments and emotions, and the mocking of mystery and allure. It is the documented story and affectionate close-up of exalted lives and furtive appetites. When Greta Garbo and Marlene Dietrich had enough of men, artifice, and glamour, they sought solace, strength, and understanding in clandestine feminine friendships. On-screen, they were incarnations of turbid fantasies. Offscreen, they depended on women who loved women, like the poet-playwright Mercedes de Acosta, whose bed they shared in succession. Catholicism and Judaism—the predominant faiths of showbiz people—are explicitly antagonistic toward same-sex love. The mores of the golden era enforced a two-way secrecy. Not only did lesbians live hidden lives, but the public at large averted its eyes. *Nobody* wanted to know.

Garbo, Dietrich, Katharine Hepburn, and Barbara Stanwyck cultivated the movies' rich territory of sexual ambiguity as insolent, direct, kiss-me-deadly females. On occasion they convinced their studios to let them play men—Marlene's dream was to play a man pretending to be a woman—and enjoyed the thrill of exposing themselves while hiding inside a character.

The gender codes of the day taught Tallulah Bankhead, Alla

Nazimova, and Garbo to think of themselves as having "dual natures," one male and one female. They were torn by these seemingly opposite sides and subcribed to the then-current theory that lesbians were men trapped in women's bodies. Garbo believed the part of her which both wanted to succeed and to love women was her male side. The sewing circle was both euphemism, readily denied, and furtive sisterhood of women in love with women. Friendship, the mysterious dynamic that unites people, was, with loyalty and trust, a greater attraction than physical passion.

Sexuality is often just another role, as arbitrary as any part a screen star is asked to play. Fear of discovery—and vanity—meant knowing how to espouse bisexuality long enough to see oneself through an offscreen bed scene. The question of whether Joan Crawford and Myrna Loy—"Gillette blades" for cutting both ways—loved women and tolerated men is less a matter of evidence than of attitude and affinity. Lesbians lie to men, said Judith Anderson, because they don't want to be rejected, even if there is no sexual attraction. A majority of Hollywood's lesbians enjoyed men as long as they didn't come too close.

Marriage was common. The most famous modern homosexual, Oscar Wilde, was married with children, and Hollywood lesbians sought protection and acceptance in "lavender" marriages to actors who were often homosexual, and with whom they could form secret alliances against hostile surroundings.

Paramount's premier costume designer Edith Head married Fox art director Wiard "Bill" Ihnen. Both were always busy, stayed out of each other's life, and lived past eighty. Crawford and Stanwyck's cracked marriages to alcoholics gave these two former chorus girls a sense of stability, while the safe and sexless marriage of Linda and Cole Porter gave his career dazzle. Laurence Olivier's marriage to Jill Esmond remained unconsummated for years as she struggled to accept her lesbianism. While living with faithful companions, Hepburn, who early on scored in near-androgynous parts, maintained the perfect front with alcoholic Spencer Tracy, who, as a Catholic, never divorced his wife. The successive marriages of Janet Gaynor, Lili Damita, and Agnes Moorehead were daisy chains of deceit. Other "tandem couples" included Charles Laughton and

Elsa Lanchester, Vincente Minnelli and Judy Garland. When they had to, lavender couples produced children.

For many, liberation had come after marriage. Since leaving their husbands, these women lived a life of travel, cultural pursuits, and leisure for the development of friendship and same-sex attachments. Some never divorced. Dietrich's unorthodox marriage to Rudolph Sieber, who lived thirty-seven years with another woman, had its roots in a 1920s Berlin accustomed to sexual ambivalence. Lili Damita, who found Marlene in a tuxedo irresistible, and Errol Flynn, Stanwyck and Robert Taylor, Berthold and Salka Viertel, were married couples with sexual independence. Unlike many working- and middle-class lesbians, none of these women sought long-term relationships with female lovers. Singles like Garbo, Katharine Hepburn, and Dorothy Arzner, Hollywood's only woman director of the 1930s and early 1940s, lived in a deeper twilight.

The focus here is Hollywood's pinnacle decades, the thirty years stretching from the dawn of the talkies in the late 1920s to the collapse of the studio system and the anticommunist witch-hunt, which was so harrowing to nonconformists. In the company of Hollywood's "odd girls and twilight lovers," the book will bed-hop to Broadway's Maude Adams, Eva Le Gallienne, and Katharine Cornell, to Natalie Barney's sapphic oasis in Paris, and to London's sewing circles, from Vita Sackville-West's aristocratic set to Lynn Fontanne's high-keyed West End *monde.*

Society condemned the love that dares not speak its name with such vehemence that Hollywood's lesbians could count on no wink of complicity from the majority of their sex. Women made up the majority in vigilante organizations such as the nonsectarian National League of Decency and, as such, were largely responsible for the 1932 tightening of Hollywood's self-censoring Production Code, which, among other strictures, forbade the depiction of homosexuality in any form.

Emma Goldman and Edith Ellis might have stormed the country for suffrage, women's rights, and, under their breaths, sapphic love, but living openly as a lesbian was fraught with danger, guilt, and anxiety. Most American women barely knew what a lesbian was, and if it was explained to them, they were quick to label such women "twisted" or, in the new Freudian vocabulary, "inverts" or "degenerates" (Russian-born "Red Emma," who was considered a monster in polite society and an advocate of "free love and bombs," was deported in 1919 as an anarchist). In many communities, female lovers caught in flagrante were institutionalized in insane asylums.

Garbo, Dietrich, Crawford, Stanwyck, Bankhead, Garland—the roll call of golden-age stars who were lesbian or bisexual may seem especially lengthy compared to what we know of contemporary movie celebrities. Since modern sex researchers agree that homosexuality is probably a constant in human evolution, and that there is neither an increase nor a decrease, proportionally speaking, the answer to why so many stars then were closeted lesbians must be found in the social context. The cinema had barely learned to talk in 1930, and everybody in the movies was young—Garbo was twenty-five, MGM's wunderkind producer Irving Thalberg thirty-one, and founding father D. W. Griffith was fifty-five. The arts and entertainment had always attracted gays, but the movies were a brand-new field. The screen catapulted a few women to unheard-of radiance and sway and gave them influence and opportunities that, with the exception of a few monarchs, no woman had ever had. Because they were the first superstars, Garbo, Dietrich, Crawford et al. seem all the more striking, and they remain, with the exception of Elizabeth Taylor, better known than the 1950s headliners. As for today's stars, who knows what we will find out about them in fifty years?

"No one loves a fairie when she's forty," said British *Vogue* in reviewing Hugo Vickers's *Loving Garbo* in 1994. Thirty-five years earlier, when such bluntness in print was not permissible, Edmund Goulding hinted that it was not Garbo's vanity that shortened her career, but her fear of being discovered a lesbian. Goulding, who directed her in *Love* and *Grand Hotel,* said that if she and the press had made up, she'd still be making pictures. "The thing she balks at," he told Ezra Goodman, Hollywood's bitter historian in 1959, "is people going into her bedroom."

In 1930s fiction and medical literature, lesbians are portrayed as neurotic, tragic, and absurd, inevitably driven toward debility or suicide. Ona Munson, the actress, and Irene Lentz, MGM's 1940s chief fashion designer, were sewing circle members who took their own lives. In contrast to today's politically charged, in-your-face sapphic literature, the writings of even a forthright lesbian such as Mercedes de Acosta are ambivalent and allusive. In Antoni Grono-wicz's controversial Garbo memoir, Garbo says de Acosta excited her physically more than spiritually. In her own memoirs, however, de Acosta's most explicit image of their relationship is a thunder-storm swelling across a beach where they lay. Modern biographers and memorialists are less reticent. In *Loving Garbo*, de Acosta is an intelligent eccentric besotted by a dull, self-centered Garbo, while in Maria Riva's *Marlene Dietrich by Her Daughter*, de Acosta appears as a tiresome figure of ridicule.

The need to feel in control at all times made it almost impossible to share fervent and touching emotions. Stars, moreover, lived in glass houses and were asked to move in the broadest circles, mean-ing few of them were ever seen in the few bars and stores catering to female "inverts." Staying in the closet was altogether satisfying, sometimes even intensely romantic.

2

The Odd Couple:
Mercedes and Thalberg

Irving Thalberg, Metro-Goldwyn-Mayer's production chief, was in no mood for jokes. The world wasn't exactly waiting for Greta Garbo to play a man, now was it?

The writer across from him, Mercedes de Acosta, smiled. To act is to assume identities. Since antiquity actors had slipped into women's clothes and painted their faces. They were still doing it in Asian theater. Admittedly, the tradition of women in men's roles was shorter, but it dated back to Cherubin in *The Marriage of Figaro*. On Broadway, a succession of actresses, from Maude Adams and Eva Le Gallienne to Marilyn Miller, had played Peter Pan. On film, Hamlet had been incarnated by Asta Nielsen.

Thalberg cut her short. *Desperate* was not supposed to be Garbo in drag, but Garbo getting out of harrowing scrapes. "We have been building Garbo up for years as a glamorous actress, and now you come along and try to put her into pants and make a monkey out of her," he snapped. "Do you want to put all America and all the women's clubs against her? You must be out of your mind."

De Acosta reeled under his unaccustomed outburst, but recovered to say Garbo knew perfectly well that to escape police and assorted villains, the plot had her disguised as a man.

"She must be out of her mind, too," Thalberg came back. "I simply won't have that sequence in. I am in this business to make money on films, and I won't have this one ruined."

"Remember Sarah Bernhardt's triumph as the duke of Reichstadt?" Mercedes asked.

Thalberg was flattered when people thought him an intellectual, and he liked to affect the airs of a Renaissance prince. She told him Paul Poiret, whose clothes were a permanent part of her own wardrobe, had designed Sarah Bernhardt's close-fitting trousers and arrogant white coat for the title role in Edmond Rostand's *L'Aiglon.* Pretending she was refreshing her own memory, Mercedes told how, on the downfall of Napoleon, three-year-old François-Charles-Joseph Bonaparte—l'Aiglon, or Eaglet, as passionate Bonapartists called him—had been recognized as emperor of France, how he had spent his short, feeble life in Schönbrunn Castle in Vienna, a pawn of his grandfather, Emperor Franz II of Austria, and his crafty chancellor Metternich. The author of *Cyrano de Bergerac* had made a strange and compelling hero of Napoleon's luckless son, who was obsessed by pathetic dreams of rebuilding the Bonaparte empire, but was unable to escape Metternich's political ruses. Eva Le Gallienne, Mercedes's longtime lover in the 1920s, had played l'Aiglon on Broadway.

"Greta will look great in uniform," Mercedes said, smiling.

The diminutive (five-foot-one) Thalberg insisted that the sequence come out. He rarely deviated from his glacial calm. He didn't have to. Power was unstated. But he was tiring of Garbo's lovers pitching asinine stories. If he had hired de Acosta, it was because her story outline promised Garbo as a "wild character," someone like Iris March in *The Green Hat.* The much-banned Michael Arlen novel was something of a fixation with him. The Production Office—the industry's self-censoring board—considered the book immoral, and Thalberg had produced a sanitized version called *A Woman of Affairs,* with Garbo as Iris March, twenty-year-old Douglas Fairbanks Jr. as the debauched brother whose death triggers the plot, and John Gilbert as the husband who, because he has syphilis, kills himself the night he marries Iris. Garbo had loved the novel, and although censorship had insisted that syphilis become embezzlement, the film was one of her most successful silents, famous for the ending in which she crashes her car into a tree rather than destroy her lover with the excesses of their passion. Thalberg wanted to remake it as a talkie with his wife, Norma Shearer, as Iris March.

De Acosta mentioned that Garbo also wanted to play the title role in *The Picture of Dorian Gray*. She quoted Dorian's lines when he first sees his portrait: "I shall grow old, and horrible, and dreadful. But this picture will remain always young. If it were only the other way. If it were I who was to be always young, and the picture that was to grow old. For that—for that—I would give everything." She added that she was herself a friend of Oscar Wilde's reckless niece.

No, Thalberg admitted, he didn't know "Dolly" Wilde, who also lived in Santa Monica.

The legend of Thalberg as the boy genius and intuitive force behind Metro-Goldwyn-Mayer's best films seems as permanently fixed in Tinseltown history as the image of Louis B. Mayer as Thalberg's and MGM's ruthless overlord. While Mayer's administration and showmanship kept the studio flourishing, Irving the wunderkind possessed, along with a sometimes canny understanding of what the public wanted, a knack for developing stars and doctoring scripts. He brought the preview to a ruthless and ritualistic perfection. All films were dry-run, returned for reediting or even reshooting, and previewed again until audiences in outlying Los Angeles areas laughed or cried on cue. He lived and worked with uncommon intensity and hired people he thought were the best and the brightest because he believed you could buy talent and that top talent cost top money. Unlike other studio bosses, he listened to arguments, although that didn't matter in the end because he always prevailed.

Shifting in his seat on this January 1932 afternoon, he knew he had to be careful. "Garbomania" was at its height. Garbo's image of European otherness, her awareness of the pleasures and vices of love, her brooding eyes, her slim, languid body and broad shoulders, appealed to both male and female audiences. Her husky, accented voice whispered the pains of passion, and in spite of herself, she snared men. Thalberg believed she was a fascinating but limited actress. "She must never create situations," he told the director George Cukor. "She must be thrust into them; the drama comes in how she rides them out."

The Garbo woman the studio developed—and the world's audiences swooned over—was a woman alone, an emotionally wounded woman with a past, who summons up the strength to march on. Garbo goes mad, drowns in frozen water, throws herself under a speeding train (in the original version of *Love*). In her movies, she said no; her leading men said yes, and in the fade-out the story had her change her mind.

In contrast to almost everybody else in Hollywood, Thalberg knew Garbo was a lesbian. He knew that women friends like Mercedes and Salka Viertel had enormous influence over his star. If Garbo didn't think a script was right, she would say, "I think I will go home," which meant that either she would ask her chauffeur to drive her to her big, rented house in the new Brentwood section of Los Angeles or, if her contract was up, that she would go to Sweden for an indefinite period.

He listened to Mercedes repeat what he already knew, that Garbo wanted stories that were different. Stars whined and begged for different roles while all their audiences wanted was for them to repeat themselves. People wanted Maurice Chevalier and Jeanette MacDonald to sing, the Marx Brothers to be funny, Johnny Weissmuller to swing from trees, and Garbo to play an emotionally wounded woman whose past will not let her be at peace, a woman who, despite great hurts, marches on until fate makes her meet her man.

Movie celebrity was based on the ability to convincingly enact love games with the opposite sex. Tens of millions of moviegoers wanted to see Garbo play the disillusioned woman hopelessly and giddily in love or the tarnished lady giving up her man or dying in the last reel. Thalberg was still angry at the way she had disdained the press on the eve of the *Mata Hari* premiere. He had let her go to New York for Christmas, and all he had got back were reports of her "high-hattin' act with New York reporters," as the *Motion Picture Herald* put it. The Depression was deepening—the same trade paper told of how even Broadway houses were going nonstop "grind," at fifteen cents a seat. And here he was planning to road-show *Grand Hotel* at $2 top. Unlike Fox, RKO, and Warner Brothers, MGM had made money in 1931. But the studio was paying Garbo $12,000 a week.[1] Her movies demanded high gloss. As for source material, Thalberg had acquired popular and expensive literary properties by Blasco Ibañez, Herman Südermann, Tolstoy, Michael Arlen, Edward Sheldon, and, for the all-star vehicle that started shooting the next week, Vicki Baum's current bestseller, *Grand Hotel.*

Of course, said Mercedes, there was always Joan of Arc or Teresa de Avila, who loved a female cousin and founded a religious order. And there was Queen Christina. Thalberg didn't mention that he had asked Salka Viertel to look into adapting the life of Sweden's Renaissance queen. He expected a good love story, not a documentary on a queen brought up like a boy.

In Thalberg's judgment, Garbo had become Garbo in *Love.* The first time her hypnotic style of acting and her classic, almost narcissistic beauty overwhelmed the popular imagination was in Frances Marion's adaptation of Tolstoy's *Anna Karenina.* Marion was currently adapting *Dinner at Eight* and was, with Anita Loos and Leonore Coffee, Thalberg's favorite screenwriter. He hired more women writers than any other production chief. Two-thirds of the Garbo films were scripted by women, and two were based on original material by women, Adela Rogers St. Johns's *The Single Standard* and now Baum's *Grand Hotel.* He worked well with female writers, although he seemed not to *like* women.

Thalberg appreciated the company of men and, perhaps because he was born a "blue baby" with a congenital heart defect and was too frail for athletics, enjoyed male distractions. David Lewis, his personal assistant, and his script doctor, George Oppenheimer, were gay. Some thought Thalberg himself was a repressed homosexual and that his 1927 glamour wedding to Shearer was a clever

1. All figures are given in vintage dollars.

The Federal Reserve calculates $1 in 1932 currency to be worth $12.57 in inflated 2001 dollars. Garbo's $12,000 a week is therefore $150,840 in today's money. It should be kept in mind that as late as 1930, federal state, and local expenditures constituted barely 10 percent of GNP, and combined taxes averaged a mere 4 percent on high incomes.

For comparison, Adrian, MGM's premier costume designer, earned $1,000 a week, while the skilled tailors and seamstresses at the studio earned between $15.85 and $21 a week ($199.24 and $263.37 in 2001 dollars).

front. Shearer quickly discovered her husband's limited sexual drive. Joan Crawford believed the marriage was just as calculated on Shearer's part. "She doesn't love him," Crawford told Rogers St. Johns, "she's made a sacrifice for what she can get out of him, knowing he's going to die on her."

Thalberg's *moderne* office on the second floor of Metro-Goldwyn-Mayer's executive building was long and bathed in shadow. His massive, shiny desk was on a platform so visitors had to look up at him. The right end of the desk was occupied by his newest contraption, the telephone-cum-intercom Dictograph, which looked like a small pipe organ and partially concealed a row of medicine bottles. As Mercedes launched into Teresa de Avila as Garbo material, the Dictograph interrupted her. A graveled voice that sounded like that of Louis B. himself called.

"Remember where we are," Thalberg admonished and left.

Being dismissed by Thalberg was routine. His days were a succession of script conferences, editing sessions, and screenings, and his front office usually harbored writers who either chafed with impatience or disintegrated through boredom. It might be days or weeks before Thalberg's office summoned a writer back. In the meantime, there was the pay envelope every Saturday night. Anita Loos claimed that while waiting for script conferences with Thalberg, she had knitted a scarf that, at her $3,500-a-week salary, must have cost the studio $85,000.

De Acosta was no mendicant scenarist hacking away nine to six in the story department. She had her own mind and money and was leading an independent existence. A few blocks from Garbo's rented villa in Brentwood, she shared a house with Thalberg's gay playwright friend John Colton. Like P. G. Wodehouse, she was allowed to do her work at home, perhaps because her black tricorn, buckled shoes, and cape were a tad too eccentric even for the writers' corridor on the fourth floor.

An expanding circle of women were intrigued by de Acosta's practice of oriental philosophy and alternative medicine, by her odd ideas about the arts, finding her cosmopolitan flair an antidote to Hollywood provincialism. She gave discreet parties attended by women in the know, even though her various rented homes never became the sisterhood's equivalent of the West

Hollywood residence of George Cukor, where the elite of gay men, boys on the make, and the occasional lesbian celebrity gathered. "George was their access to the crème of Hollywood," said fellow director Joseph L. Mankiewicz. "George was really queen of the roost." It was at Cukor's that Edna Ferber and Noël Coward both showed up wearing double-breasted suits, and to Coward's remark, "You almost look like a man," Ferber parried, "So do you."

Mercedes had deleted all colors until her wardrobe—and later her furnishings—came in black and white only. Dietrich's daughter, Maria, would describe Mercedes as looking like a "Spanish Dracula with the body of a young boy, jet-black hair cut like a toreador's close to the head, chalk-white face, deep-set black eyes permanently shadowed." Tallulah Bankhead, who did not like Mercedes but admired her dinner jackets, said she looked like a "mouse in a topcoat." Mercedes claimed she dressed whimsically to attract women—in one period she rouged her earlobes. She believed same-sex love was a life force no different from other forms of sexuality and liked to ask, "Who of us is only one sex?"

As a teenager, she had been fascinated by famous and complicated women. To please her mother, she had married, at twenty-seven. Although she refused to give up her maiden name, she made a point of dining with her painter husband, Abram Poole, whenever she passed through New York. Two of her plays, *Sandro Botticelli* and *Jehanne d'Arc,* starring Eva Le Gallienne, had been staged to indifferent reviews in New York and Paris, while *Prejudice* had been performed in London with a very young John Gielgud in the lead. During her long friendship with Isadora Duncan, she had edited and arranged for the publication of the dancer's memoirs, *My Life.*

A year before Isadora was strangled with her famous scarf, she wrote a poem to Mercedes, which, in part, read:

> Two sprouting breasts
> Round and sweet
> invite my hungry mouth to eat
> From whence two nipples firm and pink
> persuade my thirsty soul to drink
> And lower still a secret place
> Where I'd fain hide my loving face

My kisses like a swarm of bees
Would find their way
Between thy thighs
And suck the honey of thy lips
Embracing thy two slender hips.

3

Tangled Lives: Women Who Loved Women

The movies are graven images of mystery and allure. One of the pleasures of moviegoing is watching incandescent people, more interesting and riveting, more raffish, witty, and beautiful than the rest of us, defy the special gravity of the screen. Of all the stars who have fired the imagination of movie audiences, none quite equaled the elusive and unattainable Greta Garbo. She was, wrote the *New York Times* when she died in 1990, "the standard against whom others were judged."

It is one of the movies' greater ironies that Garbo's need to conceal her lesbianism added to her allure and mysticism. Her fear of discovery made her snub the press. The more she became successful in protecting her private life, the more she drove journalists to a frenzy. The more she spurned reporters, the more they pursued her. And the more the press criticized her aloofness in print, the more her fans cheered her indifference. *Photoplay,* the premier fan magazine, had to apologize for calling her "remote, retiring, unsocial, and unfashionable in dress" and, in its January 1930 issue, to admit that she could do no wrong: "Where others scrabble and squall for notice, submitting to photographers and the pawing of the herd, Garbo crawls into a hole and pulls the hole in after her.

Whether it is a trick or whether it is the nature of the lady, it is absolute perfection."

Not that she—and MGM—hadn't tried to accommodate the press. After the fan magazine *Screen Book* suggested her reclusiveness was a studio gimmick, Metro tried out different tactics. "There was nothing Garbo could do about the publicity we forced on her at first," Joseph Cohn, Metro's general manager, would remember. "We tried a lot of different poses, none of them too smart. She didn't complain, but she wasn't enthusiastic." She rarely denied anything said about her, a habit that added to her allure, and to people's impression that she had it all figured out in advance. Later in life, she came to believe *she* was the skillful manipulator, the clever seller of her own talent and legend.

Clarence Brown, who directed two of her silent films and five of her talkies, wasn't sure she even knew she possessed an ability to project thinking in action. "If she had to look at one person with jealousy, and another with love, she didn't have to change her expression," he would recall. "You could see it in her eyes as she looked from one to the other. And nobody else has been able to do that on the screen. Garbo did it without the command of English."

With five thousand people under contract, Metro-Goldwyn-Mayer was the grandest of the Hollywood studios. Paramount might have Marlene Dietrich and Mae West, and the financially troubled Warner Bros. Ruth Chatterton, William Powell, and Kay Francis, but MGM possessed Joan Crawford, Clark Gable, Wallace Beery, Jean Harlow, and, fairest of all, Greta Garbo. It was Irving Thalberg, not Louis B. Mayer, who grasped what it was that moviegoers responded to, that what constituted star power was self-identification. Audiences were not primarily attracted to the opposite sex on the screen, but projected themselves on the light-and-shadow figures of their own sex.

Male spectators imagined themselves swashbuckling like Douglas Fairbanks or imitating Clark Gable slapping around upper-class dames. Women identified with Garbo, for whom love was so often the vehicle of ruin, Harlow's vitality and humor, or Crawford's Depression-wise dames challenging men and reaching for the brass ring. Garbo's appeal to women was reflected in the Hollywood in-joke about the bridegroom getting into bed and vowing to his bride that, with one exception, he would always be faithful. If he ever had a chance to make love to Greta Garbo, he would no doubt succumb. To which the bride answered, "Me, too."

Thalberg understood that to make it big, a film must have larger-than-life players acting out a story of conflict and suspense that audiences can identify with. He had built the career of the Canadian newcomer Norma Shearer, married her, and built her some more (British *Vogue* dubbed her "the reachable Garbo"). With the efficiency of a prime-rib stock breeder, he kept his hand in the teaching, grooming, and molding of new faces on the contract list.

The studios invented the so-called standard seven-year contract, which, with options, gave the bosses all the advantages. It allowed the studio both to terminate the relationship every six months and, if a newcomer was promising, to lock him or her in for seven years. MGM usually renewed every six months, usually with an increase in salary. "Talent"—actors, directors, and any other people considered valuable enough to be under contract—benefited from the security of continual employment. The advantage for the studios was that it allowed management to favor those who behaved. Stanwyck, Cary Grant, and Charles Boyer were among the few who only signed one- or two-picture deals. Such freelancing was much admired by contractees like Bette Davis and Joan Crawford, but it was a gamble insofar as no studio had a vested, long-term interest in building up a Stanwyck, Grant, or Boyer.

The golden age was a time when actresses' menstrual periods were tracked on a posted chart, when Clark Gable's false teeth and Gary Cooper's impaired hearing were closely guarded secrets, and the studios knew whose hair was truly straw-colored. To prove herself an authentic blonde, Carole Lombard—like Jean Harlow—reportedly bleached her pubic hair. The best-kept secret, the secret Garbo took with her to the grave, was her sexuality.

Friendships and romantic relationships overlapped, and because women can openly be friends, friendships often seemed freer than love relationships. Lesbians were, in the public image, loathsome creatures. They were seen as hard, sophisticated females who seduced innocent girls or women into mysterious "perversions," or as sad caricatures of men, trying to dress and act as males, and generally aping some of men's worst characteristics. Hollywood made "butchy" women into repellent monsters, vampires, or other sub-human creatures, and the theater portrayed practitioners of the love that dares not speak its name as neurotic, tragic, or absurd. No woman in her right mind would want to be seen so negatively. No actress admitting to loving women would be a success. Because the heroine in Edouard Bourdet's *The Captive* is obsessed by another woman and refuses to be happy in her marriage, a New York City district attorney closed the play in 1926 and hauled producer, director, and cast of twelve to court on obscenity charges. The play, which was as tactful as it was audacious, met a similar fate in San Francisco, Los Angeles, and Detroit.[1]

Hollywood's lesbian and bisexual stars lived too much in a fish-bowl—and had egos too big—to be part of any for-women-only association that, to the noninitiated, was called a sewing club or sewing circle. There is some dispute as to the origin of the euphemism. Alla Nazimova, who was famous for the séances and orgies she organized, and for her *Salome* film, which, in an "homage" to Oscar Wilde, featured an all-gay cast, apparently used the term in the mid-1920s to describe a sapphic set that included Wilde's niece Dorothy, several actresses, and writers. A decade later, the sewing circle alluded to Dietrich's passel of "good-time Charlenes," and the expression came to refer to a loose network of lesbians in the performing arts. Only those who mattered "knew."

Members of the international sisterhood, who sometimes called themselves "two-spirited people," were mostly rich, well-connected, and free. While rarely letting down their guard, they entertained each other in private, often with theme parties that allowed the too familiar to be "unknown." References to lesbians were double entendres and clever witticisms supposedly above the ken of Mr. and Mrs. Joe Smith. *Vanity Fair* pictured Garbo and Dietrich in 1932 under the headline: "Both Members of the Same Club." Others referred to Dietrich and Garbo as "gentlemen at heart." Beatrice Lillie said she knew Gertrude Lawrence better than Gertrude's husband, Richard Aldrich. Of the Lawrence-Aldrich marriage in

1. *La Prisonnière* by Edouard Bourdet (1887–1935) popularized the giving of violets as the sign of knowing in sapphic circles. Between women lovers, the gift of violets was the rage for a decade, appearing in feminist literature and as an international symbol of affection. The edible flower, prized by gourmets, has a long Gallic association with sexual pleasure.

1940, sewing-circle member Constance Collier said, "Poor Richard. He thinks he has married Miss Gertrude Lawrence. He'll soon find out it's *Myth* Lawrence."

Making a circle of lesbian friends was fraught with guilt and anxiety. Those who knew would deny it even decades later or, if pressed, resort to generalizations about the inscrutability and ambivalence of human emotions. Agnes Moorehead, who thought the word *sapphic* was an improvement over *female homosexuality*, believed women could have lesbian feelings without being homosexual, that love doesn't have a sex.

The country might have been in the depth of the Depression in 1932—and Paramount filed for bankruptcy—but going to the movies remained the cheapest and, for many, the only entertainment. All-night movie houses at ten cents a seat were crowded with homeless snorers. Breadlines were getting longer than box-office queues, however, as many couldn't even afford dimes for entertainment or comfort, and cinema attendance slipped from the 1930 high of nearly 100 million a week. Traditional values resurfaced in the face of the grinding, brother-can-you-spare-a-dime poverty. The rich stopped flaunting their style, and the Cedric Gibbons movie sets scaled back on deluxe decors in favor of genteel, tasteful make-believe. The public no longer tolerated unconventional living and showy display. Eccentricities that adoring moviegoers had found endearing were increasingly seen as obnoxious—the press chided Crawford in 1934 for wondering what $100,000 per film was getting her.

Americans idolized the images of actors and never stopped asking: What are the stars really like? The studios exploited the public curiosity while making little effort to answer the question. Howard Strickling at MGM, Perry Lieber at Paramount, Harry Brand at Fox, Lynn Farnol at Goldwyn Studios, independent publicist Russell Birdwell, and the town's other ballyhoo masters portrayed the lives of their players in such free translation that the stars' private personalities were not only mostly unknown but beside the point. Concentrating on the stars—especially the women stars—to the detriment of the films themselves worked so well that instead of requesting new films by titles, theater owners asked for "two Gables" or "three Shearers." *Photoplay, Silver Screen, Modern Screen,*

Screenland, and the other fan magazines aided and abetted by enlarging stars to epic dimensions and often out of thin air, creating the Hollywood style and character.

The famous Garbo line, "I vant to be alone," was not hers, but an invention of MGM publicist Pete Smith. After Fay Wray found Tyrone Power too fond of the boys, Brand covered Ty's exuberant homosexuality with well-publicized dates with Fox contract players Loretta Young, Janet Gaynor, and Sonja Henie. When Power became world famous and under greater scrutiny, Brand publicized the star's "secret" romance with newcomer Annabella, a French actress of androgynous manners who had starred in René Clair's *Le Million.*

Strickling forbade male contractees from appearing in fashion layouts or from accepting "best dressed" awards for fear they would look effeminate. The appearance of a "blind item" intimating that William Haines, MGM's popular matinee idol, was perhaps a pansy provoked Strickling's office to flood newsrooms with the "news" that Haines had fallen in love with Pola Negri, and to follow up with photos of a king-size bed that Pola and Bill had selected for their life together as a married couple. Birdwell, who would whip the search for an actress to play Scarlett O'Hara in *Gone With the Wind* to a national frenzy in 1937, deflected rumors of the bisexual Duke of Windsor's sordid liaison with Woolworth heir James Donahue by turning it around and suggesting the Duchess was trying to convert the notorious Donahue to heterosexuality by having an affair with him. "I don't want press agentry," said David O. Selznick when he hired Birdwell. "I want imagination."

The film factories, said Selznick's father-in-law, Louis B. Mayer, were the only companies where the assets walked out the gate every night. "You put them under contract, pay them money they never in their wildest fantasies could dream of," said Brand. "You nurture them, build them, only to see 'em put everything at risk, getting drunk, screwing around." Anita Loos, who began knocking out scripts for D. W. Griffith in 1912 and became famous with *Gentlemen Prefer Blondes,* would remember the impact of actors' lives on America's standards of morality, how "casual couplings were commonplace," and how studio publicists hushed up things with "shotgun weddings, with guns wielded by studio bosses posing as papas."

Strickling took over the MGM publicity department from Frank Whitback, a former barker for Barnum and Bailey who ran Metro like a circus and was the only man, in studio photographer Laszlo Willinger's memory, who had four elephants as pets. The shirt-sleeve, circus approach went out of style when the point of press agentry was not only to blow the horn, but also to conceal, to protect both moviegoers and the stars from each other and themselves. By the high 1930s, when Strickling had a staff of one hundred publicists, the studio publicity machines had neutralized the press.

Access to stars, "exclusives," photos, handouts, lunches, all flowed with the smooth start-to-finish coverage of movies coming down the assembly lines. Less obviously, the stars came to rely on Strickling, Brand, and company, and in most cases to heed their advice. Hollywood was a company town and it was not in an actor's interest to rebel. "We told stars what they could say, and they did what we said because they knew we knew best," Strickling said in a candid moment. The Depression caused the publicity mills to modify their aim. As stage-managed by Strickling, Brand, Farnol et al., the stars downplayed their glamour a bit and told columnists and fan magazines how they wished *they* had the leisure and anonymity of secretaries to go shopping on their lunch hour.

Mayer made sure MGM films toed the Hays Office censorship line while in private he was an adulterer who maintained a brothel for visiting dignitaries where the whores were film-star look-alikes. He was implicated in stock swindles and later charged with conspiracy to violate usury laws, and, with the complicity of Strickling, he stepped in when a drunken Clark Gable killed a pedestrian, lining up a patsy from within the studio to testify that he was at the wheel at the time. Strickling not only orchestrated cover-up romances and publicized staged elopements, but also arranged abortions in Tijuana (an actress's temporary indisposition was tactfully reported, if at all, to be the result of an appendectomy). To keep the teenage Judy Garland reasonably content, Strickling assigned Betty Asher, a slim, rather unattractive publicist who not only introduced

Garland to the pleasures of same-sex love but to the drink and pills that would eventually ruin her life.

If arranging a marriage to cover up for a gay star was what it took, Mayer was accommodating. Noël Coward would describe Nelson Eddy's January 1939 lavender marriage as made in heaven and credited to Louis B. Mayer. Since *Rose Marie* had made Eddy and Jeanette MacDonald a sensational singing duo in 1936, MacDonald had married (in 1937), and Louis B. ordered Eddy to do likewise. "Eddy agreed," Coward would recall, "but he didn't want a virgin bride or some insatiable creature, and Mayer understood. Sometimes the least sexual marriages last the longest. Mayer found him an older divorcée [Ann Denmitz Franklin] who'd been married to a movie director [Sidney Franklin]—she was wise to the ways of Tinseltown, she was not sexually demanding or needful, and she was well pleased to live the comfortable life of a movie star's wife. She was satisfied. Eddy was satisfied, the studio was satisfied, the public was satisfied. At least I *assume* Eddy was satisfied. For his sake, I hope he had a very low sex drive. Or perhaps he was very, very discreet if he did step out."

If Dolores Del Rio and Cedric Gibbons, MGM's pioneering art director, were a perfectly calculated "twilight tandem," there was much innocence in Elsa Lanchester's "double-gaited" marriage to Charles Laughton. Late in life, Lanchester would write of her husband's homosexuality but not of her own and, in her autobiography, leave a touching picture of their early relationship. "There was no elements of frankness or honesty at all in our conversations," she would recall in *Herself.* "Nor was there any element of calculation or thoughts of the future for two people who were twenty-five and twenty-eight years old, who had both had previous associations. Our lack of curiosity about each other was, I would think, a sort of subconscious cleaning process, a making of space between the past and the present. Later, the past boomeranged back."[2]

* * *

2. During the filming of *The Barretts of Wimpole Street,* Laughton told Thalberg he was a homosexual. Perhaps because Thalberg's wife, Norma Shearer, was Laughton's costar, nothing came of it, although the standard "moral turpitude" clause in the actor's contract could have been evoked and his Hollywood career ended.

To act is to become someone else, someone more intense, more riveting, and more eloquent than the reflection in the bathroom mirror. Sewing circle member Janet Gaynor believed every woman puts on "acts," and that just as most men are born with an aversion to acting, women are born with an instinct for it. In coded language, she told an interviewer that, for women like her, "it has become more or less a habit with us to disguise our real feelings about things." Harry Hay, the founder of the modern gay movement in Los Angeles, said, "We're always in costume, turning on attitudes." Actors will proudly assert that they invest their understanding of both masculine and feminine emotions in their roles. Mercedes de Acosta spoke eloquently of her friend John Barrymore's androgyny as the source of both "his great gifts and his equally great destructiveness."

Classical Hollywood was a company town, and the actors' fear of rejection was easily manipulated by the bosses, whose approval the actors not only craved but without whom there was no acting. For Cedric Gibbons and Dolores Del Rio, Barbara Stanwyck and Robert Taylor, marriage not only provided deep cover, but gave them poise and rank in the community. If the celebrity was a gay woman, there were enough men, as comedienne Patsy Kelly would say, ready to tie the knot in order to get on the gravy train.

Stars were always talked about, even though fame erected barriers that kept lesser mortals at bay. The studios had the power to silence cops and newsmen, but they had no way to still the rumors that leaked through the service trade. Lurid details had a way of spreading through the hired help and the nether-world of prostitutes and racketeers to people who paid for this kind of information—private detectives, showbiz attorneys, Hedda Hopper, and her fellow columnist Louella Parsons. Stars cringed before the peephole columnists while wooing them with corruptive flattery and often self-defeating cooperation. The ears of Hopper, Parsons, Cal Young, and a host of lesser gossips were always perked, and to be sure they were always au courant, they employed networks of informants while affecting a stewardship of public morality. Nothing was more provocative of course than the misdemeanors of the privileged. Then as now, to see them spanked in public was both edifying and entertaining.

* * *

Garbo's husky voice and accented English only added to her stature. Style and reticence make for larger-than-life fantasy, and her aura of unattainability bewitched her public and made her life a source of intense curiosity. She had a fanatical following in the United States, and her international renown was unequaled. The public imagined that her haunting beauty was a reflection of inner perfection. Her presumed love affairs were the subject of endless speculation, not all orchestrated by Strickling or breathlessly rewritten by fan magazines and columnists. There were reports of an abortive elopement with her costar John Gilbert, and reports of a wedding ceremony at which she failed to appear.

Sapphics had little trouble figuring her out. The word *lesbian* was abhorred, and women in love with women preferred a more fluid terminology or no labels at all. They thought of relationships in the singular and couched an attraction as a nonsexist friendship.

"They hate lesbians even more," Louise Brooks would say of Hollywood's loathing of gay men in remembering how Mayer fired Haines after he refused to put distance between himself and his boyfriend by marrying Negri or some other actress. Although Garbo was the least bisexual of the actress stars in love with women, that is, the one who in private referred to herself as a man ("When I was a young man"; "Oh, what a funny man I am"), and never sought refuge in a lavender marriage, she was the one who was never found out.

4

In Love: Garbo and Mercedes

Garbo was twenty-four and living at 1717 San Vicente Boulevard in Santa Monica when she met de Acosta in 1929. Mercedes, who was thirty-six, had only been in Los Angeles three days when Salka Viertel invited her to tea and, on the telephone, said Garbo just *might* stop by. Within walking distance of Garbo, Salka lived on a tiny dead-end street overlooking the Pacific—a gypsy had once told her she would escape heartbreak and misfortune as long as she lived close to water. Mercedes dressed with care for the afternoon. She slipped a heavy bracelet onto her wrist. She had heard Garbo liked modern, chunky bracelets.

Salka was forty and the central attraction of Mittel Europa intellect and vitality. The house she shared with her often absent husband, Berthold, and their three growing sons was the end station for onrushing exiles from the German-speaking arts. As an actress, she had known everybody in Berlin and Vienna, and as darkness descended over Germany, she would see them all—from Max Reinhardt, Arnold Schoenberg, and Thomas Mann to Bertolt Brecht—trek to 165 Maberry Road in search of contacts, reassurance, and *Kaffeekuchen*. The Viertels had come to Hollywood in 1928, Berthold to write movies for German émigré director F. W.

Murnau. Since Salka had helped her husband with scripts in Germany, he suggested she become another researcher-writer for Thalberg. The Viertels met Garbo at a black-tie affair and spent a multilingual evening with her and their French director-actress friends, Jacques Feyder, and his wife, Françoise Rosay. The next day Garbo came to Maberry Road and spent the afternoon with Salka. In her autobiography, Salka would remember that "the observations [Garbo] made about people were very just, sharp and objective."

Garbo was also one of eleven brave souls who attended F. W. Murnau's funeral. The forty-two-year-old Murnau liked very young men. On March 11, 1931, he was in the passenger's seat of his Packard going down on Garcia Stevenson, his fourteen-year-old Filipino "boy" at the wheel, when the big car leaped off the road, killing the director. Garbo commissioned a death mask of Murnau and kept it on her desk during her years in Hollywood.

Garbo showed up wearing a tennis cap pulled down to hide her eyes for her introduction to de Acosta. "To have Garbo in the flesh before me instantly seemed the most natural thing in the world," Mercedes would recall decades later. "As we shook hands and she smiled to me, I felt I had known her all my life; in fact, in any previous incarnations." Garbo owed much of her success to the excitement her intoxicating beauty, jutting nose, and periwinkle eyes provoked in people. She had a way of making the person she was with feel that nothing in life existed outside the present moment. Others might remark on the way she walked with the thrust of her shoulders, but Mercedes thought the real Garbo was more beautiful than the screen idol.

While Garbo never penned her life story, Mercedes wrote, and rewrote, hers. In her published memoirs, she would recall her first impression of Garbo:

> She was dressed in a white jumper and dark blue sailor pants. Her feet were bare and like her hands, slender and sensitive. Her beautifully straight long hair hung over her shoulders and she wore a white tennis visor pulled well down over her face in an effort to hide her extraordinary eyes, which held in them a look of eternity. When she spoke, I was not only charmed by the tone and the quality of her

voice but also by her accent. At this time she spoke English quite in-correctly with a strong Swedish accent, and her mispronouncements were enchanting. That afternoon I heard her say to Salka, "I trot-teled down to see you." Oddly enough, the words that she said were often more expressive than the correct ones.

In due course Garbo—she hated to be called Greta—noticed de Acosta's bracelet. "I bought it for you in Berlin," said Mercedes, slipping it off her wrist and handing it to the star. The gesture sealed an intimate attachment that would last for decades. However different they, and a little later, Marlene Dietrich were, the longevity of these three women's love, rivalries, and on-and-off ardor and devotion can be seen as the overriding arch of sapphic and bisexual love in Hollywood.

Garbo didn't stay long. Two days later, however, Salka telephoned Mercedes to ask her to come for breakfast, saying Garbo had sug-gested she be invited.

It had been a busy year for both Garbo and de Acosta. In the middle of filming *Wild Orchids,* Louis B. had come to the set with a telegram telling Garbo of Moshe (Mauritz) Stiller's death in Stockholm. A man of delicate features, foppish manners, and tor-mented creativity, the homosexual director who had discovered her and brought her to America had not been a success in Hollywood. When, in defeat, he had returned to Stockholm, Garbo had promised to follow him. Mayer and Thalberg, however, had kept her busy, and Stiller died before she made it back to Sweden. Mercedes sensed how guilty Garbo felt.

De Acosta had attended rehearsals of her play *Prejudice* with John Gielgud, Gwen Ffrangcon-Davies, and Ralph Richardson in London and was motoring through France and southern Germany with friends when she had been called to her beloved sister Rita's deathbed in New York. It was thanks to the sewing circle that she was now in Hollywood. A few weeks earlier Bessie Marbury had called her to say RKO was looking for a story for Pola Negri. "It might just as well be you," Bessie had cooed.

This evening, Mercedes told Viertel and Garbo over muffins and coffee, she was invited to dinner at Negri's—a dinner for six.

"More like six hundred," said Garbo. Whether she meant that

Negri always invited too many or that people habitually crashed her dinner parties, Garbo didn't say.

Mercedes went to the dinner, and as Garbo had predicted, the guests were numerous. Negri was Paramount's answer to Garbo. Her mansion featured a Roman bath in the living room, and her dinner parties were pseudo-aristocratic affairs. Mercedes could feel flattered to have been chosen to write a picture for the Polish-born screen vamp, who had come on the coattails of Ernst Lubitsch, the director of her Berlin triumphs. Women copied Negri's chalk-white face, kohl-rimmed eyes, slinky gowns, and ropes of pearls. Like Garbo, she was supposed to have been the mistress of her Svengali, but Tallulah Bankhead, for one, called her "a lying lesbo, a Polish publicity hound." Negri had been married twice, by her own account, once to a Baron Popper and once to a Count Bomski (evil tongues said her real name was Schwartz), and, with Gloria Swanson and Mae Murray, belonged to the film colony's *nouvelle* nobility.[1]

Over dessert, a houseboy called Mercedes to the telephone. Picking up the receiver, she immediately recognized Garbo's husky voice asking her to sneak out and come to her house.

Garbo scattered blossoms for her new friend to walk across the threshold, only showed her the garden, and told her she would have to leave soon. On her second visit, Mercedes found the living room gloomy. Garbo told her she never used the room, that she lived in her bedroom, and took her upstairs.

Beyond a living room and her bedroom, Garbo didn't bother to furnish the various West Los Angeles villas she rented because she moved each time fans discovered her address. Even Mayer and Thalberg didn't always know where she lived. Two of her friends saw deeper meanings in the constant moving. Alice Glazer, whose husband, Benjamin, wrote two Garbo pictures, said the star's constant moving to different, rented homes wasn't just to escape fans and journalists but had its roots in a deep-seated sense of inadequacy. Anita Loos believed Garbo's awe-inspiring beauty made her

---

1. Gloria Swanson married Henri, the indigent but very real Marquis de la Coudraye de la Falaise in 1925, a year before Mae Murray married the equally destitute Prince David Mdivani, whose ancestral "château" turned out to be little more than a heap of ruins in the Russian-Persian borderlands.

feel like a freak and therefore seek solitude. Such beauty, Loos would write, "creates a disadvantage, which is almost impossible to overcome." Others were stunned by her beauty. After Thalberg sent Lenore Coffee to see *The Temptress* so she could help write the next Garbo picture, Coffee came back saying, "She makes them all look like thirty cents."

Garbo told Mercedes that what she liked about the house was the tall cypress trees and bushes that shielded the house not only from the neighbors but also from the street. Mercedes found the bedroom to be more like a man's room, but was somehow sad when Garbo said, "You must go now."

De Acosta celebrated her first screenwriting assignment by giving a party at the house she and Colton rented. She invited Garbo in the hope of impressing her guests, who included her former lovers Alla Nazimova and Katharine Cornell, and lovers' lovers Laurette Taylor, Constance Collier, and newcomer to Hollywood from the London stage Diana Wynyard. When Garbo called to say she had caught a cold and couldn't make it, Mercedes said she treated colds with a mixture of orange and lemon juice—Buddha's gift of sun and energy—and insisted on coming over. Garbo replied that she had already consumed enormous quantities of oranges, that in her dreams she sometimes saw faces of people she knew on oranges. De Acosta abandoned her guests and, within the hour, appeared at Garbo's front door with two bags of oranges and lemons.

In the kitchen, Mercedes squeezed oranges and lemons into a row of glasses where the proportion of orange to lemon juices was progressively less. The last glass was almost pure lemon juice. After three glasses, Garbo begged off, promising she would drink the rest later.

While Mercedes would remember walking the hills overlooking the silvery Pacific Ocean, Antoni Gronowicz, Garbo's less-than-reliable biographer who claimed to have been her lover in 1938, would write a fuller account of the two women's first night alone. In his version, Mercedes impressed Garbo by insisting that what a person needs besides a good diet and sensible exercise is meditation and love. Meditation and vegetarian habits would reconcile humanity and turn lovemaking between people of the same sex into passionate renewals of the soul.

"I'd like to stay with you longer," Mercedes said, "and show you the proper attitude toward life."

Garbo smiled, "You mean I will live forever."

"Not forever, but very long, until your life will have no sense for you and no excitement for others. Then you will pass into immaterial immortality." Garbo thought her new friend's philosophy was both puzzling and somehow convincing. Garbo liked Mercedes's kohl eyes, her throaty voice, and guessed her to be five, six years her senior.

A few hours later they were lovers.

Mercedes stayed the night. "I knew she was almost as excited as I was," Garbo would tell Gronowicz. "She possessed vivacity, charm, and a great knowledge of love. She had excited me in everything she did."

5

"In America, Men Don't Like Fat Women"

Greta was four or five when, pretending to be asleep in her corner bed one afternoon, she witnessed her drunken father refuse to hump his wife. It was a hot summer's day, and the alcoholic Karl Gustafsson was on the conjugal bed, fully dressed, sleeping off his *brännevin*. Whether Anna Louise was feeling amorous or the heat in the two-room apartment was too much, she took her clothes off. Anna was a big woman. She went into the kitchen, came back with a shot of brandy, crossed to the bed, tapped Karl on the shoulder, and handed him the drink. The booze, not the sight of Anna, got him up on an elbow. He asked for another glass. Anna obliged. He gulped down the second schnapps, and Anna went into the kitchen to put down the empty glass. When she returned, Karl had turned his face to the wall and was snoring. She woke him up, hung over him, her big breasts in his face.

Greta thought she was witnessing some sort of parental reconciliation until, in the absence of a response from her father, her mother jumped off the bed, grabbed a chair, and smashed it on his back. Running screaming through the apartment, she yelled, "You're a drunkard and a fraud! You can do it with other women but not with me."

Greta sat up. Blood trickled down her father's left cheek. Without a word, he shuffled to the door and left the apartment. Anna avoided her daughter's gaze and stood seething, staring at the wall. After a while she put her clothes back on, fetched a coal sack, and methodically filled it with the sticks of the smashed chair. She tied the top of the sack in a knot and threw it under the bed for next winter's kindling wood. When Sven and Alva, Greta's older brother and sister, came home and asked where Dad was, their mother said that, as usual, he hadn't arrived yet and was probably out drinking. From her bed, Greta yelled, "You're lying."

Anna pounced on her daughter. In her retelling of the episode, Greta would say Sven and Alva managed to pull their mother off her.

Garbo's Stockholm childhood was Dickensian and Strindbergian, squalid and tormented. Her parents were fresh off the farms, living in working-class misery in a tenement in the city's Södermalm district. The cold-water flat was four flights up a dark stairway. Outhouses in the back served for the whole building. In the winter, families huddled for warmth, and tuberculosis was the dread disease that had plagued Karl in his youth and, for periods, kept Alva bedridden.

No marriage certificate ever turned up, but Karl and Anna were probably married shortly after they met in 1897. Sven and Alva followed, four years apart, and Greta was born September 18, 1905. Her father's profession, when he had one, seemed to have been butcher and seasonal city day laborer. Anna cleaned houses in richer neighborhoods, and Sven and Alva were barely out of childhood before they started working. Alva's tuberculosis kept her coughing in bed a lot of the time, but when she could, she worked as an office girl.

In family quarrels, Greta took her father's side and accused her mother of favoring Sven and Alva. Anna, in turn, insinuated that there was something unnatural in Greta's attachment to her father.

Greta found school boring and gave herself attitudes. She loved to read stories and act out characters, but told her father she had neither talent nor desire for learning. She carried out imaginary conversations with actors whose photographs she cut out of magazines and hung over her bed. On sober days, Karl asked his daughter to read *Gösta Berling's Saga* to him. Father and daughter loved this tale of a fateful year in a village where imagination and whimsy overpower the forces of law and order, and both beauty and chaos results. Greta imagined herself a writer like Selma Lagerlöf, who, paralyzed as a child, wrote about her childhood world and won a Nobel Prize in 1909. There were also times when Karl took Greta to the theater district so she could see the names on the marquees and, with luck, get a glimpse of actors at the stage door. Increasingly, alcoholism and recurring TB kept Karl from getting up in the morning. He was forty-eight when he died one summer morning two months before Greta's fifteenth birthday.

If her father had taught her anything, she would remember, it was to count on no one. Her mother found her a job as a "lather girl" in a local barbershop. Against Anna's wishes, Greta began to go out at night and haunt two local theaters, sometimes slipping backstage. Too shy to talk to actors, she sometimes followed them in the street. At home at night, she hid under the covers with a photo of her favorite actor. Her mother caught her masturbating and forced her to see their pastor, Hjalmar Ahlfeldt. Greta used the interview to ask him to help find a job at Bergström's, Stockholm's largest department store. When the Reverend Mr. Ahlfeldt asked if she didn't want to be an actress anymore, she replied, "First I have to have money enough to get my mother off my back."

It was sometime later that she discovered the pastor was her mother's lover. She found the idea of her mother and the graying Ahlfeldt performing the sex act revolting. Later in life Greta would say she was always afraid of sex and, after the act, never felt fulfilled. "If I were to analyze myself, I would say that the source of all this confusion was the relationship that existed between my parents."

Greta proved herself a perky salesgirl at Bergström's millinery department. She was striking if a tad chubby and modeled five different hats for the store's 1921 spring catalog. She spent her evenings in theaters, grew bolder, and, from her first-row seat, one night shouted, "I love you," to Carl Brisson, an elegant and handsome Dane. In his dressing room after the performance, he made her read Shakespeare, gave her a chaste kiss, and told her she had talent but needed to go to drama school. Erik Petschler, the Mack

Sennett of Sweden, made her a bathing beauty in a romp about a mayor, his wife, and three daughters. Greta was a few months shy of her seventeenth birthday, when, after trying in vain to seduce her on his casting couch, Petschler suggested she apply for a scholarship at the Dramaten, the Royal Dramatic Theater. She was one of six accepted.

Greta felt uneducated and unsophisticated. She dutifully studied and played her assigned scenes from J. M. Barrie, Victorien Sardou, Ibsen, and Shakespeare, and in fellow newcomer Mimi Pollock found a friend. The two girls stayed up late, smoked cigarettes, and discussed everything. In a class photo, Greta and Mimi stand apart from the others, holding hands.

It was neither Miss Gustafsson's grasp of the classics nor her stage deportment that overwhelmed the movie producers and directors who regularly checked out the drama school for fresh talent. "You are tall and have a beautiful face and shoulders," one teacher said. "Those qualities and your smile will charm them." In the spring of 1923, she was introduced to Mauritz Stiller.

Since Stiller was Jewish and Russian-born like Louis B. Mayer, MGM publicists would dream up a touching story of his fleeing St. Petersburg in 1918 to escape czarist military service (and never mind that the Bolsheviks overthrew Nicholas II in 1917 and Lenin had signed a separate peace with Germany). In fact, Stiller was born in Helsinki in (Russian-occupied) Finland and had been making movies in Sweden since 1912. When he was introduced to Greta Gustafsson in the corridor of the Dramaten, he was preparing *Gösta Berling's Saga,* his forty-fourth movie.

Stiller was five when his musician father died of an incurable disease and his Polish mother committed suicide. Brought up by relatives, Moshe was brilliant in school, spoke Swedish, Russian, German, and Polish, fell in love with the stage, and, at eighteen, organized amateur theater. He found Helsinki to be a cultural tundra, left for St. Petersburg, where, half-starving and living in a rat-infested cellar, he was diagnosed tubercular. A friendly Jewish doctor offered to arrange for his stay in a sanatorium in the Crimea, but Moshe said he would prefer to be helped on his way to Stockholm or Paris, where he promised he would take care of his health.

With a thousand rubles tricked out of the good doctor and a wealthy patient, Stiller landed in Stockholm in 1912, purchased two elegant business suits, and at the Strand Hotel registered as a German filmmaker. He bought everybody drinks, talked of not having time to meet important people, and startled theater and filmfolk by speaking of the *many* movies he planned. He spoke a charming mixture of Swedish and German, found work acting and directing at Strindberg's old theater, and snatched Svenska Bio's first offer to write and direct a potboiler in which he played a seducer. A few months later, the company hired another small-theater actor-director, Victor Sjöström. Over the next ten years, Stiller and Sjöström led the fledgling Swedish cinema toward international recognition.

While Sjöström's films were restrained, solemn, and ponderous, Stiller made vivid, technically virtuoso melodramas, whodunits, and vaudeville flicks that gave him a reputation as a sensitive, effeminate creator capable of profound poetry. His leading ladies helped him meet people with influence and money. He maintained the success of a film of his was proportionate to how enamored his leading lady was with him. He became a Swedish citizen in 1920.

On New Year's Day, 1923, Axel Esbensen, the Danish set designer of all Stiller and Sjöström movies, committed suicide after a violent quarrel with Stiller. It was never established that they were lovers, and the suicide was hushed up. After Sjöström went to Hollywood, where his name was Anglicized to Seastrom, Stiller was the king of the Swedish cinema. By the time he invited Greta Gustafsson to meet him, he was the arrogant homosexual in fur coat and diamond tie clips who saw to it that his unconventional persona was a topic of gossip.

Stiller cast Greta in *Gösta Berling's Saga.* Impulsive and often cruel, he told her she didn't know how to behave or how to think, that she had a good figure, graceful shoulders, fair legs, an unusual face, beautiful eyes with long eyelashes, and a husky voice, but that she was fat, didn't know how to walk or talk. Since he estimated there were a million Gustafssons in Scandinavia, he decided to change her name. "After this film, your new name will be known all over Europe. You will be publicized in the Swedish press and in newspapers all over the world. Don't bother about your friends.

When I finish with you, you will have no friends, but admirers everywhere." She would be Greta Garbo, he declared. "The name is simple and hard-hitting, and it suits you. Even though it is derived from Polish, it's pronounceable in any language."

She was not yet eighteen; he was forty.

The March 1924 premiere of *Gösta Berling* was a cultural event. Members of the royal family, Lagerlöf, director, and cast attended a swank reception. When the sixty-six-year-old Lagerlöf said she thought the movie cheapened and distorted her work, Stiller saw to it that she got drunk and was taken home before members of the press could interview her. The reviews were lackluster, the box office strong. Trianon Film, Berlin, bought the German rights and invited Stiller and cast to Berlin for the German premiere. Ernst Lubitsch, Joe May, Georg Pabst, and Fritz Lang were making artful, caustic movies that turned Emil Jannings, Asta Nielsen, Pola Negri, Conrad Veidt, and Lil Dagover into international stars. Stiller decided his future was in the vibrant German cinema.

Gösta Berling was a greater success in Germany than in Sweden (in four weeks, Trianon earned back its investment), and Stiller signed with the company. Trianon suggested a screen adaptation of *Hotel Stadt Lemberg,* but Stiller wanted to do Vladimir Sanityev's story of an aristocratic Russian girl fleeing the Crimean War, only to be sold into a Turkish harem. Trianon approved *The Girl From Sevastopol* and with Garbo and crew, Stiller left to scout locations in Istanbul. Germany's hyperinflation, however, bankrupted Trianon and reduced the million-mark budget to pennies. The Swedish consulate in Istanbul advanced money for train tickets back to Berlin for Stiller, cast, and crew.

Between Prague and Berlin, an assistant to director Georg Pabst recognized Garbo, as she sipped coffee in the dining car, and once in Berlin told his boss the gorgeous actress from *Gösta Berling* was in town. Pabst, who would later find the Nazis easier to handle than the Warner brothers, had people try every hotel until they found Garbo (and Stiller) living on credit at a Tiergarten pensione.

For $4,000 in American money, Pabst offered her the role of an honest girl in his brutally realistic *Freundlose Gasse (The Streets of Sorrow).* Stiller told her to say no. When she said yes, he accused her of sleeping with her new director. To avenge himself, Stiller found a syphilitic prostitute who spoke a little Swedish and introduced her to Pabst in the hope he would contract her disease. What really irked Stiller was that on-screen Pabst revealed Garbo at her most exquisite.

Louis B. Mayer came to Berlin on one of his scouting expeditions. MGM was Hollywood's largest employer of Nordic talent, and Stiller was quick to arrange a meeting. Mayer was noncommittal but cabled Sjöström in Hollywood. By return telegram, Sjöström confirmed that Stiller was a capable director. In one retelling, Mayer had his eyes on Garbo and, in order to get her, signed her director to a one-picture deal. In another version, it was Stiller who insisted his pretty but slightly pudgy protégée be part of any package. Reluctantly, Mayer agreed, supposedly muttering, "In America, men don't like fat women."

Stiller and Garbo arrived in America in September 1925, a few days before her twentieth birthday. Victor Sjöström was in New York and obtained invitations for them to the world premiere of Charlie Chaplin's *Gold Rush* and the glittering reception that followed. Stiller thought Chaplin might consider Garbo for his next film, but the comedian decided she was too tall for him. At Stiller's initiative, society photographer Arnold Genthe agreed to do a session with Garbo. Struck by her face, he brushed back her hair, threw a shawl over her shoulders, and produced a series of extraordinary photographs. One of them appeared on the November 1925 cover of *Vanity Fair.*

A studio photographer snapped Stiller and Garbo politely smiling as they got off the train in Los Angeles. Stiller rented a small beach house in Santa Monica, and Garbo moved into the nearby Miramar Hotel. Garbo was often a startled fawn in the presence of strangers, and totally dependent on Stiller. Pola Negri would remember a dinner where Garbo constantly looked to Stiller for permission before uttering a word. Leaving the men to their cigars and brandy, Negri took Garbo into her drawing room and told her to be shocking, audacious, egocentric. Anything but shy. Three years earlier when Ernst Lubitsch had brought Negri to Hollywood, she, too, had imagined she owed everything to her director. "I did succeed. Soon you will have to do the same—without Stiller."

Garbo sighed, "I hope so."

Irving Thalberg was not overwhelmed by her first screen test. At Stiller's insistence, however, a second test was made, and this time the production chief was more favorably impressed. He recommended a diet to slim down the five-foot-seven newcomer and sent her to the studio dentist, and to the studio hairdresser. After ten weeks, she was summoned to his office, handed a script, and told to study the role of Leonora, a beautiful Spanish peasant girl who falls in love with the wealthy Don Rafael Brull. The dark, handsome Ricardo Cortez, whose real name was Jacob Krantz, would play Don Rafael. He was MGM's answer to Paramount's Rudolph Valentino and, to Garbo's relief, didn't know Spanish and had never been to Spain. *The Torrent* was an adaptation of a novel by Vicente Blasco Ibanez, and it was expected to do for Cortez what Ibanez's *Four Horsemen of the Apocalypse* had done for Valentino. The daily rushes revealed Garbo's gift for conveying emotions for a camera, and before the movie was even released, Mayer raised her salary. *Variety* pronounced Garbo "the find of the year."

She was such a completely new phenomenon that the flapper, successfully played at MGM by Norma Shearer and Colleen Moore, disappeared from the screen. Any actress worth her salt wanted to copy Garbo—Constance Bennett came closest. The follow-up to *The Torrent* was a variation called *The Temptress*. Garbo thought her role silly and told Thalberg, "I cannot see any sense in getting dressed up and doing nothing but tempting men in pictures." Repeated arguments with Mayer and Thalberg led to Stiller's dismissal from the picture. For her third film, *Flesh and the Devil*, MGM teamed Garbo with its leading man, John Gilbert. At a time when movie houses changed playbills twice a week and a film running a full week was a success, *Flesh and the Devil* broke month-long records. The Garbo-Gilbert love scenes, peppered with suggestive gestures, were electrifying. As directed by Clarence Brown, Garbo played the faithless wife of an elderly count (Marc McDermott), sitting in a church pew between husband and lover (Lars Hanson), preening, as the preacher, looking straight at her, lashes out at the sins of the flesh. At the Communion rail, she forcibly turns the chalice so that her lips will touch the same spot as her lover's. For an encore, MGM had costarred Garbo and Gilbert in a 1927 modern-dress, happy-ending version of Tolstoy's *Anna Karenina*. Mayer changed the title to *Love* because he thought nobody could pronounce the original.

With his coal black hair and flashing, dark eyes, the jovial, high-strung, thrice-divorced Gilbert was, after Rudolph Valentino's premature death in 1926, the embodiment of silent-screen masculinity. Garbo thought him conventional and sexually unattractive. Always intensely ambitious, Gilbert (né John Pringle) suffered from an inferiority complex that Garbo did nothing to ease. Thalberg and the MGM publicity department fabricated offscreen echoes of the on-screen Garbo-Gilbert attraction. With the studio's encouragement, they were seen together. He was her introduction to tennis games with Aileen Pringle, astrology with Dagmar Godowsky, Valentino's former leading lady. After Garbo told the press she had no time for men, Tallulah Bankhead became her friend. The bawdy, outrageous Tallulah baited the world with her antics and got Garbo to smile with her imitations of Charlie Chaplin.

It was at Gilbert's Tower Road mansion overlooking Beverly Hills that, one winter evening in 1927, they became lovers. Near the height of their ecstasy, Gilbert froze and whispered, "Get up quickly." With Garbo grabbing her clothes and running after Gilbert out on a cold terrace, he whispered that he could hear Stiller quarreling with the butler at the door. Gilbert jumped into his clothes and smoothed his hair and told her to get dressed while he went to greet Stiller and explained he was showing her the view from the terrace.

Gilbert took his uninvited guest on a ten-minute tour of the mansion. From room to room, Garbo could hear Stiller yell, "Where's Greta?" When she reentered the living room, the jealous director was hitting Gilbert in the face, shouting, "It's time to go home!" She jumped between them. Stiller dragged her out of the house.

In Stockholm, Greta's sister died of tuberculosis, and when Stiller begged Greta to return with him to Sweden, she promised she would. After Stiller left, she began to depend on Salka Viertel, who cultivated her insecurities and, after suggesting movie ideas, began developing story lines that Garbo took to Thalberg. They plotted a talkie version of *Sapho*, Alphonse Daudet's 1884 novel about the moral and spiritual collapse of a young artist who falls under the sway of his model. Thalberg said yes, and Clarence

Brown directed the picture as *Inspiration,* with Sapho rechristened Yvonne, and Robert Montgomery's role changed to that of a young diplomat.

Garbo was filming *Wild Orchids,* based on an original story by John Colton, when Louis B. himself came to the set to hand her the telegram telling her Stiller was dead. The cause was attributed to tuberculosis. He was buried in Stockholm's North Cemetery, November 9, 1928. Aside from his attorney, Hugo Lindberg, nobody attended the burial. Garbo blamed herself for his death.

Mayer and Thalberg kept her busy. After *Flesh and the Devil,* Garbo made two more pictures in 1927, three the following year. After another trio of films in 1929, she declared herself exhausted and left for her homeland. She met the Count and Countess Wachtmeister on board the Swedish-American oceanliner and had a shipboard romance with the socially prominent countess, a tall, vigorous woman nine years her senior who was related to the royal family. In Stockholm, Garbo asked about Stiller's grave but didn't visit the cemetery. Instead, she talked about him as if he were still alive.

Garbo never let go of him. Her life and career would have been so much richer, she came to feel, if he had lived. Twenty years later when she enjoyed a brief, but physically satisfying, affair with Cecil Beaton, the photographer and stage designer noted in his diary:

> An intimate dinner in which she talked of the inadequacy of her career—the high hopes she had had as a girl when first under the spell of Maurice [sic] Stiller (only of course she did not mention him by name). She could never get over the great influence he had had over her, because in her family life there was never any interest in the things that she liked. It was a sudden revelation to know him. She talked about the manner people should conduct themselves. If their sex desires are in a certain direction, they should not be obvious to the world.

6

Lover to the Stars

Until a boy challenged her to show *her* penis, Mercedes de Acosta was convinced she was male. Her eccentric mother had wanted a son and called her daughter Rafael. Micaela de Acosta dressed her child in Eton suits and encouraged her to play with boys as a boy. Mercedes/Rafael was seven when a neighborhood boy she challenged to a fight took her behind a bathhouse, unbuttoned his pants, showed *his* penis, and asked if she had one like that. In an early, unpublished version of her memoirs, de Acosta would describe her horror:

I had heard about grown people and children being deformed. These stories now leapt to my mind.

"You're deformed," I shouted.

"If you are a boy and you haven't got this, *you* are the one who is deformed," he shouted back.

By this time the other boys had joined us, each boy speedily showing me the same strange phenomenon the first boy had exhibited. They were like menacing and terrible judges! They demanded that I produce the same "phenomenon."

"Prove you're not a girl," they screamed.

In that one brief second everything in my young soul turned monstrous and terrible and dark.

She ran home to her nurse and, when she confronted her mother, was told that, yes, she was a girl.

Little in de Acosta's background destined her to give meaning to the lives of some of the romantic women idols of stage and film, and to deal with the wild egos and opposite natures of Hollywood stars. Mercedes was the youngest of eight children, one of whom was already dead when she was born in 1893. Since her parents always summered in France, she liked to stress that although she was born in New York, she was *conceived* in Paris. Her father and mother were blue-blooded Spaniards who never ceased to be haughtily Castilian.

She wrote in her memoirs, "My mother and father, both transplanted from Spain to America, communicated to my brothers and sisters, and to me, a consciousness of a sort of homelessness—that is, of not actually belonging to America. But having acquired a modern way of life there, we could not feel when we returned to Spain that we belonged to that country either."

Mercedes's father, the distant, gray-eyed Ricardo de Acosta, was one of life's miscasts. Although born in colonial Cuba, he spent most of his childhood shuttling between Havana and Madrid. As a young man, he joined a student uprising in Havana. He was arrested and with twenty others was lined up on a cliff to be executed by firing squad, their bodies to be fed to the sharks in the ocean below. He escaped the bullets by hurling himself into the sea and fleeing to the United States aboard a Boston schooner. Mercedes's mother, Micaela Hernandez de Alba y de Alba, was a descendant of the Duke de Alba.

The de Acostas lived in a house on Forty-seventh Street between Fifth and Sixth Avenues. The area was fashionable. Former president Theodore Roosevelt owned a house across the street; future ambassador to Britain Joseph Choate lived next door. Maude Adams, famous for the spiritual quality of her acting, for never marrying, and, in the parlance of the time, for exhibiting a calculated coolness toward men, lived for a while on the street. Mercedes was twelve when her mother took her to see Adams play J. M. Barrie's beguiling Peter Pan. When the thirty-three-year-old actress advanced to the footlights and asked the audience if it believed in fairies, theatergoers invariably roared, "Yes." With the rest of the audience, Mercedes happily suspended her common sense and accepted Peter Pan as a living person. "Every child was hysterical about her as the little boy who never grew old, and I was no exception," she would remember. "To me she *was* Peter Pan, and when I saw her in the part, I was thrown into a state of ecstasy."

One of Mercedes's earliest memories was of seeing her eldest sister, Rita, on her wedding day. Rita wore a princess gown of cream lace, a sable boa, and black hat. She was a striking beauty, painted by Sargent and Boldini, and Mercedes would never forget Rita coming downstairs in her wedding gown on her way to marry William Earl Dodge Stokes, a millionaire twenty years her senior. "Rita was my first conscious glimpse of beauty, and all through my life she symbolized beauty to me."

Like the rest of the de Acosta children, Rita was brought up in strict Spanish Catholic tradition, which didn't prevent her from divorcing Stokes and marrying Philip Lydig. It was as Mrs. de Acosta Lydig that Rita became famous for her extravagances, her clothes, patronage of the arts, and her traveling with a staff of seven. Rita treated her kid sister as an adult from the time Mercedes was ten and introduced her to the luminaries of the day, from Rodin and Bergson to Yvette Guibert, D'Annunzio, Edith Wharton, and Sarah Bernhardt. Ethel Barrymore was a friend of Rita's, and Catherine Harris, John Barrymore's first wife, was Phil Lydig's first cousin. Baba, another sister of Mercedes's, married a cousin of George Bernard Shaw.

Ricardo never lived down his youthful escape from death. Why had none of his twenty comrades followed him over the cliff? When Mercedes was fourteen, he killed himself by jumping off a high rock. In the first manuscript of her memoirs, she would write that she understood her father. "I knew this gesture was, in his mind, an expiation at last to his comrades for having escaped with his life so many years before."

After encouraging her daughter's boyishness, the widowed Micaela decided Mercedes should be taught femininity, and to that effect sent her to a Catholic boarding school outside Paris.

It didn't take. Mercedes told a nun that because she was neither girl nor boy, she would always be unhappy and never fit in anywhere. As an adult she would come to appreciate her ambivalence:

It has made me understand the halftones of life, and like the halftone light of dawn and twilight, whose vibrations are ever more mystical and romantic, so, too, I have come to regard these halftones of life and the people who walk their rhythm as the most beautiful. . . . To the outward form of sex which the body has assumed, I have remained indifferent. I do not understand the difference between a man and a woman, and believing only in the eternal value of love, I cannot understand those so-called "normal" people who believe that a man should love only a woman, and a woman only a man. If this were so, then it disregards completely the spirit, the personality, and the mind and stresses the importance of the physical body. I believe in many cases this is why the "normal" people are usually much less inspired, seldom artists, and much less sensitive than the "halftone" people. They are held down and concerned so much with the physical body that they cannot see beyond the outward form of male and female.

Known for slicking back her jet-black hair with brilliantine, Mercedes was a vivacious, bold teenager drawn to the theater, its women, and the secrets of sapphic love. She discovered the soon-to-be-famous "little theater" Washington Square Players, where she met and fell in love with Katharine Cornell, and on Broadway became part of the life of Peter Pan herself—Maude Adams.

Cornell, who would become a tradition of the theater and spurn innumerable offers for screen stardom, was five years younger than Mercedes. Maude Adams Kiskadden was twenty years her senior. Maude Adams's name was enough to pack theaters, and although she shunned both press and followers, her worshipers could not resist her soft, elusive charm. "Only a few people penetrated the wall of air with which she surrounded herself," wrote Broadway historian and critic Brooks Atkinson. Mercedes would admit to an awkward moment when she was alone with Adams for the first time.

Kitty Cornell was tall, dark, not classically beautiful but compelling. She was winning notices for her ability in long speeches, and, offstage, for her sharp tongue. She introduced Mercedes to Elisabeth ("Bessie") Marbury, the doyenne of sapphic Broadway.

Marbury was a socially prominent professional woman, theatrical producer and agent, and powerful figure in the Democratic Party. She represented Europe's leading playwrights from George Bernard Shaw and James M. Barrie to Victorien Sardou and

Georges Feydeau. When Oscar Wilde was in prison, Bessie had secured some money for him by selling his *Ballad of Reading Gaol* to
the Pulitzer newspapers. She weighed over two-hundred pounds
and was a chain-smoker and an insomniac who read three to five
plays and manuscripts daily at all hours. She lived with the stylishly
slim and witty Elsie de Wolfe, an actress turned avant-garde interior
decorator who flew with Wilbur Wright, marched for suffrage,
backed Cole Porter's first musical, and would teach the Duchess of
Windsor how to run a home for a king. When their friend Anne
Morgan, J. P. Morgan's daughter, was included, they were known as
the Three Graces. The parties they gave at Morgan's Sutton Place
town house were so stylish they supposedly made lesbian households not only acceptable but chic. When she was sixty, Elsie would
astonish everybody by marrying Sir Charles Mendl.

Bessie was old enough to have known George Eliot and, in successive retellings, told Mercedes of how her meeting caused the
novelist to adopt a more masculine wardrobe. Of Bessie, Mercedes
would write that she "used to refer to herself as my grandmother,
but at quite an early age I made her laugh by saying she seemed
such a man to me that I felt she was more like my grandfather. She
was so delighted that afterwards she often signed her letters to me
'Granny Pa.' "

Rita introduced Mercedes to John Barrymore, who introduced
her to Kahlil Gibran. Spending time with the Lebanese poet-
philosopher made Mercedes question her Catholicism, her "blind
belief." She would think more for herself, she decided.

In the spring of 1917, she became a fan, a friend, and lover of
Isadora Duncan. To escape the ardent wooing of Paris Eugene
Singer, the heir to the sewing-machine fortune, the witty, liberated
dancer took a house for the summer on Long Island and invited
her new friend to come and stay with her. Duncan, who was sixteen
years older than Mercedes, was the sex symbol of intellectuals, at-
tracting painters, literary figures, and wealthy patrons to her art.
On elfin summer evenings, she danced for Mercedes, once hum-
ming Wagner's entire *Parsifal* score.

Ten years later, Mercedes came to Duncan's financial rescue
when, loaded with debt and out of favor, Isadora lived in a Paris
hotel without food. Mercedes helped her with her autobiography
and was rewarded by a deep friendship and sensual poems. On the

Riviera a few months later, the dancer died when her scarf wound itself around the axle of a Bugatti taking her to a new amorous adventure.

The entry of the United States into the Great War in 1917 stirred patriotic fervor and gave Mercedes her first job writing for the stage. The occasion was a large war benefit held at the Madison Square Garden.

Bessie gave Mercedes a matinee ticket to see Alla Nazimova in *War Brides* at the Princess Theater. The Russian-born Nazimova was Broadway's most daring lesbian and most exotic actress, famous for her interpretations of Ibsen and Chekhov. In *War Brides*, she represented Imperial Russia in a thrilling tableau, coming onstage dressed as a cossack and waving the czarist flag.

"She had thick black hair which stood out from her head, and her eyes were the only truly purple-colored eyes I have ever seen," Mercedes would recall. "Her lashes were black and thick, providing a setting for the intense purple they surrounded. I was always fascinated and conscious of Nazimova's eyes, and at the first meeting they made a great impression on me. She held out both her hands to me and said she had heard a lot about me from Bessie."

Nazimova asked Mercedes to walk her home and told her she, too, was of Spanish blood. She was the daughter of Spanish Jews who had emigrated to Russia, and her real name was Lavendera. She had taken Nazimova as a stage name because *zima* meant winter in Russian. Because of her crush on Alla, Mercedes devoured Dostoyevsky, Tolstoy, Gogol, and Pushkin.

Mercedes celebrated the Allied victory in November 1918 by dancing at the Ritz Hotel with Ivor Novello. She thought the actor-playwright-composer the handsomest man in a British officer's uniform. Abram Poole was another man in a captain's uniform with whom she danced. His family were wealthy Chicagoans, and, he admitted, he had grown up spoiled by four adoring sisters. He wanted to be a painter; his brother Ernest was a novelist. He asked if he could see her again. Mercedes was going on twenty-six, and before she could say no, her mother said yes on her behalf.

Mercedes was more interested in meeting Bessie's friends. Hope Williams was a promising actress who had seduced Tallulah Bankhead when Tallulah was sixteen and Hope nineteen. "Why don't you write a play for Hope?" Bessie asked Mercedes. An amateur society group performed the result. Meeting Eva La Gallienne was of greater consequence. Eva was nineteen and the star of *Liliom*. After Mercedes saw her in the Ferenc Molnár play, she wrote a formal letter of admiration inviting the actress to dinner. They discovered they were both devoted admirers of the Italian diva Eleonora Duse. Le Gallienne's biographer, Robert A. Schanke, would write that "they began their arranged lunch at the Ritz by comparing notes on Eleonora Duse's brooding intensity, and ended by returning to Mercedes's apartment." They became soul mates and, for five years, lovers.

In May 1920, Mercedes married Poole in her mother's apartment. None of her friends were present (the excuse for the stealth wedding was that Abram was a Protestant). Mercedes appeared in a gray chiffon dress instead of a wedding gown and barely allowed her sister Rita to hire a small band to play Mendelssohn's "Wedding March" in an adjacent room. Carrying his bride over the threshold to their new apartment, Abram saw Mercedes's sad face. When he asked why, she said she was thinking of her mother. Abram said this was probably the saddest night in her mother's life. He phoned for a cab and told his bride to go home and be with her mother. Mercedes would always cherish him for this gesture.

Abram was a heterosexual and the marriage was consummated, although in the coded language of her memoirs, Mercedes would admit they were incompatible in bed. Le Gallienne was jealous of Abram and, while on tour with *Liliom,* wrote Mercedes that it was unbearable to think of him or anyone else lying in Mercedes's arms.

Marriage was a way out for several of Mercedes's high-profile theatrical friends. A year after she married Abram, Katharine Cornell married her gay director Guthrie McClintic, and Lynn Fontanne married Alfred Lunt.

While pretending to be the newlywed of her society-painter husband, Mercedes's emotional life was concentrated on Le Gallienne, who gave herself totally. Eva was the daughter of the British literary critic and poet Richard Le Gallienne and the Danish journalist Julie Nörregård, a pair of marital misfits who from the beginning lived apart and divorced when their daughter was four. Eva's half sister Gwendolyn Le Gallienne was a lesbian painter who in 1930s Paris lived a quarrelsome life with Yvette Ledoux. Eva was brought up in Paris and, at fifteen, made her acting debut in London. A year later, she had come to New York.

When on tour, Eva wrote as many as three letters a day to Mercedes. When in New York, they met in her apartment. They spent evenings with Stark Young, the editor of *The New Republic*, and his lover, and in foursomes ventured up to Harlem, where the Park Avenue after-theater limousine crowd looked for new thrills. They went for the basement speakeasies like the Drool Inn and the Clam, where transvestites performed and lesbians flaunted themselves. One night, they were introduced to Jeanne Eagels, high on opium and clinging to Libby Holman. Eagels was an actress of irresistible freshness and strange corrupt beauty; Holman was an actress-singer who, at twenty-five, was "rotten ripe," as her gay friend Clifton Webb said. Eagels told Mercedes that she, too, was Spanish, that her real name was Aguila.

We do not know what Abram knew of the two women's relationship, but when his wife fell ill in May 1922, he immediately alerted Eva. After Mercedes recovered and left for Europe, Eva followed, to see her mother in London and, in Paris, to be with Mercedes. Far from prying families, they lived near the Luxembourg Garden at the Hotel Foyot, where Casanova and T. S. Eliot had once stayed. American-in-Paris bookseller and James Joyce publisher Sylvia Beach, who shared her life with Adrienne Monnier, reserved rooms for visiting sapphic couples at the Foyot. Shakespeare and Company, Beach and Monnier's bookstore in nearby Rue de l'Odéon, was the most famous expatriate address, and a few years later Mercedes persuaded Beach to carry her published poems. The stay was the happiest moment in de Acosta and Le Gallienne's life together.

Prince Igor Agoustinsky befriended the two young women. He had been fabulously rich before the Bolshevik revolution, but had arrived in Paris without a penny. He made a living selling other Russian nobles' icons, paintings, books, furniture, and gold tea sets. Mercedes thought he looked like a pasha sitting on the floor among his fellow exiles' hoards and asking her and Eva to admire a particular treasure.

The idyll was temporarily interrupted when Eva's mother came over from London. Mercedes discreetly left for Munich. By midsummer, however, the lovers were together again, traveling by themselves to Genoa, Venice, Vienna, and Budapest, where Molnár greeted the star of the American version of *Liliom* with a brass band and welcoming banners on the façade of the Dunapalata Hotel. All too soon, Abram joined them, however, and while Eva returned to London, the Pooles traveled to Istanbul, to stay at the Pera Palace, the celebrated hotel whose guests included Agatha Christie.

Mercedes and Abram were in Turkey for ten days in August 1922. In her published memoirs, Mercedes would remember how she met, but never talked to, Garbo. Perhaps inspired by Thomas Mann's *Death in Venice,* she would write how in the Pera hotel lobby she saw "one of the most hauntingly beautiful women I had ever beheld. Her features and her movements were so distinguished and aristocratic that I decided she must be a refugee Russian princess." The hotel porter didn't know the woman's name, but said she was an actress who came with the Swedish film director Mauritz Stiller. Mercedes would claim she followed the woman in the street several times, haunted by her eyes, but somehow never had the courage to talk to her. For the Trianon film project that fell through, Stiller and Garbo were indeed in Istanbul, but in December 1924, more than two years later. In the first draft of Mercedes's life story, Garbo was more a vision and a portent, the "person who would one day mean more to me than anyone in the whole world."

Mercedes and Eva were reunited in London. Abram, however, made demands. Mercedes threatened suicide, and Eva left for New York.

The following year, the two women were back in Paris. As diehard admirers of Eleonora Duse, they stood in the Rue de Rivoli under the aging diva's windows, moved to tears when they saw her sit wrapped in a blanket on the balcony. They wrote missives asking for interviews, but were turned down by la Duse's companion, Desirée. They walked through Brittany like a pair of tramps, bunked with a fisherman and his wife, and once back in Paris were invited to Friday-afternoon tea at Natalie Barney's.

Barney was the doyenne of the wealthy American women who felt freer in Paris. Her three-hundred-year-old Left Bank house in Rue Jacob was the oasis for "odd girls," onrushing expatriates, and native intellectuals. It was in her garden that Isadora Duncan danced and Anita Loos mingled with Willa Cather, Djuna Barnes, and Hemingway's sister-in-law Virginia Pfeiffer. It was here that Janet Flanner, who under the pen name Gênet wrote a "Letter from Paris" column in *The New Yorker,* fell in love with fellow writer Solita Solano.

Before the Great War, Barney had entertained her guests by having the naked Margaretha Geertruida Zelle, a dancer borrowed from the Folies-Bergère, ride a white horse. The Dutch woman passed as a dancer from Java and used the stage name Mata Hari. Since she had hardly any breasts, she was wearing a bra, but, wrote Colette, her "back and thighs are of the finest order." When Dolly Wilde was in Paris, she gave Barney's 20 Rue Jacob residence as her address.

When Eva and Mercedes learned the incandescent Duse would make a farewell appearance in London, they cabled for tickets. Shortly after Mercedes's thirtieth birthday, they were in London, enchanted by the sixty-five-year-old actress in *Cosi Sia.* Back in New York, Eva was chosen over Billie Burke to star in the Broadway production *The Swan,* Molnár's romantic comedy about a prince, a princess, and a commoner. Mercedes wrote *Sandro Botticelli* and, with Eva, raised money for a showcase production. Basil Sydney of West End *Strange Interlude* and *Dinner at Eight* fame, played the Renaissance painter and Eva the ravishing noblewoman Simonetta Vespucci, who, as the model for Botticelli's *Birth of Venus,* was his unrequited love.

Sam Lyons, Eva's agent, feared whispers of lesbianism would destroy her career. "You gotta get a fella," he thundered. She found one in her British costar, Basil Rathbone, but three weeks after sleeping with him the first time she thought she was pregnant. When she told him, he broke off the affair. Duse died on her American farewell tour in Pittsburgh, and when the body lay in state in a small Manhattan chapel before being taken to Italy for burial, Eva and Mercedes held a vigil. Eva felt she had betrayed la Duse and herself by taking a male lover.

Jehanne d'Arc, Mercedes's second play for Eva, was a costly flop in New York and in Paris. Together they raised $12,000—and eventually found another $28,000—and hired Norman Bel Geddes to direct. Mercedes's Joan was a simple girl who dies on the stake because she refuses to compromise. Not trusting the material, Bel Geddes overproduced the play with elaborate movements of crowds that didn't so much color the story as asphyxiate it. With their director, they went to Paris in early 1925. The sets were too large for the Paris stage, and a second, larger theater had to be rented.

Failure, irritation, and Eva's need for new conquests ended the affair. On the ship back to America, Eva fell in love with Gladys Calthrop, Nöel Coward's set designer. In 1926 LeG, as Eva was known in theater circles, established a populist theater of classical acting in New York. She called it Civic Repertory Theater and turned down leading roles on Broadway for the sake of performing Shakespeare, Ibsen, and Chekhov at cut-rate ticket prices. Mercedes became interested in spiritual matters and after meeting Jiddu Krishnamurti began to explore Buddhism. The handsome, solemn guru, who was supposedly the incarnation of all deities past and future, cut an elegant figure in London and New York. The London Theosophical Society claimed him to be the Messiah.

Three books of de Acosta's verse were published, *Moods, Streets and Shadows,* and *Archways of Life.* She stayed close to the theater and was always about to write a play for Eva. She spent the summer of 1927 with Bessie Marbury in Maine. A year later, when Mercedes's former lover Hope Williams starred in *Holiday* with Donald Ogden Stewart on Broadway, and at the 14th Street Playhouse Eva shared the stage with Nazimova in Chekhov's *The Cherry Orchard,* Mercedes met Cecil Beaton. She thought the twenty-four-year-old Englishman's slender and willowy physique gave an impression of fragility. He found her "a kind & clever friend & guide without any false show of affection & effusion." Were it not for his affair with Adela Rogers St. Johns, he bragged, he would have liked to go to bed with her. When they met again in Palm Beach in January 1930, Beaton noted in his diary how he enjoyed gossiping with Mercedes about "the dreary crowd of New York Lesbians & we made fun of their boring loyalty to one another, their earnestness, squalor, poverty, and complete lack of humour." The de Acosta–Beaton friendship, and infatuation for the elusive Garbo, would last forty years.

51

* * *

Bessie thought of Mercedes when RKO scouted for talkie screen material for Pola Negri. Mercedes wrote an outline of a story and showed it to her gay playwright friend John Colton and suggested they write it together. Colton was famous for having shared a Los Angeles hotel with Somerset Maugham in 1920 and one night asking if Maugham had anything Colton could read. Maugham had given him the galleys of his short story "Miss Thompson." The next morning, an excited Colton said he wanted to make a play out of it. With Clemence Randolph, Colton turned Maugham's classic story of repressed sexuality into the sensational Broadway play *Rain*. Starring Jeanne Eagels as the South Seas harlot, *Rain* electrified Broadway for four years.

Bessie sold the Colton–de Acosta story to RKO. Negri came to New York and, after reading it, recommended that the two writers be put under contract. In January 1929, Mercedes, John, and British ballerina Marjorie Moss boarded the Century Limited for the first leg of the three-days-and-four-nights trip to Los Angeles. As the train crossed the Colorado River, Marjorie cried that she would die in California, which she did four years later.

7

The Perfect Sapphic Liaison

The January 14, 1932, editions of the Los Angeles newspapers reported two noteworthy events. It snowed in Hollywood, and John Barrymore and Garbo met for the first time on the set of *Grand Hotel*. MGM publicists contrived to have Garbo at the main studio gate to welcome Barrymore. Half an hour went by before someone ran down to inform her that the actor had arrived early with the intention of escorting *her* to the set. To wring an "item" out of the contretemps, a publicity release reported that, after their opening scene together, Garbo impulsively kissed her costar, saying, "You have no idea what it means to play opposite so perfect an actor."

De Acosta went to see Thalberg with less fanfare. She had rewritten her Garbo-in-disguise story to his specifications, and a week after Edmund Goulding started filming *Grand Hotel*, MGM registered *Desperate*. It told the story of a girl whose mother committed suicide by jumping off a cliff. The way Mercedes characterized her heroine could have been a description of Garbo or perhaps herself:

One feels in her a strange, wild nature, with the conflicting struggles of her mother and father combined—of the old world and the

53

new—from an early age this inner battle had raged. One feels in her sadness and gaiety, sanity and neuroticism, vitality and listlessness, reticence and restlessness, shyness and daring—all of these mixed in a mad contradiction that spends her own strength and throws her back upon herself—that makes her forever a mystery to the ordinary mortal. In her eyes one already sees the doom that comes from the soul rather than outward events—unmoved eyes, holding in the depth that look of eternity.

Two years into their liaison, star and writer lived a rich, if sometimes stormy, relationship. Garbo was willful, instinctive, spoiled, and quick to dispose of people. Mercedes saw this trait in Garbo the first time she brought Ivor Novello over to meet her. Garbo was pleasant to the handsome gay actor-writer who was the most popular figure in the British musical theater. Novello was in Los Angeles on a short-term contract to adapt his society comedy *The Truth Game* for Thalberg. In a stance Garbo would repeat, notably at her first meeting with Cecil Beaton, she suddenly stiffened and bade Novello goodbye.

De Acosta was a sometime victim of the darkest depressions, enduring what she called "the dark night of the soul." Garbo possessed a genius for making things difficult for herself and everyone around her, Mercedes for smoothing things out. Garbo surrounded herself with people she could dominate—housekeepers, gay men, starstruck matrons—and demanded total devotion. De Acosta and Garbo didn't so much define their relationship in terms of sex but as an emotional involvement, although Garbo found Mercedes erotically stimulating. Neither categorized her sex partners as being more or less important, and each thought of herself as single.

Garbo avoided all appearances of being coupled. Mercedes lived a continent away from Abram Poole and took her freedom for granted. Wishing her husband the best, she advised him to seduce Janice Fair, a model he was fond of, a suggestion, he wrote back, that he considered immoral.

There was more to de Acosta than sex, elegance, Buddhism, and vegetarianism. She gave Garbo a measure of self-confidence that was new and introduced her to literature, music, poetry, and painting. George Cukor credited Mercedes with teaching Garbo "beautiful" English. "I have been like a ship without a rudder, lost and very lonely," Garbo told the Associated Press without saying *who* was making her feel less forlorn. She provoked a sentiment of protection in people that made them want to defend her, although they weren't sure exactly what they were defending her against.

Mercedes discovered less likable sides in her friend. As a devoted animal lover, Mercedes was appalled to see Garbo burn insects she found in the house or on the lawn. There were odd corners of secrecy between them. To Thalberg, Mercedes suggested Garbo play Joan of Arc. He approved the idea and Mercedes spent nine months developing a script. One night Thalberg called her at home to tell her Garbo no longer wanted to play the virgin warrior. Mercedes suspected Garbo was being influenced by somebody, but never had it out with her.

Garbo cultivated an exaggerated sense of her own frailty. She often described herself as depressed, less depressed, or more depressed; ill, very ill, or recovering from an illness. She claimed she was eternally exhausted, but stunned Mercedes by the vigor with which she could swim and row. She was a regular at Cedric Gibbons and Dolores Del Rio's tennis court. As MGM's art director, Gibbons was the undisputed arbiter of style and arrived every morning in his gleaming white Duesenberg invariably dressed in a dark blue suit, gray homburg, and matching gloves to lord over a staff of two hundred. Dolores was called the most beautiful woman to grace the screen, a banker's daughter born in Durango, Mexico, brought up in a convent and married at sixteen to a gay writer who committed suicide. One afternoon at the poolside, Gibbons found Dolores fondling Garbo's breast.

Garbo was MGM's highest-paid star, and to justify her $12,500 a week, Louis B. Mayer and Thalberg tried to make three Garbo movies a year. She hated the pace. Mercedes felt that instead of agonizing over each of these pictures and over her reticence, Garbo should take chances.

When filming, she insisted on closed sets. William Daniels was the only cameraman she trusted with her face. She felt his innovative style and mood effects made him only a little short of a genius, and when he filmed her in close-ups, black screens were placed around her and the camera. Asked why she objected to visitors, she answered that when people watched, she felt she was just someone making faces. There were days when she said she needed to be alone and dismissed Mercedes, and days when she summoned her back and told her how much she admired her sensitivity and ability to listen. Garbo gave in to moods, holed up alone for days at a time, or taking off for nature hideaways to play the role of a nymph. When Wallace Beery offered her the use of his log cabin on an island in the middle of Silver Lake, Nevada, she left with James, her chauffeur, only to telephone Los Angeles and beg Mercedes to join her.

Once at the lake, James was sent home, and the two women spent six weeks by themselves. They bathed and told each other about their early lives until all hours of the night. Garbo cooked mountain trout and astonished Mercedes with her sense of humor. In photographs Mercedes took, Garbo is seen topless in beret and shorts, gym shoes and white socks, or wearing a shirt that barely covers her breasts.

They loved violent weather. On the few occasions when diluvian rain, thunder, and lightning hit Los Angeles, they drove up on Mulholland Drive or along the Pacific Coast Highway to Decker Canyon for a view of the sky and the ocean. "We would rush to the highest peak overlooking the sea to watch the lightning break through the sky like great cracks of fire and hear the thunder crashing down on us," Mercedes would recall. "We were always happy and stimulated in a storm."

Christmas, 1929, was exceptionally warm in Los Angeles. To put themselves in the mood at Garbo's house, they closed the curtains and lit a fire. "To know Greta one must know the North," Mercedes would write. "She may live the rest of her life in a southern climate, but she will always be Nordic with all its sober and introvert characteristics. To know her one must know—*really know*—wind, rain, and brooding skies."

In January 1931, Thalberg and Garbo beat RKO and Pola Negri to the Mata Hari story. *Mata Hari* was an imitation of Paramount's *Dishonored* and a movie both Garbo and her director, George Fitzmaurice, would soon prefer to forget. Thalberg, however, thought Garbo as Mata Hari was surefire. Mercedes knew the story.

Her brother-in-law Philip Lydig had been the lover of the real Margaretha Zelle, who spied so clumsily for the Germans that they betrayed her to the French. Ramon Novarro played the Russian lieutenant whose information she was supposed to steal, and Lionel Barrymore her former lover (and Novarro's superior). She shoots Barrymore and, true to life, faces the French firing squad.

Garbo's wardobe was by Adrian. The slender designer (né Adolph Greenberg in Naugatuck, Connecticut) was responsible for the ravishing clothes that defined Metro's glamour. He dressed Garbo in suits and, to take attention away from Joan Crawford's hips, created the shoulder pads that became the Crawford hallmark. Garbo's face fascinated him, and he liked to draw attention to her eyes with eye-catching headgear. Garbo trusted his taste—Mercedes thought he looked like an Arab boy—and went on shopping sprees and often lunched with him. For *Mata Hari,* he created spare-no-expense clothes that featured the same accent on broad shoulders as those shown in the 1931 Paris collections. Mercedes hated *Mata Hari,* but found Garbo facing the firing squad enchanting: "In a long cape with her hair brushed straight back and her face unrelieved, she never looked more beautiful or more stirringly dramatic."

Offscreen, she preferred turtlenecks, plain skirts or slacks, and flat-heeled shoes, but since *A Woman of Affairs,* Adrian was in charge of her film wardrobe. For fittings, lighting checks, and extreme long shots, the studio gave her two doubles, Chris Meeker and Geraldine de Vorak. De Vorak was such a look-alike in face and figure that Howard Strickling sent her to smart restaurants and nightclubs wearing Garbo's gowns. It all went to her head. She let people believe she *was* Garbo, began signing autographs and living as a celebrity. Frustrated over not being able to interview the real Garbo, one Hollywood reporter wrote, "Geraldine has everything that Garbo has except whatever it is that Garbo has."

Salka Viertel remained very much in the picture. So much so that the press sometimes confused Garbo's two vestal attendants. In its January 28, 1932, edition, the *Hollywood Reporter* told how Viertel had gone to the Pasadena railway station to greet Garbo returning from New York after Christmas:

Mrs. V came into the station in very tailored attire, flat-heeled shoes, etc., and was immediately swamped with reporters who, too, were waiting for the glamorous one. They asked her if she was meeting Garbo, and she said, "Yes." Whereupon all the cameramen asked Mrs. Viertel to pose for some pictures. Flattered, this lady smiled and posed for several minutes. When it was all over the reporters said, "Thank you very much, Miss d'Acosta [sic]."

De Acosta had met Viertel through Eleonora von Mendelssohn. The immensely wealthy granddaughter of the composer—named Eleonora after her godmother, Duse—had married Dietrich's gay hanger-on Hans von Twardowsky, but lived in her family castle near Salzburg, unimpressed by Adolf Hitler's agitation next door. During the Great War, Salka had fallen in love with the beautiful Eleonora when they both acted in a repertory company in Dusseldorf. Mercedes and Eva Le Gallienne had been guests of von Mendelssohn. Eleonora shared her life with Alice von Hofmann-sthal and included among her friends Arturo Toscanini and Max Reinhardt. Of the beautiful Eleonora, Mercedes would say she had "a violent fixation on both men and women."

Tangled lives. Glamorous Garbo
and intriguing de Acosta.
Photos: (1) author's collection
(2) Library of Congress

Boy genius and intuitive force. Irving Thalberg understood that audiences are not primarily attracted to the opposite sex on the screen, but projected themselves on the light-and-shadow figures of their own sex. *Photo: The Motion Picture Arts and Sciences*

1717 San Vicente Boulevard. Garbo scattered blossoms for Mercedes de Acosta, her new friend, to walk across the threshold.
Photo: Axel Madsen

Anna Gustaffson and her daughter, 1928. Greta's mother insinuated there was something unnatural in Greta's attachment to her father. *Photo: National Archives*

Mrs. Philip Lydig. Mercedes' sister Rita was famous for her extravagances, her clothes, patronage of the arts, and her traveling with a staff of seven. *Photo: Library of Congress*

The doyenne of Sapphic Broadway. Elisabeth ("Bessie") Marbury as painted by William Rankin in 1932. *Photo: Library of Congress*

Eva Le Gallienne as L'Aiglon. As de Acosta's lover, Eva wrote it was unbearable to think of anyone else lying in Mercedes' arms.
Photo: Library of Congress

Author, playwright, poet. Mercedes de Acosta in 1925. "Say what you want about Mercedes," remarked Alice B. Toklas, "she had the three most important women of the twentieth century." De Acosta bragged that she could get any woman from any man. She let the sewing circle know about her affairs with Garbo and Dietrich, and a wag speculated the third conquest Toklas alluded to was either Gertrude Stein or Eleanor Roosevelt. *Photo: Library of Congress*

Were it not for his affair with Adele Rogers St. Johns, Cecil Beaton claimed he would have liked to go to bed with Mercedes. Cecil was known as the society photographer in 1924. *Photo: UPI/Bettman*

Garbo at twenty-eight. Willful,
instinctive, spoiled and quick
to dispose of people.
Photo: author's collection

Garbo by de Acosta. Mer-
cedes photographed Garbo
topless, clad only in beret and
shorts, gym shoes and white
socks during their solitary six
weeks at Silver Lake, Nevada.
Photo: author's collection

Adrian and Crawford. MGM's chief costume designer dressed Garbo in suits and to take attention away from Joan Crawford's hips, created the shoulder pads that became the Crawford hallmark.
Photo: author's collection

Joan Crawford was an earthy bisexual who went through men and, when they were available, young women with the same ruthlessness she used to reach the top. Photos of her and an unidentified woman circulated in the pornographic underground.
Photo: author's collection

© 1913.

OLIVER MOROSCO.

Alla Nazimova taught Broadway's Laurette Taylor Sapphic love and how to hold out for great roles. *Photo: Library of Congress*

Lavender romance. Stanwyck and Robert Taylor in *His Brother's Wife* (1936). *Photo: author's collection*

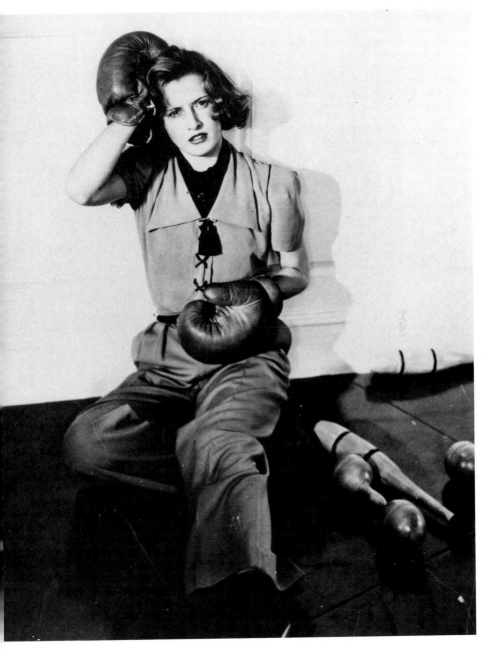

Lady with a punch. The way Barbara Stanwyck related to men in her films made her the role model for young, insecure lesbians.

Photo: author's collection

"What right has she to live." Dietrich smashes the life-sized statue of herself in the melodramatic ending of *Song of Songs*. *Photo: Museum of Modern Art Archives*

Alla Nazimova was the executive producer, cowriter and star of *The Brat* (1919). Metro Pictures paid her $13,000 a week and billed her the "woman of a thousand moods."
Photo: author's collection

The marriage was a sham. Jill Edmond married Laurence Olivier when she was twenty-two. By the time she was thirty, she was exclusively lesbian.
Photo: Library of Congress

688-139-13

Story conferences honed down the queen's love of women. Garbo as
Queen Christina. *Photo: Museum of Modern Art Archives*

"I long to hold you in my arms and pour my love into you," Ona Munson wrote Mercedes in 1940.
Photo: The Academy of Motion Picture Arts and Sciences

Marlene, husband, and daughter in 1931. The 1967 caption to the period photo of Marlene, Rudy and Marie Sieber coming to America added: "Dietrich is wearing the mannish garb that became her trademark during this era." *Photo: UPI/Bettmann*

Sincerely yours Katharine Cornell

Katharine Cornell concealed her love of women in her longterm marriage to the bisexual Broadway producer-director Guthrie McClintic. She surprised Garbo and de Acosta one Sunday morning and cattily delayed her departure. *Photo: author's collection*

8

Enter Joan Crawford and Katharine Cornell

While Garbo was playing the faded ballerina John Barrymore falls in love with in *Grand Hotel,* and Harry Edington, her agent, got Mercedes an assignment at RKO, Salka struggled with the Queen Christina story. Thalberg first said the studio had no intention of paying for her cinematic treatment since Christina (1626–89) was a historical character and therefore in the public domain. He eventually paid Salka $7,500 for her story line and hired her at $350 a week. To work with her on the screenplay, he assigned Bess Meredyth, who had scripted two silent Garbo-Gilbert pictures.

People expected a good love story, he told Viertel and Meredyth at their first story conference. He wondered whether the bachelor queen's affection for Countess Ebba Sparre, her lady-in-waiting, was not similar to the teacher-student relationship in *Mädchen in Uniform.* A censored version that glossed over the German film's already veiled lesbianism had opened in New York, and Thalberg thought of offering Leontine Sagan, its director, a Hollywood contract. Salka was an old friend of Leontine's—they had shared the stage in an Ibsen play in Dresden. If handled with taste, Thalberg told the two writers, Queen Christina's fondness for her lady-in-waiting could result in "interesting scenes." Salka left Thalberg's office impressed by his broad-mindedness. Bess was certain he would eliminate any originality they came up with.

Grand Hotel was Garbo's second film with Edmund Goulding. The Nöel Coward look-alike writer, director, bisexual, and idea man of wit and confidence was the director most actresses wanted because he made them believe they had a touch of greatness in them. He welcomed temperament so he could cut it down to size, and on *Love* had had the pleasure of doing so to Garbo. No one could do her hair right, she had complained to him in her dressing room. With no time for finding a new coiffeur, Eddie stuck bobby pins in his mouth and went to work on her hair. Within a minute, the stunned Garbo got off her high horse. On *Grand Hotel,* he was in top form and steered the all-star picture with such authority that Thalberg scheduled a preview for the end of March.

In a gesture that his friends found poignant, Goulding had married the dying Marjorie Moss, with whom Mercedes and John Colton had come to California. At their Santa Monica beach house, the Gouldings entertained a savant mix of fellow Brits, natives, and various strays that on occasion included Garbo. During the last weeks of filming, the Gouldings' houseguest was Cecil Beaton.

Beaton, whose sexual leanings were principally toward men and whose appetite for glamour was insatiable, was on one of his many Hollywood assignments for fashion magazines. He had photographed Marlene Dietrich and the Marx Brothers, Dolores Del Rio and "Tarzan" Johnny Weissmuller, but Garbo eluded him. Anita Loos, who was among his first "facilitators," introduced him to John Gilbert and Ina Claire and secured an invitation to William Randolph Hearst's San Simeon. That Beaton had never managed to meet—and photograph—Garbo didn't prevent him from gossiping about her. Since Goulding worked with Garbo every day, Beaton begged his host to invite her. When she phoned one Sunday and heard that Beaton was there, she wouldn't come. "No," she told Eddie, "he speaks to newspapers. I don't want to meet him."

Beaton retired to his room to soothe his pride with a long, hot bath.When he reappeared downstairs, Garbo was there. He pretended to tiptoe out of the room, but was called over by Marjorie and introduced. In his diaries, he would describe how Garbo complimented him on his youth and beauty, how they played charades and drank Bellinis, and how, when he invited her to his room to see his photographs, he kissed her. He quoted her as telling him, "You are a Grecian boy. If I were a young boy, I would do such things as you."

The party lasted all night. Lights were turned off and "our bacchanalia became wilder in the firelight." When Garbo left at dawn, Beaton cried, "Then this is goodbye."

"Yes, I'm afraid so," she answered, climbing into her big automobile. *"C'est la vie."*

They would not see each other again until after World War II.

Goulding and William Daniels, Garbo's favorite cinematographer, invented tricky camera angles to underscore her romantic performance as the fading Russian ballerina. John Barrymore played a penniless baron who wants to steal her jewels but instead loses his heart to her. Lionel Barrymore was cast as a shabby bookkeeper whose importance grows with the expanding adventures in the luxury hotel. Wallace Beery was a pompous but pathetic industrialist on the skids who hires Joan Crawford as his secretary and plaything. Crawford as the secretary was not the most inspired casting, but she wanted to be in a film with Garbo even if they had no scenes together.

Crawford was three years younger than Garbo, and as Mrs. Douglas Fairbanks Jr. was bent on proving she was a serious actress. To escape her flapper image, she imitated Garbo's aloofness, hairstyle, and makeup and tried to copy her dramatic intensity. Her mouth was wide and generous, and as Fairbanks Jr. would say, "She put on lipstick with broad, brave strokes." To give herself racier features, she had her back teeth removed. The operation was painful, but George Hurrell, the studio photographer, told her she had the closest face to Garbo's perfect proportions.

On a stairway one morning, she managed to meet Garbo. "What a pity; our first picture together and we don't work with each other," Garbo said. She took Crawford's face in her hands and added, "I'm sorry. You have a marvelous face." In recounting this stairwell meeting for publication years later, Crawford would comment, "If there was ever a time in my life when I might have been a lesbian, that was it."

Crawford was an earthy bisexual who went through men and, when they were available, young women with the same ruthlessness she used to reach the top. Intimates called her Billie. More than one young woman reporter would tell of interviews at Crawford's home when the star, under the pretext of needing to change, invited the journalist to continue the conversation while she dressed for dinner. Once in the bedroom, Crawford made remarks about the color coordination of the reporter's clothes and, picking designer dresses from her closet, suggested the visitor slip out of her dress and try out several outfits. Christina Crawford, Joan's adopted daughter, would say that her mother tried to sleep with a hired nurse. "I knew about my mother's lesbian proclivities," Christina would write in *Mommie Dearest,* "and this only added to what I had already figured out for myself."

Louise Brooks thought Crawford belonged to the dark side of golden-age Hollywood and said of her that she didn't approve of her own life. "To feel that Hollywood does not, and the public could not, approve of her private self," Brooks would say of Crawford, "makes for a deadly state of confusion." Crawford had a knack for dramatizing herself, for communicating with her fans and, in purple language, for speaking the truth. At nineteen, she had appeared in a pornographic movie that, in 1935, led black-mailers to extort a reputed $100,000 from MGM in return for the negative. Photos of a reclining naked Crawford, eyes heavenward in real or fake ecstasy, a woman between her spread-eagled legs, circulated in the pornographic underground.

De Acosta didn't like working at RKO. The picture she was writing for Negri was called *East Side.* Mercedes called the assignment of no consequence, and by the time *Grand Hotel* finished filming, she was quietly terminated. On his own, Colton finished *East Side.* Paramount purchased it from RKO as a Marlene Dietrich vehicle, but soon dropped it.

A March 11, 1932, preview in Santa Barbara told Mayer and Thalberg that they had a hit in *Grand Hotel.* "Lionel Barrymore, as Kringlein, walks away with the acting honors," the *Hollywood*

Reporter glowed the next day. "The glamorous Garbo is as glamorous as ever. Joan Crawford does her best work as the stenographer and looks more beautiful than at any time since her advent in pictures."

Money, not sex, consumed Garbo during the spring of 1932. Fame gave her leverage, but behind the hype of petulant mutiny, she was in fact the acquiescent studio employee. She never demanded to work with great directors, and her closest professional relationship was with William Daniels, the gay cinematographer who filmed most of her movies. MGM had slimmed her down, capped her teeth, adjusted her hairline, just as Paramount saw to it that Dietrich's wisdom teeth were pulled to allow her cheeks to sink, her ankles massaged until they were fat free, her eyebrows plucked, and her breasts lifted with surgical tape. It was money, not roles, that sent Garbo and Dietrich into sulks and suspensions. Neither was ever just a brainless twit, and both had Harry Edington as their agent.

Shortly after Garbo finished *Grand Hotel,* she became a victim of one of the many bank failures that deepened the Depression. In *Here Lies the Heart,* Mercedes would tell how she dreamt that Garbo came to her in distress to say the bank in which she kept her savings had failed. In her dream, Mercedes ran to the attic, found an old handbag, got Garbo out of bed, and had her chauffeur rush them down to the bank. Police were outside to keep angry depositors at bay. With Garbo in tow, however, Mercedes managed to get in through the back door, commandeer the manager to open Garbo's safety box, and scoop her securities and valuables into the handbag.

In reality, Mercedes was no less resourceful. In the face of rumors that the Beverly Hills Bank was failing, Mercedes phoned a New York banker friend, who advised her to grab Garbo, rush to the bank, and retrieve whatever they could. James chauffeured Garbo and her friend down to the bank. The two women managed to get past irate depositors in front, security guards in the back, and to rescue the valuables in Garbo's safety box. However, a million dollars she had on deposit were lost.

Mayer and Thalberg squeezed another film out of Garbo before her contract ran out. *As You Desire Me* was an adaptation of Luigi Pirandello's new play, *Come tu me vuoi.* Garbo plays a cabaret star suffering from amnesia, and Erich von Stroheim the man she is never sure is her husband. Salka was responsible for getting Garbo and von Stroheim together, and Garbo for getting him hired as her costar. At their get-together at Salka's, Mr. von Stroheim—nobody called him Erich—told Garbo he was interested because he had heard the role was a caricature of Ferenc Molnár. For the ambitious picture, Garbo bleached her hair and Von, as his friends called him, shaved off his. It was a painful time for the man who had once lorded over such MGM productions as *Greed* and *The Merry Widow*, but Garbo protected him. If there were days when he felt he couldn't report to work, she told him to phone her so she could inform Thalberg that *she* was indisposed. At home, she rehearsed one of her most difficult scenes with Mercedes.

If Garbo had one offscreen talent, it was for wresting more money out of Louis B. Mayer. The contract that had brought her and Mauritz Stiller to Culver City in 1925 had paid her $600 a week, but as soon as she discovered that the studio paid her costar, John Gilbert, $10,000 a week, she had informed Mayer she wanted a raise and that $5,000 a week would do. Louis B. exploded. Such ingratitude! He had brought her to America, given her a chance to become a star, spent money building her up—and this was the way she thanked him! Unmoved, she walked out of his office.

Their standoff had lasted seven months. Mayer cut off her salary and had the publicity department issue news releases that wondered whether the Immigration Department could grant a visa extension to this unemployed alien. Gilbert told her to wring every penny out of Mayer. More importantly, he introduced her to Harry Edington, a former MGM accountant who had set himself up as a business manager to the stars and included Dietrich among his clients. Edington had demanded a five-year contract paying Garbo $5,000 a week, fifty-two weeks a year, whether she worked or not. To undermine her bargaining power Thalberg imported Eva von Pletzner from Austria, renamed her von Berne, and put her in *Mask of the Devil* with Gilbert. The picture bombed and Eva was sent back to Vienna.

This time, Louis B. Mayer had until the end of July to make Garbo a contract offer, and in advance of the negotiations, both sides sharpened their tactics. To undercut her expected demand for more money, Mayer showed Edington what he called the less than smashing figures for *Mata Hari*. In rebuttal, Edington showed the January 7, 1932, issue of the *Hollywood Reporter* with its *"Mata Hari* Hits $80,000 for 4 Days" headline and the trade paper's January 14 front page, saying that in its third week the film was still packing New York's Capitol Theater. To make the point that Garbo was uncooperative, Mayer invited her to the *Grand Hotel* West Coast premiere at Grauman's Chinese Theater, knowing full well she wouldn't come.

Garbo's—and de Acosta's—counterploys were no less calculated. While Mercedes spread rumors that Garbo might not renew, Garbo returned Salka's *Queen Christina* outline without comments, as if she had not read it. To keep Mayer further off-balance, she let him know she planned a visit to her homeland. Since her contract expired July 31 at midnight, she had booked passage from New York to Göteborg aboard a Swedish-American liner scheduled to sail during the early hours of August 1, 1932.

It seems impossible that Mayer and Thalberg didn't know she had lost a fortune in the bank collapse, but in her memoirs de Acosta would claim they did not. "If MGM knew the position she [Garbo] was in, it was quite possible they would reduce their offer, knowing full well that being pressed for money she would have to accept the reduction."

To cut down her expenses, Garbo vacated a $1,000-a-month home on San Vicente Boulevard and moved into de Acosta's rented house. For appearance sake, Mercedes rented a house half a block away on Rockingham Road for herself and her roommate, John Colton. Rockingham Road lost itself in the as-yet-unsettled canyons of the Santa Monica mountains. On days off, Mercedes and Garbo rented horses from the Bel Air Riding School and rode up into the hills.

The sewing circle grapevine—if not Mercedes's own letters to far-flung friends—led to surprise visits. Katharine Cornell rang the doorbell, unannounced, one Sunday morning. Garbo fled upstairs. Cornell, who concealed her passion for women in her long-term marriage to the bisexual Broadway producer-director Guthrie McClintic, was on the first leg of a national tour, the star of a company of forty that included the young Orson Welles. She no doubt guessed *la divina* was in the house and that Mercedes was actually dying to introduce her, because she cattily delayed her departure and, for old times' sake, asked for breakfast. Since their time together, she had triumphed in *A Bill of Divorcement* and reached stardom in *The Green Hat* as Iris March, on whom Thalberg had wanted Mercedes to pattern her *Desperate* heroine. United Artists was after Kitty to repeat her stage success in the screen version of *The Barretts of Wimpole Street*, she sighed, but the movies were just not for her. Garbo finally came down to be introduced.

A few weeks before Garbo's scheduled departure for New York and Stockholm, she and Mercedes took a long hike on the beach. On the spur of the moment, Garbo decided they should look in on Ernst Lubitsch.

"Mein Gott, mein Gott," shouted Lubitsch when he saw Garbo in the doorway.

Ona Munson, the actress he was living with, nearly dropped the two cocktails she was carrying in from the kitchen, but had the presence of mind to offer one to Garbo.

Lubitsch pulled Garbo down on the sofa next to him and asked, "Vhy don't you tell those idiots in your studio to let us do a picture together. *Gott,* how I vould love to direct a picture with you."

She smiled. "You tell them, Ernst. I am far too tired to talk to studio executives."

While Lubitsch told her how stupid Mayer and Thalberg were, Munson took Mercedes into the kitchen, and said, "I've always wanted to meet you. Nazimova told me a lot about you."

Born Owena Wolcott in Portland, Oregon, Munson had been in vaudeville at fourteen. She had rocketed to fame in musical comedies, playing the title role in *No, No Nanette,* and made her film debut opposite Edward G. Robinson in the film *Five Star Final.* She collected the works of Picasso, Dalí and Braque. Mercedes found her extremely pretty. "The thing that struck me," Mercedes would write, "were her eyes. They were very sad, and there was something about them that touched me deeply."

They didn't meet again for another seven years, but became lovers in 1940. "I long to hold you in my arms and pour my love into you," Ona wrote Mercedes that year. In a letter six years later, Ona wrote of having shared "the deepest spiritual moments that life brings to human beings" and "created an entity as sure as though [we] had conceived and borne a child."

* * *

The weeks leading up to Garbo's departure were quarrelsome for her and Mercedes. Echoes of their fights reached the ears of Anita Loos, who, three months later, spread the gossip in a letter to Cecil Beaton:

> There has been so much going on in our set here that every time I think of writing I am swamped with the idea of trying to tell it all. The Garbo-Mercedes business has been too amazing. They had terrible battles, and Garbo left without saying goodbye. Then Mercedes flew to NY to see her and Garbo wouldn't. Mercedes flew back, despondent—lost her job with MGM and is in the most awful state. Also says she is broke—can't get a break and it's too terrible.

De Acosta would never say whether she went East with Garbo, but in Gronowicz's retelling, the lovers left for New York together. They eluded the press waiting for the Twentieth Century Limited to pull into Manhattan's Grand Central by getting off the train at the 125th Street station in Harlem and checking into the Hotel Gramatan in the Westchester County suburb of Bronxville.

Masquerading as Harriet Brown and Lilyan Tashman, Garbo and Mercedes went shopping in New York. They were on Fifth Avenue a few days before the oceanliner's departure when, while Mercedes was gazing at a window display, a man who looked strikingly like the late Mauritz Stiller stepped in front of Garbo and told her to commit suicide on his grave.

The man disappeared as Mercedes turned around, caught the deathly pale Garbo by the waist, got her to the curb, and flagged down a cab. Lying in bed back in their hideaway hotel, Garbo told Mercedes how she had been born into shabbiness, how she had adored the alcoholic laborer who was her father and hated her mother. She had left school at thirteen, a year before her father died. She lost her faith when her mother had an affair with their pastor and experienced her first gush of sexual pleasure one summer when her older sister, Alva, tickled her between the legs and invited her to do the same to her. After a boy's clumsy attempt at penetrating her, Greta dreamed about a man with experience, and about women who were lovers. A new life had begun when Stiller picked her out of a lineup of drama-school students. Until the day

Thalberg fired Stiller, the director had been in absolute command of her life.

It was dark in the hotel room when Garbo finished telling Mercedes how an old gypsy had foretold her and Stiller's future, saying he would die like a rat, lonely and far away from her, while she would live among many people but have no friends. Mercedes extracted small statues of Saint Francis of Assisi, the Virgin Mary, Saint Teresa, and Buddha from her trunk. Exorcism, she said, was the only way to drive away Stiller's evil spirits. Because Stiller was suffering in hell, he had sent a devil to meet Garbo on Fifth Avenue and demand that she kill herself. Mercedes placed the statues in the four corners of the room, lighted aromatic candles in front of them, knelt in the middle of the room, and took her clothes off.

"Come here, kneel beside me, and get undressed," she said. "Let the fragrant smoke and my prayers touch your naked body and protect you."

The two naked women knelt on the floor. Mercedes spoke in tongues, in turn addressing Mary, Francis, Teresa, and Buddha. After a while Garbo felt free, peaceful, and sleepy. In a trance, she saw herself floating in a church, surrounded by the faces of a thousand young girls. When she awoke, she and Mercedes were lying in bed. Mercedes touched her and said the spirit of Mauritz Stiller would no longer haunt her.

Garbo's decision to go to Sweden alone forced them to discuss the nature of their relationship. The trip to her homeland was the first of several well-publicized trips, and Garbo wanted no company. Mercedes accused her of being a slave to her career, sacrificing the happiness of those who loved her, and caring for nothing besides fame and money.

"God accepts me as I am," Garbo would remember saying. "So should you."

Mercedes snapped, "I am sure you're afraid of being accused of having sapphic inclinations."

"You're right."

Eluding a thousand fans, Garbo slipped on board the SS *Gripsholm* the morning of July 31 and locked herself in her stateroom. An hour before the midnight sailing, two representatives from Loews,

MGM's parent company, knocked on her door and presented her with a contract draft. They also handed her an expensive watch from Mayer. Other bon voyage gifts included a gold cigarette case from cameraman Bill Daniels, and from John Gilbert, an antique bracelet she suspected the studio had made him buy. There was also a package containing books on Queen Christina.

When a steward announced the ship's imminent departure, she accompanied the representatives to the gangplank. She would need time to consider the contract, she told the disembarking Loews men. Off the Long Island coast, she read the contract proposal. She was to receive $250,000 per picture, and her insistence on making only two films a year was negotiable.

Mercedes returned to Los Angeles, where Thalberg had a job for her, and on the rebound became the lover of Marlene Dietrich. In Stockholm, Garbo resumed an affair with Countess Wachtmeister.

9

Dietrich on the Rebound

Marlene Dietrich would remember finding Mercedes sobbing in the Thalbergs' kitchen during a party. After being told Garbo's cruelty was the reason for the tears, Dietrich wrote to her husband in Paris:

> Thalberg had one of those very grand parties. I met a writer, Spanish, very attractive, named Mercedes de Acosta. They say Garbo's crazy about her. For me, she was a relief from this narrow Hollywood mentality. Here they should build all the churches in the shape of a box office. Kisses.

There would be no tears in Mercedes's recollection. In her memoirs, they both attended a performance by the German dancer Harald Kreutzberg, Mercedes sitting a row behind Dietrich and her escort, Cecil Beaton. At one point, Marlene turned in her seat and introduced herself.

Mercedes was at her writing desk the next day when her maid, Anna, entered with a large bouquet of white roses and announced Dietrich was downstairs. Mercedes went to greet her guest. Shaking her hand, Marlene explained she knew few people in Hollywood and had brought the white flowers "because you looked like a white prince last night." She found Mercedes to be sad and said she was herself unhappy and lonely. With some exaggeration she went on to say Mercedes was the first person she had felt drawn to. "Unconventional as it may seem, I came to see you because I just could not help myself."

Florist vans delivered bouquets of roses, carnations, and rare orchids flown in from San Francisco for days until the maid despaired of finding enough vases. When Mercedes let her admirer know of Anna's desperation, Marlene sent Lalique vases instead, followed by dressing gowns, scarves, pajamas, slacks, and lamps from Bullock's department store.

"The way Marlene looked and dressed was different," Ruth Albu would recall. Albu and Dietrich played chorus girls on a Berlin stage in 1927. "I was eighteen, six years younger than Marlene, and, like everybody else, I found her startlingly beautiful and fascinating." The play was a German-language edition of *Broadway*, George Abbott and Philip Dunning's spicy story about chorus girls and a vaudevillian's climb to stardom. "The first time I saw her walking across the stage, I knew she was different. When stage johnnies knocked and came into our dressing room, we all scurried into dressing gowns. Not Marlene. She didn't care what men saw. I always thought this denoted a lack of interest in sex."

The young Dietrich was a good-natured girl with no particular ambition or talent. She was at times touching and endearing, even though stardom gave her an ego that was enormous, perhaps pathological. She was challenging and ironic, sentimental and impressionable, someone for whom nothing is unimportant, and liked to make herself believe that deep down she was a woman in love with married bliss. Albu and Dietrich reached California at the same time in 1930, Albu as the wife of Heinrich Schnitzler, and daughter-in-law of Viennese playwright Arthur Schnitzler. In Hollywood, interest in sex was no less than in Berlin. "One was aware that everything was going on, bisexuality, of course," Albu would remember. "What was different was the drinking egged on by the Prohibition. Hollywood parties rarely ended in sex orgies, because the men got drunk."

Albu might think Marlene sentimental, impressionable, endearing, and careless. To the early 1930s threadbare audiences who demanded creatures of dreams on their silver screens, the Dietrich face, name, stance, and presence spelled mystery and allure.

Dietrich came out of the social chaos of post–World War I Berlin, an army widow's daughter with theatrical aspirations. Like the teenaged Garbo and de Acosta, Marlene was in love with theater celebrities. As a teenager she not only plucked her eyebrows to resemble Henny Porten, Germany's first movie star, but on her violin serenaded the actress under her Berlin window and, when she discovered Henny Porten's name among Alpine resort guests at Garmisch, pursued her with more early-morning fiddling.

From her earliest appearances in cabaret, onstage, and in film, Dietrich toyed with a libidinous cool that audiences found provocative. She was a star by 1927, her name above the title in films in which she played larcenous amours or courtesans giving men love lessons. In *Ich küsse ihre Hand, Madame* (I Kiss Your Hand, Madame) she was a heavy-eyed divorcée who, when an obese little lawyer offers to do anything in the world for her, replies, "All right, you can walk my dog." *Das Schiff der verlorenen Menschen* (The Ship of Lost Men) had her as an American aviatrix rescued twice—first when her plane crashes at sea and she is picked up by a ship, second when its lustful crew is about to have their way with her. The plot allowed her to be attractive in men's clothes. Surviving stills show her in borrowed seaman's pants and sweater on deck and surprising Fritz Kortner and Gaston Modot, who are ready to fight over her. In the sketch comedy set in a department store, *Es liegt was in her Luft,* Dietrich and Margo Lion, the openly bisexual French actress, created a sensation with a number called "Sisters." In similar black dresses and huge hats, they sang a duet, Lion singing in a falsetto and Marlene in a smoky, low register, about two girlfriends buying underwear for each other.

Dietrich was a young mother constantly working in film and cabaret when *The Blue Angel,* her first film with Josef von Sternberg, fashioned the image that became legendary—the sensual blonde with her provocative legs and bracing insolence singing through clouds of cigarette smoke in an overcrowded dive. Each of the six Hollywood movies Sternberg and Dietrich made together would include a scene of her dressed as a man.

Much of what Garbo suggested on the screen, Dietrich showed. Unlike the reclusive Garbo, Marlene was a shimmering and vibrant hedonist who frolicked in Hollywood night after night, sipping champagne with a trademark single white rose petal floating on the surface. Lesbians propositioned her in restaurant and night-club rest rooms. During World War II, Dido Renoir, the Brazilian wife of director Jean Renoir, would remember Marlene asking her to come to the ladies' room with her. Dido assumed the reason was that the actress wanted to show off her famous legs, but Marlene told her she needed protection from women who assailed her.

While she was being drawn to lovers, male and female, Marlene's lifelong commitment was to Rudi, the husband she supported in style in Paris. "Papilein," as she and their daughter, Maria, called him, never spied or accused, and in her unending stream of letters, telegrams, and transatlantic telephone calls to him, she was, in her own way, obsessively honest. Falling in love with Mercedes was no exception. In a follow-up letter the next day, Marlene wrote:

> Papilein,
> I saw Mercedes de Acosta again. Apparently Garbo gives her a hard time, not just by playing around—which by the way is why she is in the hospital with gonorrhea—also she is the kind of person who counts every cube of sugar to make sure the maid isn't stealing or eating too well. I am sorry for Mercedes. Her face was white and thin and she seemed sad and lonely—as I am—and not well. I was attracted to her and brought an armful of tuberoses to her house. I told her I would cook marvelous things for her and get her well and strong.

Dietrich's missives to her husband are to be taken with a grain of salt. Marlene was a law unto herself, and her information, when relayed to Papilein, acquired the power of truth. It is hard to imagine her crawling into bed with de Acosta if she knew Mercedes to be the lover of the venereal-diseased Garbo. By August, when Marlene joined Rudi and his mistress in Paris and he suffered a kidney-stone attack, she wasn't sure whether it was Garbo or Erich von Stroheim who had had urinary problems during the filming of *As You Desire Me*. "Mercedes, sweetheart," came her familiar voice over the transatlantic telephone, "Rudi has kidney stones—I have to find a great doctor. Didn't Garbo have some trouble with peeing—

or was that Stroheim when she made that awful picture with him, where she looked like a bleached chicken?" Marlene was off the phone before Mercedes could suggest remedies.

Dietrich was noted for performing fellatio on her male lovers—it gave her the power to direct the scene—but preferred to go to bed with women. Women were better in bed, she said, "but you can't *live* with a woman." She would dismiss most of the actors who starred in her films as having "a peanut where other humans have a brain."

Her affair with Mercedes was sensual. Mercedes wrote Marlene:

> Wonderful one,
> It is one week today since your beautiful naughty hand opened a white rose. Last night was even more wonderful and each time I see you it grows more wonderful and exciting. You with your exquisite white pansy face—and before you go to bed will you ring me so that I can just hear your voice.

"Say what you want about Mercedes," remarked Alice B. Toklas, "she had the three most important women of the twentieth century." De Acosta bragged that she could get any woman from any man. She let the sewing circle know about her affairs with Garbo and Dietrich, and a wag speculated the third conquest Toklas alluded to was either Gertrude Stein or Eleanor Roosevelt. In the 1950s when Truman Capote became Mercedes's friend and coaxed stories about her sex life from her, he invented a game called International Daisy Chain. Its goal was to connect people sexually through as few beds as possible, and the author of *Breakfast at Tiffany's* maintained the best card to hold was Mercedes because "you could get to anyone—from Cardinal Spellman to the Duchess of Windsor."

As concocted by Sternberg, Dietrich's screen persona of a listless woman who was the equal of a man, even in gallantry, metamorphosed her into a temptress of no particular gender. Less peculiar than Garbo about who watched her act, Marlene was no less narcissistic. She knew every angle of her face, taught herself lighting techniques, and had herself filmed with a mirror next to the camera so she could watch her own make-believe. She insisted on wearing trousers everywhere, and when her pants caused a sensation, she was promoted—in the mercurial spirit of the studio system—as "the woman even women can adore." Clothes were important enough for her to seduce Irene (née Irene Lentz), the designer who took over when Adrian left MGM in a huff in 1941.

Sternberg and Dietrich were yoked at the hip. The Viennese-born writer-director was a pale, fragile man with brooding brown eyes, a shock of dark hair, and a drooping mustache who gave himself the airs of a fop and affected the fake "von," asserting power over others by staring at them under heavy, snakelike lids and wondering aloud about the abysmal depth of human stupidity. The son of poor Orthodox Jews, he had come to New York at fourteen and, after a patchy education, started to work as an assistant film editor. Dietrich was already a name in German jazz-age movies when Sternberg came to Berlin in 1929 and chose her to play the fleshy Lola-Lola in *The Blue Angel*. Marlene hated the part, and her relationship with her director remained fierce, obstinate, and fractious.

She also hated Los Angeles and never really unpacked. Her various rented homes were as impersonal as the movie sets they imitated. She liked a black-and-white decor, and in her affection for zebra and leopard rugs more than one slick magazine found an echo of her monkey suit in *Blonde Venus*. Her lovers came to worship in her bed, but because of The Child, as she called her daughter, Maria, no stranger ever appeared at the breakfast table in a dressing gown. "It must have been exhausting and uncomfortable for everyone," Maria would write in her memoirs sixty years later, "those predawn maneuvers of getting up, dressing, and driving home, only to return a few hours later as though nothing had 'transpired.'"

Marlene had just been through a traumatic experience. The kidnapping and murder of Charles and Anne Lindbergh's two-year-old son, Charles, in March 1932 triggered copycat attempts. The Depression had wiped out one out of four 1929 jobs, and for criminal minds, the movie colony was a choice target. A month after little Charles Lindbergh was found murdered, extortionists threatened to kidnap Marlene and Rudi's seven-year-old Maria.

The extortion note was made out of pasted-up newspaper letters and read, "Your daughter will be kidnapped unless you give us $10,000. Have the money by May 16. Leave your car in front of your home and put money package about six inches from rear on bumper. Keep silent. Don't be crazy. Quick action. Want only $5 and $10 bills. Lindbergh business." Beverly Hills police were alerted. Marlene told Maria everything.

During waking hours Marlene never let her daughter out of sight. She telephoned Rudi in Paris and told him to come. He set off immediately, but to get from Europe to Los Angeles took at least ten days of continuous travel. In the meantime, Marlene hired detectives to roam the rented house and surrounding garden around the clock. Iron bars were added to the windows, an electric alarm system installed. Maria slept on the floor near her governess, who was armed. During the day, Marlene brought the girl to the studio where other guards stayed with her at all times. Rudi arrived as quickly as he could.

The story grew as the deadline approached. Paramount issued a statement in her name, saying "necessary measures were taken to safeguard the child as well as myself." On May 16, FBI detectives put a bag of fake money on the bumper and staked out the parked automobile. Nobody came to collect the money. The incident led Marlene to rent and fortify the North Roxbury Drive residence of Charles Mack, a vaudeville comic popular on radio. Incongruously, neighbors, fans, and would-be kidnappers knew she was home when her blue Rolls-Royce roadster was in the driveway. Her meeting Mercedes made her move again, this time renting Marion Davies's beach house at 321 Ocean Front Avenue in Santa Monica.

Dietrich's letters to her husband documented their affair. Marlene and Mercedes became lovers on September 16, 1932, and when Mercedes drove her back to her beach house at the end of their afternoon tryst, Marlene got out of the car in a hurry so that her daughter would not see her. A few days later, however, Marlene had Mercedes over to meet Maria. One evening when Sternberg insisted on seeing Dietrich, she apologized to Mercedes for not joining her for dinner and asked her to wait in bed. Maria didn't like Mercedes and, behind her back, called her Dracula.

Mercedes called Dietrich her "Golden One" and signed her letters to her by her childhood name, Rafael. She composed a love verse, "For Marlene":

* * *

> Your face is lit by
> moonlight
> breaking through your
> skin
> soft, pale, radiant.
> No suntan for you glow
> For you are the essence
> of
> the stars and the moon
> and
> the mystery of the night

Marlene made fun of two German homosexuals who were houseguests overstaying their welcome. Martin Kosleck was a character actor who would specialize in playing Goebbels in World War II Hollywood movies. Hans von Twardowsky was married to Salka's and Mercedes's friend Eleonora von Mendelssohn. To add to the merriment—and little Maria's confusion—Rudi Sieber came from Paris with his Russian mistress, Tamara Tamul. While he worked to unravel the mess Marlene always made of their finances, "Tami" taught Maria to swim with the result that the girl fell in love with her father's lover. There were pool parties and ocean swimming, and moments when Rudi patiently listened to Mercedes telling him how she was dying of love for his wife.

Mercedes was busy working for Thalberg. She happily plunged into the story of Grigory Rasputin, the monk whose pathological influence over Czar Nicholas II and Empress Alexandra contributed to the Romanovs' overthrow and the establishment of Lenin's Bolshevism. It was all recent history. Prince Felix Yusopov, who, to save the monarchy, had killed the monk in December 1916, was living in London, a naturalized British subject. Mercedes had met him in Paris through Prince Agoustinsky, the erudite nobleman who eked out a delicate living selling fellow exiles' heirlooms.

The way Thalberg explained it, casting the *three* Barrymores was the gimmick that would make the story of the last days of czarist Russia work. Lionel Barrymore would chew up the scenery playing Rasputin. Sister Ethel, who hadn't been before the cameras in fourteen years, would be the empress, and Jack Barrymore, Rasputin's murderer. Mercedes's friend Diana Wynyard was cast as the czarina's lady-in-waiting. Mercedes had no trouble imagining the story of the mad monk and the troubled Romanovs in the grip of destiny.

As had happened on *Desperate,* she was summoned to Thalberg's office. When he had her in the low chair across from his desk, he told her he had an idea. He wanted her to write a scene in which Rasputin tries to seduce Princess Irina. "It must be a very violent and terrific scene," he said.

Mercedes objected that Rasputin and Princess Yusopov never met.

"Who cares?" Thalberg answered. "Putting this scene in gives strength to the whole plot."

"But this is history. History in our time with the people living who enacted it. Such a sequence would be absolutely unauthentic and probably libelous."

Thalberg rose impatiently. "I don't need you to tell me a lot of nonsense about what is libelous or what is not. I want this sequence in and that is all there is to it."

With that he walked out of his office and slammed the door.

Mercedes went home deeply disturbed. She realized that if she refused to write the scene, Thalberg would fire her. That night she sat down and in her big handsome scrawl wrote a letter to Prince Agoustinsky. She asked him to tell Prince Yusopov that she was writing this scenario for MGM and wanted to know how much she could use of the story he had told her about Rasputin and his murder. For further advice and comfort, she went to see Krishnamurti. The guru suggested she give up the job rather than write the sequence.

It took Thalberg several weeks to summon her back. When he did, she went to see him with a cable from Yusopov saying he trusted her with the story but forbade her to mention Irina.

When she handed Thalberg the cable, he exploded, "How dare you consult anyone about this picture?"

She answered that she had probably spared the company a lawsuit. To see if he could fire her on the spot, Thalberg summoned a messenger to bring in her contract. Before it arrived, she fired herself by saying her friends came before the industry. When the contract arrived, he tore it up. Charles MacArthur finished the script, with Ben Hecht blocking out the action. To cover himself just in case, Thalberg had MacArthur fictionalize Yusopov as Prince Paul Chegodieff. Charles Brabin started filming *Rasputin and the Empress* during the 1932 Los Angeles Olympics, only to be fired for incompetence and replaced by Richard Boleslawski. Thalberg—or people in his entourage—made sure de Acosta was ostracized by other studios. Again and again, Harry Edington reported back to her that he couldn't get her a job anywhere.

Dietrich was also under pressure. *Blonde Venus,* her fourth American movie with Sternberg, had been a flop, and both the studio and her director—but not Marlene—felt it was time for a change. At a stormy meeting at her house, Sternberg told her that after five films with her he was drained, that, as Paramount demanded, she should make *Song of Songs* with Rouben Mamoulian. Feeling betrayed, Marlene froze in anger and, after Sternberg left, locked herself in her bedroom for twenty-four hours. Her finances didn't allow her to pout any longer.

Marlene's lifestyle was as extravagant as Garbo's was miserly. Besides supporting the Ocean Front Avenue menagerie, that is, the rented villa, the staff, bodyguards, and assorted hangers-on, her earnings kept Papilein in style in Paris and on transatlantic wanderings with Tami, and Marlene's mother in Berlin. In early September, Paramount laid down the law, knowing full well she could not afford to say no: report to Mamoulian for *Song of Songs* or forfeit her $300,000 salary and be sued for the $185,000 it had cost the studio to turn Hermann Südermann's 1908 novel *Das hohe Lied* (Song of Songs) into a Dietrich vehicle. Marlene consented to meet the director.

Ironically, Rouben Mamoulian, specifically imported from Broadway to transfer stage successes to the screen, became one of Hollywood's leading directors by revolting against "canned theater." By appreciating the use of the close-up, and by making his camera pick out what was dramatically fresh and illuminating in a scene, he broke with his own theatrical brilliance. Lured from Broadway by Paramount's Jesse Lasky in 1929, he was, by his third film, *Dr. Jekyll and Mr. Hyde,* in full control of his new medium.

He and his wife, Azadia, were Georgians, he a Tbilisi banker's son who had spent part of his childhood in Paris, studied criminology at the University of Moscow, and trained for the stage at the

Moscow Art Theater under Konstantin Stanislavsky. Garbo fell in love with Azadia, and although the feelings were not reciprocated, they continued to see each other long after Mamoulian and Garbo finished *Queen Christina*. The thirty-four-year-old director was a forceful presence behind his horn-rimmed glasses. He mollified Marlene by telling her his approach to the romantic nonsense called *Song of Songs* would be theatrical and center on the development of her character.

The precocious Maria believed her mother would soon tire of Mercedes, but the two women showered each other with attention and affection. For Sunday tennis matches, Marlene decreed that she, Maria, and Mercedes wear similar creamy flannel trousers, shirts, and polo necks. *Song of Songs,* however, gave Marlene a new love interest. He was Brian Aherne, her costar. "Why do you, an important actor from Broadway, come here to make this silly picture?" Marlene asked him the first time they met. "I have to do it, because Mr. von Sternberg has walked out, and I am left without any protection. But you! Are you crazy?"

Aherne, who was English and therefore "cultured" in Marlene's mind, came to the house to meet his leading lady. For the duration of the visit, de Acosta was told to take eight-year-old Maria across the highway to the beach and watch her play and swim. Lionel Atwill was cast as the lecherous old baron.

As Marlene and Aherne became lovers, Mercedes came less and less to the house, but continued to send missives to Dietrich. Rudi and his mistress arrived from Europe. Marlene read aloud to her husband from Mercedes's letters:

> To try to explain my real feelings for Greta would be impossible since I really do not understand myself. I do know that I have built up in my emotions a person that does not exist. My mind sees the real person, a Swedish servant girl with a face touched by God—only interested in money, her health, sex, food, and sleep. And yet her face tricks my mind and my spirit builds her up into something that fights with my brain. I do love her but I only love the person I have created and not the person who is real. . . . Many times when I am away from you I desire you terribly and always when I am with you. I know you have felt my desire because I have known you when you felt it.

I only am as I am, and God knows I would give anything in my life to be different. You will see I shall get over this "insanity" and then perhaps you will love me a little again. But if I get over it what then shall I pray to? And what will then turn this gray life into starlight.

Another letter offered to bring anyone to Marlene's bed. Many years later when Maria discovered the letters, she wondered what would have happened had her mother taken Mercedes up on her offer and said, "Bring me Garbo."

The country was in the middle of an election campaign. President Herbert Hoover, who wanted to use the government's power sparingly, was so unpopular that mounted police had to protect him in several big cities, while Franklin D. Roosevelt crisscrossed the country in his special train, telling everybody he was ready to intervene directly to pull the country out of the Depression. On October 25, FDR gave his "four horsemen" speech in Baltimore. "Destruction, delay, deceit, and despair" were the horsemen of the Republican leadership.

Mayer and Thalberg were doing everything to defeat FDR and, for governor of California, Upton Sinclair. Faced with the state's gigantic unemployment and relief problems—three hundred thousand were unemployed in Los Angeles alone and destitute "Okies" were still pouring in—the novelist urged heavier taxes on high-income Californians and on movie studios. At MGM, word went out that everybody earning over $100 a week was expected to contribute one day's pay to the campaign of the Republican candidate for governor, Frank Merriam. For good measure, Mayer and Thalberg turned out a fake newsreel showing hordes of grimy vagrants entering California, ready to seize private property the moment Sinclair was elected. The "vagrants" were studio extras, and the pseudonewsreel, entitled *The Inquiring Reporter,* was distributed free to cinemas. Roosevelt was elected, winning forty-four out of forty-eight states. Sinclair was defeated. One of Governor Merriam's first acts was to pass an income tax law.

Rudi and Tami left for Paris—Tami with a trunk of Marlene's hand-me-down clothes. *Song of Songs* started filming in January 1933, as Hitler became Reich chancellor and a first wave of German liberals and Jews—among them the cream of Germany's intelligentsia—began the exodus that would eventually turn Los Angeles into a New Weimar on the Pacific. Mamoulian gave deft touches to the film. On Marlene's first visit to Aherne's studio, she is appalled to see his imaginary sketch of her ("Oh, I haven't any clothes on"), but nevertheless allows herself to be coaxed into posing, bashful and blushing, in the nude. When he watches her silhouette as she takes her clothes off, he caresses the statue he is making of her. As she leaves, she meets Atwill, who has commissioned the statue and mutters, "She interests me very much . . . *very much.*" Aherne's careless rejoinder, "She means nothing to me," provokes her to marry the baron, only to be finally reunited with the guilt-ridden sculptor. The visual titillation of the film is a life-size nude statue that, in the melodramatic ending, Marlene smashes with a sledgehammer.

De Acosta missed Garbo. The visit to her homeland had been another flight from crowds. Fans in Stockholm broke the window of a limousine she was riding in, and she escaped to the Tistad estate of Count and Countess Vilhelm Wachtmeister.

Count Vilhelm was a royal equerry and Tistad one of the largest and oldest estates in Sweden. Garbo spent most of the fall of 1932 at Tistad. With the countess, she visited the university town of Uppsala, saw the castle where Queen Christina gave up her throne in 1654, and studied portraits of the bachelor queen by Van Dyck and Velásquez. The countess persuaded the royal family to give Garbo access to its archives. Christina's life had not ended with her abdication, as Salka's script had it, but continued another thirty-five years. In exile in Rome the queen had surrounded herself with writers, painters, and musicians. Garbo read Strindberg's *Christina,* a play every Stockholm theater had rejected. When it was finally performed in 1908, seven years after he wrote it, it was savaged by critics as a ragbag of schoolboy howlers, insolent contentions, and insane distortions that had nothing to do with Swedish history. Living in the Renaissance queen's shadow and reading about her gave Garbo new insights into her. Christina, too, she found out, had disguised herself as a man and referred to herself as male.

Ivor Novello arrived from London and took Mercedes to dinner at the home of Joan Crawford and Douglas Fairbanks Jr. Mercedes saw other British friends, including Laurence Olivier and Jill

Esmond. Their marriage was a sham. On the wedding night, she had turned away from her husband in revulsion. The two had appeared in the Broadway production of Nöel Coward's *Private Lives* and were now in Hollywood, where RKO had signed them to a forty-week contract. Olivier was cast opposite Lili Damita and Adolphe Menjou in *Friends and Lovers,* and Esmond was loaned out to Paramount to appear with Ivor Novello and Ruth Chatterton in *Once a Lady.* They were staying at the Garden of Allah, a raffish if pricey collection of bungalows around a large swimming pool on Sunset Boulevard patronized by actors and writers in transition. Jill had discovered the sewing circle, and its newest member, Cheryl Crawford, the theatrical producer and cofounder, with Lee Strasberg and Harold Clurman, of the new Group Theater in New York.

Diana Wynyard was a new sewing circle member. She was one of the first of the Hollywood English ladies. She had repeated on Broadway in 1932 her London triumph opposite Basil Rathbone in *The Devil Passes* and came west the same year, bringing allure, poise, and patrician good looks to early Fox and MGM talkies. She found Tinseltown quite mad as she was simultaneously cast in the film of Nöel Coward's *Cavalcade* and in *Rasputin and the Empress,* winning an Academy Award nomination for the former. Wynyard shared a beach house in Santa Monica with a lady friend, who was lying in the bathtub when the 1932 Long Beach earthquake hit. The woman ran screaming from the agitated tub before floorboards gave way and sent water cascading. Mercedes rushed over to help mop up.

Mercedes spent a mundane Christmas Eve at Adrian's, bringing Dietrich. Lots of money had transformed a former Spanish-mission house of stucco and overwrought ironwork into a suite of airy rooms with blue shadows. Adrian's guests gathered under a pepper tree on the patio with a family of monkeys in a two-story wire cage forming the backdrop. Constance Collier made a grande-dame entrance, Basil Rathbone recited a scatological limerick, and everybody sat down for an exquisite dinner. Mercedes was introduced to Hedda Hopper, but didn't rate a mention in the next day's column. When Mercedes got home, she found a telegram from Garbo, wishing her a merry Christmas and telling her she would soon be back.

10

Queen Christina

Garbo came back—the long way through the Panama Canal—in March 1933. Salka Viertel, whose husband was with the Soviet cinema's gifted Sergei Eisenstein in Mexico on the doomed *Que Viva Mexico* shoot for Paramount, greeted the returning star when the freighter docked. Mercedes found a new rental home for her on San Vicente Boulevard.

Dietrich prepared to depart as Garbo arrived. We don't know whether de Acosta was the cause, but Marlene's daughter would intimate that her mother was tiring of Mercedes's "cloying emotionalism," and her need to explain her feelings for Garbo.

Marlene, her husband, and her daughter were German citizens. Hitler's ascension to chancellor on January 30, 1933, and the burning of the Reichstag three weeks later, convinced Rudi this was no time to go to Berlin. From Paris, he cabled his wife that if she returned to Germany, she might not be allowed to leave again unless she was in possession of a new American film contract. If she wanted to see her mother and sister, they could all rendezvous in Austria.

Marlene signed the Paramount contract Harry Edington had negotiated because, in addition to a sizable salary increase, it gave her script and director approval. She decided to forgive Sternberg.

He, in turn, convinced himself he should make another film with her. What did he have in mind? The story of the rise of a guileless young princess to a mocking and ruthless empress. He would spend the summer writing a fantasy on the love life of Russia's Catherine the Great.

Dietrich gave her approval, and with her daughter left for Paris.

In signing *her* contract, Garbo agreed to star in *Queen Christina,* and to have Rouben Mamoulian direct her. As previously noted, the new contract paid her $250,000 per picture. She had approval of directors, cameramen, costar. If a film took longer than twelve weeks to shoot, she was paid an additional $10,000. A special clause gave her days off during her menstrual period.

After directing Dietrich, who else would be Mamoulian's next step up but Garbo. He could afford to be difficult, and as a condition for signing on with MGM, he asked for a rewrite of the Viertel-Meredyth script.

The rewrite man Mamoulian brought to the project was S. N. Behrman. Sam Behrman, with his squat body and large head, thought himself physically ugly. The son of a rabbi in Worcester, Massachusetts, he had written seventeen plays before the first one was produced on Broadway. With Dorothy Parker and her gay husband Alan Campbell, Robert Benchley, and Donald Ogden Stewart, Behrman belonged to the sophisticates who sat in writers' offices, all a little too clever for their own good, telling each other they were going to seed in the California sun, although in the best possible style. In "buzz sessions," as story conferences were called (at Warners', the conference room was called the "echo chamber"), they talked pulp into formula, each trying to add, as one wit had it, "to the compost heap."

Thalberg liked to keep writers laboring on the same project unaware of each other's input. Salka was not to see the new man. Behrman traipsed into her office, however, told her to call him Sam, and struck up a friendship that lasted for years.

Salka and Garbo made a habit of dropping in for tea on Sundays at Behrman's rented Beverly Hills house. One day he felt emboldened enough to ask the star how she got mixed up with an alcoholic like John Gilbert. Behrman would write, "Very slowly, in her cello voice, she said, 'I was lonely—and I couldn't speak English.'"

In the final script, Queen Christina is first seen as a child being introduced to her Parliament as their future ruler and, in a speech written for her, promising to continue the war that killed her father. Fifteen years later, members of her Parliament clamor for the adult Christina to continue the war and to marry a military hero. The story line has her distressed at the thought of a political marriage. She wanders through her country in men's clothes and falls in love with Don Antonio de la Prada, the Spanish ambassador, who had come to woo her for his king only to fall in love with her himself.

Story conferences honed the queen's love of women down to one audacious scene. Here, Countess Ebba Sparre bursts into the queen's chambers, and the two kiss passionately on the lips. Ebba suggests they go for a sleigh ride, but Christina says Parliament awaits her. They will see each other in the evening. "Oh, no, we won't," Ebba pouts, "you will be surrounded by musty old men and musty old papers." The queen caresses Ebba's face and promises they will soon go to the country together "for two whole days."

Legend would have it that it was Garbo's idea to play most of the film in drag. Adrian, not she, was in charge of costume design, and she liked his sketches of her Renaissance wardrobe. She fell in love with a tall fur hat that flopped down coquettishly to one side and told him the clothes looked better than the designs he had done for *Mata Hari*.

Behrman wrote crisp dialogue, but the cross-dressing posed problems: How would Don Antonio know the man he's (1) washing hands with, (2) tossing a book to, and (3) asking to open a window is a woman? They decided the queen would betray her true gender when Don Antonio, asking for help in unlacing an obstinate boot, catches the outline of her breast beneath her thin shirt as she kneels to untie the knot.

Elizabeth Young, a New York socialite and a member of the film colony's smart set, was cast as Ebba Sparre. The part of Chancellor Axel Oxenstierna was given to Lewis Stone, with whom Garbo had made seven pictures. As for her leading man, Garbo turned down Leslie Howard, Franchot Tone, Nils Asther, and Bruce Cabot, but agreed to Thalberg and Salka's choice—Laurence Olivier.

After wooing Olivier for several months, MGM had signed the promising new actor to a $1,000-a-week, three-month contract. With his wife, Jill Esmond, Olivier came out from New York. He reported for work August 1, to be introduced to an impatient Mamoulian and a sullen, withdrawn Garbo.

For their first scene together, Mamoulian selected a boudoir setting in which Don Antonio embraces the queen with such passion that she gives up her boyishness. On the set, Mamoulian told the actor to come forward, hold Garbo by the waist, look her in the eyes, and in gesture and monologue awaken the passion for which she will be willing to give up her throne. "I went into my role giving it everything I had," Olivier would remember, "but at the touch of my hand Garbo became frigid. I could feel the sudden tautness of her, her eyes as stony and expressionless as if she were marble."

After three days' shooting, Garbo went to see Mayer and asked for John Gilbert. Mayer exploded. They had just gotten rid of Jack and certainly didn't want him back. As usual, Garbo let the boss rant. When he calmed down, she went home and sent word she was too ill to report to work, even for scenes that did not involve her leading man. Mayer got the message. Olivier was fired, and Gilbert was Don Antonio. Shooting resumed August 4 before Gilbert had time to dry out.

While Marlene, her husband, daughter, and Tami were sightseeing in France, Switzerland, and Austria—and, at Rudi's insistence, avoiding Germany—Mercedes and Garbo made up. Garbo was a changed person, warm and pleasant toward her lover. Still, when Mercedes had a car accident that disfigured her face, it was not Garbo, but Dietrich, who, on the transatlantic telephone from Paris, found L.A.'s best plastic surgeon, told him to spare no expense, and to charge her friend's surgery to her. The procedure was primitive, and Mercedes's face underwent a series of painful surgeries and recoveries.

If Mercedes needed a lift, she got it with the aftermath of *Rasputin and the Empress*. Although Charles MacArthur was nominated for a best screenplay Academy Award, Prince Felix Yusopov's lawsuit generated more drama than the movie. When attorneys representing Yusopov asked if de Acosta would come to London to testify that the prince had cabled his objections to seeing his wife impersonated and that Thalberg had seen this cable, MGM suddenly hired Mercedes again.

Thalberg called Edington to say her joblessness was "a big mistake," invited her to see him, and at their first meeting asked her what she would like to do. He agreed Joan of Arc would be a marvelous vehicle for Garbo, put Mercedes on payroll, and, two months later, pronounced himself delighted with her first draft.

Prince Yusopov's libel action went to trial in London in February 1934. Without Mercedes's testimony, Yusopov won record damages of twenty-five thousand pounds ($1 million in 2001 money). As MGM realized it would have to settle with other aggrieved parties, it did so. The film was a net loss.

Thalberg was never man enough to apologize to Mercedes.

Garbo and Gilbert played their best scene almost silent. They are in a room at the inn after their first night together. As the ambassador watches, bemused and beguiled, the queen moves slowly around the room, touching and caressing the furniture as if to burn the memory of the night into her mind. Mamoulian called the scene a sonnet. "This has to be sheer poetry and feeling," he told her. "The movement must be like a dance. Treat it in the way you would do it to music."

For Gilbert, *Queen Christina* was the big picture he had been praying for, even if it paid him only one-seventh of his previous salary. Garbo's patronizing behavior toward her old flame did little to boost his confidence. She would claim that by insisting on his being her costar, she wanted to save his foundering career. On his first day on the set, however, she told him this would be his last film with her, perhaps his last film ever. He no longer looked like the man who a few years ago drove Garbo into raptures, and between takes, he drank in his trailer. He felt Garbo was the only person who wanted him there, that because she had rammed him down the throat of Mayer and Thalberg, they hated him more than ever. Worse, the spark between them was gone, and his dazed performance as Antonio was appalling.

Garbo, on the other hand, felt she *was* Christina.

In movement, voice, and manner, she was distinctly androgynous. For the first third of the film, she strides about in tunic, pants, and boots, kisses Elizabeth Young, and, when told she cannot die an old maid, swears to "die a bachelor." When she begins to wear dresses, the decision to soften and reveal herself is hers, not

imposed by outside forces. By telling Garbo to underplay everything, Mamoulian brought out the queen's conflicting impulses,
the inner struggle between her dauntless tomboy and her wish to
be loved. Bill Daniels was the cameraman again, and director and
cinematographer worked well together.

Garbo liked her director's personality and found working with
him stimulating, although they disagreed over her male disguises,
which she wanted less glamorous and more authentic. The studio
wouldn't let her coarsen her face with massive, masculine eyebrows, but her first appearance as an adult was decidedly virile. In
this scene, what appears to be two men ride furiously through the
open countryside and into the castle. One dismounts and runs up
the stairs, accompanied by two dogs. A wide-brimmed hat hides the
face until it comes off and reveals Garbo.

Garbo began to date her director. Los Angeles newspapers reported Garbo and Mamoulian were seen dining at popular Sunset
Strip clubs, and gossip columnists hinted at a star-director romance. De Acosta's first humiliation came when, instead of a long
weekend in northern California that she and Garbo had planned,
Garbo went away with Mamoulian. Garbo refused to see de Acosta.
Mercedes was jealous and furious at Garbo's double betrayal of
going out with someone else who was also a man. Mercedes posted
herself on the sidewalk outside Garbo's house, watching her com-
ings and goings.

Mamoulian was horrified when, picking up Garbo one night,
she slipped onto the floor of his car while he backed out of her
driveway. She got back up in the passenger's seat once they were a
block down the street. Her explanation: she didn't want a lady
friend watching her coming and going. When it happened a second time, Mamoulian was furious. "I will not drive this car out of
the gate until you behave like a human being," he told her.

"But I don't want her to see me," she protested.

If MGM had Garbo as Sweden's Renaissance queen, Paramount
had to have Dietrich as Catherine the Great. As soon as Josef von
Sternberg finished *The Scarlet Empress* script, the studio summoned
Marlene from Europe. Because the marine air rusted her sewing
needles, she cabled Sternberg to find her another house. Rudi

took the boat train to Le Havre to inspect their stateroom. Before they sailed, he told his wife to give his regards to Sternberg, Edington, and de Acosta, and to concentrate on the work awaiting her. Sternberg rented Colleen Moore's house in Bel Air for his returning star.

Marlene found de Acosta out of favor with Garbo and told her husband on the transatlantic telephone that Mercedes was "tragically sulking."

The Scarlet Empress told the story of the German princess Sophia Frederica (1729–96), her marriage at sixteen to the Grand Duke Peter of Russia, and the insurrection that led to her becoming the new empress Catherine. The young Catherine quickly learns the value of her sexual powers as a means of self-preservation at the court in St. Petersburg and, by the end, gallops up the palace steps, totally depraved by absolute power. Sam Jaffe was cast as the crippled half-wit Peter, John Lodge as her long-haired, swaggering love interest, and Louise Dresser as the corrupting old empress, Elizabeth.

Dietrich squabbled with Travis Banton, Paramount's alcoholic head designer, over the furs, feathers, veils, and chiffon ensembles he created for her. Banton feared a fur hat Marlene wanted would look like a knockoff of Garbo's headgear in *Queen Christina,* but Marlene assured him that no one ever remembered what Garbo wore. Fittings delayed the shooting start until Thanksgiving, when Dietrich wrote to Rudi:

> Dearest Papi,
> Here it is Thanksgiving, so we are not working. Mamoulian is supposed to have made a very bad film with Garbo. Saw secret sketches—so it can't be the clothes. Tomorrow, they start to shoot retakes and a new end [*sic*].

Marlene had it halfway right. A massive coronary had felled the driven Irving Thalberg and put *Queen Christina* in jeopardy. Doctors disclosed his weak heart had been further damaged and recommended a long convalescence. Thalberg felt betrayed when Mayer hired his thirty-one-year-old son-in-law, David Selznick, to head a production unit of his own and gave him his pick of stars, directors, and stories—plus a $4,000-a-week salary. Selznick didn't like what he saw of *Queen Christina*. He wanted the picture reshot and asked Ben Hecht, the prolific screenwriter and script doctor, to do a complete rewrite.

Nothing came of it. With less than two weeks of shooting left, Mamoulian ignored Mayer's son-in-law and shot the ending. The contretemps provoked Garbo to veto Selznick's suggestion that she star in a screen adaptation of the George Emerson Brewer Jr.–Bertram Block play *Dark Victory*.[1]

The Scarlet Empress became the pinnacle of the Sternberg-Dietrich collaboration, an eccentric, dramatically insubstantial but visually brilliant homage to a star. Sternberg shot almost all the action in close-ups, showing faces degraded or exalted by primal passions. He and Marlene made film history with a sequence in which Catherine, in tall mink cossack hat, inspects her personal guard, a line of men she has all possessed. She tilts her head, looking slowly down the row of lovers while sucking on a piece of straw held rakishly between her teeth.

Garbo and Mercedes resumed their affair as if the fling with Mamoulian had never happened. MGM launched *Queen Christina* in December 1933 with a New York premiere at the Astor Theater, and an all-out publicity campaign that, besides the traditional press ballyhoo, included department-store promotions advertising Queen Christina sleeves, collars, and necklines. Paris fashion designer Elsa Schiaparelli picked up on the idea and, for 1935 daytime wear, came out with severe and military looks—fitted, square epauletted suits, drummer-boy jackets, plumed hats, and gauntlet gloves. The *World-Telegram*, the Hearst chain's New York City flagship newspaper, was the only daily chiding the film's disregard for "the intensity of the queen's devotion to [her] Countess."

Gilbert blamed Mayer for his downfall. Virginia Bruce, his fourth wife, filed for divorce after a marriage that lasted eighteen months. One day Adela Rogers St. Johns, Gilbert's Malibu neigh-

---

1. Stanwyck considered the heroine in *Dark Victory* an actress's plum and for several years tried to convince Selznick to her cast her, but he sold the property to Warners. Bette Davis's portrayal of the young woman dying of a brain tumor earned her a 1939 Academy Award nomination.

bor, asked where he was going when he furiously backed out of his garage. "I'm going to kill Louis B. Mayer," he shouted.

She jumped up on the running board. "Take me with you. You shouldn't be alone on a mission like this. Besides, you can't drive in this condition. You've been drinking."

St. Johns, whose father had died an alcoholic, talked Gilbert out of his act of desperation. Years later she would say, "It killed him. It was too much for a man of his ego to accept the charitable offer of a role from Garbo and then to be ignored."

Gilbert made another picture and was seen everywhere with Dietrich. He died, bitter and broke, at thirty-eight, felled by a heart attack and his inability to realize that as a screen lover he had gone out of fashion. Salka Viertel got to write *The Painted Veil* for Garbo. Dietrich and Sternberg made *The Devil Is a Woman,* an uncommercial folie à deux, totally outside mainstream Hollywood that, perversely, they both called their favorite film. It was their last together.

Behind Thalberg's back, Louis B. Mayer tried to hire Darryl Zanuck as production chief, but the convalescing Thalberg returned to work. When Salka came to see him, she suggested Garbo's next movie should be the life of Marie Walewska, Napoleon's enduring mistress. As the wife of Alexandre Colonna, Count of Walewski, Marie bore Napolean an illegitimate son, and since the Hays Code forbade adultery, it seemed futile to try to bring the story to the screen. Thalberg, however, thought it could be finessed and encouraged Salka to dig deeper into the story.

Dietrich's mass popularity began to wane after *The Scarlet Empress;* Garbo's after *Queen Christina.* By the time the two pictures were released, movie audiences were drifting away from costume epics. People wanted glitzy, brassy musicals to cheer them up or gangster flicks to thrill them. The picture to see was Frank Capra's breezy *It Happened One Night* with runaway heiress Claudette Colbert and laid-off newspaperman Clark Gable meeting on a long-distance bus.

Garbo was still the screen's most miraculous face, but John Meehan and Salka Viertel's soulful adaptation of Somerset Maugham's

Painted Veil, with Garbo between George Brent and Herbert Marshall in epidemic-ridden China, was confused and slow. The film's less than triumphant December 7, 1934, premiere left her depressed and humiliated. She left for Sweden.

Dietrich's follow-up to *The Scarlet Empress* was called *The Devil Is a Woman.* Pierre Louys (1870–1925) was a French writer admired by lesbians for his *Chansons de Bilitis,* celebrating the poetess Bilitis, who supposedly lived on Lesbos at the time of Sappho. *The Devil Is a Woman* was the third screen version of his mockingly erotic 1898 novel, *Le femme et le pantin* (The Woman and the Puppet).[2] It was Sternberg's last film with Dietrich, and with Lionel Atwill as the older Spanish nobleman she degrades and ruins, director and star came up with a clever, styled farce. They had Marlene sing a masochistic number called "If It Isn't Pain Then It Isn't Love," which, along with seventeen other minutes of screen time, ended up on the cutting-room floor after objections by the Production Office. The *New York Times* called *The Devil Is a Woman* "one of the most sophisticated films ever produced in America," the *New York Sun* found it "the dullest picture of the season," and the *New York Herald-Tribune* thought it "almost entirely devoid of dramatic substance."

In March 1935, *Photoplay* started a Garbo versus Dietrich war, calling Garbo the silent Swede whose throne was threatened by the "lush Teuton with slumberous eyes." After Paramount's ads for *The Devil Is a Woman* announced just "Dietrich" twice as big as the title, MGM gave Garbo similar billing. And if Marlene was "the most glamorous woman in the world," Garbo was "divine."

However much the rivalry was played up by their studios and an eager press, there was no truce offscreen. Perhaps because the one person they had in common was absent, Garbo and Dietrich studiously avoided each other. Mercedes de Acosta, who had loved them both, was in New York and in Europe. Abram Poole, her husband, asked for a divorce in 1935. She thought they were the best

2. Reginald Barker filmed *La femme et le pantin* in 1920 with Geraldine Farrar, and Jacques de Baroncelli directed a French version in 1928 with Conchita Montenegro. After the Josef von Sternberg edition with Dietrich, Julien Duvivier directed a fourth version with Brigitte Bardot in 1958, and Luis Buñuel a fifth rendition in 1977 as *Cet obscur objet de désir* with *two* Conchitas: Carole Boquet and Angela Molina.

of friends and refused to seek a Nevada quickie divorce. Since it was his idea, she forced him to take up thirty-day residence in Reno among the routine crowd of aggrieved wives. She left for Italy and Austria, spent time in a convent of twelve nuns, and in Salzburg was a houseguest of Eleonora von Mendelssohn. By cable, Garbo suddenly summoned Mercedes to come to Stockholm. After a sentimental evening at the Grand Hotel, they went to stay with Count and Countess Wachtmeister, and Garbo took Mercedes to see the Södermalm tenement where she was born.

Mercedes remained Dietrich's on-and-off lover through the 1930s and, when Marlene received no movie offers between 1937 and 1939, offered to stay with her. None of the three women pretended to be bothered by promiscuity. The two stars would not meet until 1945.

11

The Flaming Twenties

"Really," exclaimed Dietrich reading Brian Aherne's letter telling how the British press complained about her trousered look, "he thinks I invented trousers. Hasn't he ever heard of George Sand?" To stereotype people and their behavior makes for a kind of order that not only pleases psychiatrists and statisticians, but most people. It makes the acceptable bearable and the exceptional unacceptable. Research in the 1990s has raised the hypothesis that sexual identity is not set in stone, that sexual behavior may evolve, and our desires change.

The gender codes of the day taught lesbians to think of themselves as having "dual natures," one male and one female. Garbo was torn by these seemingly opposite sides and believed the part of her that both wanted to succeed and to love women was her male side. Modern psychoanalysts—as opposed to feminists who reject Freud's assertions about women—tend to believe that by adopting masculine clothing and postures, lesbians borrow men's culturally accepted urge to conquer women.

When Garbo and de Acosta dressed and acted in ways they conceived as being masculine, there was an added sense of provocation that no longer exists. "Garbo in pants!" shouted a wire-photo caption, mimicking the *Garbo talks!* screamer that launched her first talkie. "Innocent bystanders gasped in amazement to see Mercedes de Acosta and Greta Garbo striding swiftly along . . . dressed in men's clothes."

A few days later, MGM sent out a press release under Garbo's name, in which she apologized for inflicting her "trousered attitude" on hostesses, escorts, and maître d's.

Marlene Dietrich fended off charges that she was wearing male attire to get publicity by telling *Screen Book* magazine she wore trousers before coming to America. "In fact, I used to dress up in boys' clothes when I was a little girl. I have always liked the freedom of men's garments."

Lesbianism might have been tolerated in France, but transvestism was not. French police warned Dietrich she might be subject to arrest if she dressed like a man in Paris. Katharine Hepburn's bosses at RKO objected so much to her trousered look that they threatened to suspend her unless she switched to skirts. She, in turn, threatened to walk around in her underwear, and when the studio carried out its threat and confiscated her clothes, she carried out hers and went from her set to the commissary in her underpants.

It is hard for a modern person to fathom yesteryear's dress taboos. Afghan women may be stoned for exposing any part of their bodies in public, but at a time when most Americans don't know what to wear at a funeral, few people are even conscious of the strictures of dress. Despite her high-profile affairs with Igor Stravinsky, the Duke of Westminster, Pierre Reverdy, and Paul Iribe, Gabrielle "Coco" Chanel was rumored to prefer women to men. She started feminizing men's wardrobes on the eve of World War I. Throughout her life she championed a nervy tomboy look, although she hated women in pants. Until the end of the 1930s, the very notion of a women wearing trousers was frowned upon in conventional households, and with the exception of Ina Claire's satin pajamas for intimate dinners and World War II work overalls, pants did not appear in fashion magazines until Yves Saint Laurent's pantsuits in the early 1970s.

"Though a person may recognize attraction to both sexes, and may have adopted a fixed sexual identity, something else is needed to fully explain sexual preference: the social structure in which these dual desires can be realized," wrote Martin S. Weinberg, Colin J. Williams, and Douglas W. Pryor in *Dual Attraction*. "These structures—for example, open relationships—not only show us how bisexuality actually works in everyday life, but also illustrate the wide range of bisexualities that exists." Bisexual couples, these researchers established, tended to distinguish between primary heterosexual and secondary homosexual relationships. Jealousy was strongest when a person's secondary relationship was with someone of his or her own sex.

Establishing a public persona in the lesbian subculture is important, writes Pat Califia in *Sapphistry: The Book of Lesbian Sexuality*. "It used to be taken for granted that a young lesbian would decide whether to emphasize the masculine or the feminine aspects of her personality and appearance. This whole process still exists though in slightly altered form. The costumes have changed, the social mannerisms and etiquette have altered, but the continuum of masculinity and femininity continues to have meaning in the lesbian world. Most modern lesbians can tell you (if pressed) which of their acquaintances are butch and femme. . . . It is infinitely more desirable to be known as a woman who is sexually active and experienced than to have a reputation for passivity and naïveté. Femmes are suspect. They may not be real lesbians. They are viewed as being more prone to emotional upsets and more likely to defect than butches."

With Janet Flanner, the Paris-based journalist, Diana Fredericks cited the freedom from fear of conception as an incentive for sex between women. As she wrote in her putatively autobiographical 1939 novel *Diana*:

> It was natural enough that the homosexual would approach intimacy more quickly than the normal person. The very lack of any kind of social recognition of their union gave it a kind of informality. Normal love, having to consider property and children, had to assume responsibilities that were of no consequence to the homosexual. Fear of conception, a deterrent to the consummation of normal love, was no problem to homosexuals.

The flaming twenties were a period of experimentation for women. The decade was a rich cocktail of society and the avant-garde, of verve, jazz, the automobile, Hollywood, and the headlong pursuit of freedom. Sports and physical activity firmed the feminine ideal, sunbathing changed skin tones, the taste for faster living modified elegance. "The love affairs were romantic instead of critical," Anita Loos would recall. "We hadn't yet heard of that old Viennese spoilsport Sigmund Freud." The quintessential 1920s woman—slim, sophisticated, streamlined, and modern—didn't so much demand a fashion that was boyish as one that was youthful. On the screen, vamps, career gals, chorines, and flappers flouted the taboos. Until the end of the Great War, Western women were considered nonsexual, by men and by themselves. To enjoy sex was considered "unladylike."

Lesbians were seen as either sick or sinful, and as Lillian Faderman noted, "no one would want to be considered one." In 1928, Djuna Barnes wrote that same-sex love remained "as daring as a Crusade," and few women who had only affectional relationships with other women were part of any fledgling lesbian subculture. A lesbian often grew to adulthood afraid of her sexual feelings, and in many instances, unaware of how to cope with them. While many women admitted to intense emotional relations with other women, they usually saw such relationships as isolated experiences and expected to marry and live as heterosexuals.

Women in love with women met at the Big House on Hollywood Boulevard or the Lakeshore Bar near Westlake (today MacArthur) Park, less than a mile down Wilshire Boulevard from the Ambassador Hotel and its Coconut Grove.

"The bars were about the only place you could go when you were a lesbian where people wouldn't point and laugh if you were tattooed or wore pants," said dancer-actress Iris Adrian. "They were the only places you could go and be comfortable." The bars featured one or two female artists every week, from belly dancers to lesbian comedians and musicians. The clientele stretched from the gender blurred to working-class bull dykes and their femmes. The Golden Bull and SS Friendship were nearby gay bars, the If Club and the Open Door lesbian hangouts.

Mercedes de Acosta, Viertel, and their friends were more likely to visit the Hotel Brevoort for a poetry reading and a séance than to cruise bars. A few would be invited back to "open houses." Cecil

Beaton was a companion of de Acosta, Garbo, and Edmund Goulding at several such outings. Goulding was a voyeur host of very private libidinous weekend saturnalia that had echoes of the Arbuckle case.

Sin was mostly in the eye of the beholder. When the movies came west in 1913, Los Angeles boardinghouses had advertised, "Rooms for rent—no dogs or actors allowed." As late as 1919, the Garden Court apartments still held out against "picture people." By 1923, however, the $32 million the new studios spent annually in salaries and services softened attitudes. Eighty percent of the world's motion pictures were made in Los Angeles, yet the *New York World* could write that "Hollywood has no art galleries, no institutions of learning aside from primary schools and kindergartens—nothing that makes the slightest pretense to culture, civic or otherwise." As late as 1927, the sarcastic H. L. Mencken could write that the wildest nightlife he had encountered in Hollywood was at Aimee Semple McPherson's tabernacle. "And no wonder, for they are worked like Pullman porters or magazine editors," he said. "When they finish their day's labors, they are far too tired for any recreation requiring stamina. Immorality? Oh, my God. Hollywood seemed to me to be one of the most respectable towns in America. Even Baltimore can't beat it."

In Alla Nazimova, however, the flaming twenties lived up to their name. The legendary star of the Russian and American stages and of many silent Hollywood films was one actress passionately attached to women who threw caution to the wind and produced and starred in an all-gay *Salome*.

Nazimova was born in Yalta, Crimea, in 1879. She studied music at the St. Petersburg Conservatory and was an accomplished violinist when she made her stage debut at nineteen. She played leads at the Moscow Art Theater under Konstantin Stanislavsky and emigrated to America in 1906. On Broadway, she was so prominent she had her own theater. Young George Cukor would remember going three times to see the dark, intense star in a smoldering Hungarian drama. In 1921, she became Nancy Reagan's godmother when newly divorced Edith Davis toured with her. Nazimova's nephew, Val Lewton (Vladimir Ivan Leventon), was a prolific novelist and author of *Yasmine,* a book of pornography that sold under the counter. He became David O. Selznick's story editor and in the 1940s a director of horror movies.

From the beginning, a top-ranking star provided almost fool-proof budget insurance because the public responded to determined starmaking. It was Selznick's father, the former jewelry dealer from Kiev, Lewis Selznick, who in 1917 not only paid Nazimova a thousand dollars a day to star in *War Brides,* but made sure every newspaper knew he paid her a thousand dollars a day. A year later, Metro billed her as "woman of a thousand moods," paid her $13,000 a week, and on movie posters listed *Revelation, Toys of Fate, Eye for Eye, Out of the Fog,* and *The Red Lantern* as Nazimova productions. Some of her boldly conceived and often bizarre and haunting screen vehicles were directed by Charles Bryant, an Englishman and friend of William Desmond Taylor, to whom she was variously said to be married or, for obscure reasons she never revealed, unable to marry. Her first picture with Rudolph Valentino was *Cambial.* In 1923, she presented *Salome.*

In 1896, Oscar Wilde adapted for the stage the biblical tale of Salome, who so pleased Herod Antipas, governor of Judea, by dancing at his birthday feast that he granted her wish to have the head of John the Baptist on a platter. Henny Porten, the movie star Dietrich had pursued and serenaded as a teenager, played Salome in the first film version of Wilde's drama in 1902. Three years later, Richard Strauss used the play as the basis for his opera *Salome.*

Nazimova, who counted Dolly Wilde, Oscar Wilde's niece, among her lovers, retained Aubrey Beardsley's sets and costumes from Wilde's play. Her lover Natasha Rambova wrote the screenplay under the name Peter M. Winters. Rambova's real name was Winifred Shaughnessy Hudnut. She was the adopted daughter of Richard Hudnut, a cosmetics tycoon, but pretended she was Russian. Charles Bryant directed Nazimova in the title role, and Mitchell Lewis and Nigel de Brulier in supporting roles. The stylized silent *Salome* was a financial and critical failure. Modern film anthologies call it almost unendurable, a movie that looks better in stills than on the screen.[1]

---

1. For a 1980 revival, the *New Yorker* noted: "The movie looks better in stills than when one actually sees it, but a folly like this should probably be experienced."

Nazimova bought a mansion surrounded by three and a half acres of poplar, cedar, and fruit trees, at 8080 Sunset Boulevard at Crescent Heights Boulevard, and christened it the Garden of Allah. Her guests called her Madame and were forbidden to bid her good night because she believed the words brought her bad luck. She created a "moon parlor" and had the swimming pool shaped in the form of the Black Sea. The Garden of Allah was a notorious rendezvous for celebrity trysts. Mary's, also owned by Nazimova, was a dyke bar on the Sunset Strip opposite Café Gala, a gay bar that by the 1930s was home away from home for Cole Porter.

Until Jesse Lasky imported England's Elinor Glyn, a widowed author of sinful books and an intimidating presence, no one had more influence than Nazimova. And if her movie reign was brief, her influence was long-lived. Bungalows erected around her Garden of Allah swimming pool not only became the place of randy assignations but the first Hollywood residence of onrushing sophisticates like Lili Damita. In succession, Nazimova induced two of her lovers, Jean Acker and Natasha Rambova, to marry Rudolph Valentino.

Rodolfo Raffaelo Filiberto Guglielmi di Valentina d'Antonguolla shortened his name to Rudolph Valentino and became the most electrifying male star of the silent screen. Jean Acker was a dancer. She and Valentino married a year after he became a living legend. The film that made him was the 1921 screen version of Blasco Ibáñez's *Four Horsemen of the Apocalypse,* in which he played an Argentine aristocrat turned Parisian playboy who on the battlefield meets his death at the hands of his German cousin.

"After the ceremony we had supper and danced until two A.M.," Valentino said of the wedding night. "Then we parted." Together, they applied lacquer to the Chinese furniture they both liked. When he sued for divorce, Acker said their marriage had never been consummated.

Valentino impetuously married Rambova in Mexico without waiting the full year for his interlocutory divorce from Acker to take effect. An ambitious district attorney had the star jailed for bigamy and made sure reporters were informed ahead of Valentino's lawyer.

Rudy and Natasha made a striking couple. Mercedes de Acosta would remember them dancing together. They summered on the French Riviera where Natasha owned a château near Juan-les-Pins. Paramount decided to have Valentino make *The Sainted Devil* at its New York studio in Astoria, Queens. With her mystical inclinations and belief that she was guided by supernatural forces, the new Mrs. Valentino imposed her ideas on everything and soon found the story, the players, the sets, the costumes, and the director to be impossible. For once her astral bodies were right. *The Sainted Devil* was awful. For Valentino's next film, she hired Adrian, whose sketches and graceful looks she liked. The twenty-three-year-old designer traveled west with Valentino, Rambova, and their retinue of maids, valets, cook, business manager, Natasha's monkey, and three trunks of tea gowns.

The marriage foundered in 1926 when the costly Valentino–Bebe Daniels *Monsieur Beaucaire* was a box-office disappointment. Rambova let it be know that the marriage had never been consummated, but after Valentino died in 1926, claimed she was a straight spiritualist.

Recognizable actresses with sapphic interests almost never took chances in bars, or even on movie sets, and the Garden of Allah was a place where friendships were initiated. It was at Nazimova's swimming pool in 1928 that Lili Damita met Dolores Del Rio and Ann Boyar, the fiancée of J. L. "Jack" Warner of the studio-owning brothers.

Damita was a Frenchwoman of great beauty who radiated style, wit, and intelligence. In the mold of foreign sophisticates like Garbo and Dietrich, she was a leading lady of silents and early talkies whose tempestuous marriage to Errol Flynn made bigger headlines. Née Liliane Carré in Bordeaux, she got her stage name by being the mistress of Alfonso XIII. *"Petite dame"* was what the king of Spain called the former chorus girl. Diane Vreeland, who met the king before he was exiled in 1936, called him "the most exciting man I've ever seen."

Liliane was the daughter of an actress who spent years on the road and kept her child as near to her as possible. Liliane's education, such as it was, was minimal, transient, and multilingual in Spanish, Portuguese, and Greek convents that took in children of traveling troupers on a month-to-month basis. Mother and teenage daughter spent World War I entertaining wounded soldiers whose only thought was that they might die tomorrow and never kiss another girl.

Liliane attracted attention when, at nineteen, she was selected to succeed Mistinguett as the star of the Casino de Paris revue. Within a year she was performing for the king of Spain and was courted by Louis Ferdinand, the son of the deposed German crown prince. She became a friend of Dietrich's while working in Berlin among clever people with nervy tastes. These movie and theater people spent money prodigally, indulged themselves, considered homosexuality perfectly in order, and ridiculed those who refused to sleep with their own sex.

Samuel Goldwyn imported Liliane in 1928 to play a tempestuous married beauty opposite Ronald Colman in an adaptation of Joseph Conrad's novel *The Rescue*. She went on to play a fierce dancer in Warner Brothers' *Bridge of San Luis Rey*. Although her accent was too French, she managed to make nine more early talkies. "Everything about her was arrogant, and the more arrogant the more beautiful," Errol Flynn would write in *My Wicked, Wicked Ways* of their meeting aboard a transatlantic oceanliner taking him to America for the first time. "She rustled when she walked. Lili always seemed to rustle; it was one of her wonderful traits," he would add, without mentioning her bisexuality. He was eight years her junior, and although an enthusiastic bisexual himself, he was intimidated by Lili's superior knowledge of matters sexual. They met again in Mexico City where Lili was with Carmen Figueroa, a young woman Flynn would call "extraordinarily attractive."

Lili was living at the Garden of Allah in 1935, enjoying exhibiting her body and surrounded by gays, when, on a dare, she married newcomer Errol Flynn and, with her friends Dolores Del Rio and Jack Warner's fiancée Ann Boyar, persuaded the studio chief to give her new husband a break. The improbable marriage lasted six years and produced a son, Sean Flynn, who was to become the most famous Vietnam War photographer to disappear, on an assignment in Cambodia.

12

Stanwyck: The Best-Kept Secret

For young women in love with women, growing up in loneliness, fearing parental shock, and despairing of finding examples to emulate, the star they thought of as one of them was Barbara Stanwyck. The reason was not any coded message in gestures or delivery, but the way Stanwyck's screen characters defined themselves on their own terms. There was no subliminal I'm-Jane-you're-Tarzan wink of the kind Bette Davis and Rosalind Russell used. Stanwyck was emotionally honest, and the way she related to men was different. In the dark anonymity of a movie theater, lesbians didn't care that the plot demanded Stanwyck be attracted to a man. They told each other that for them the women she played in such Columbia and Warner Bros. B movies as *Ladies of Leisure*, *Ten Cents a Dance*, *Baby Face*, and her women-in-prison drama, *Ladies They Talk About*, "worked." Later generations would see her spinster roles as closet lesbians.

This intensely private, most closeted of independent actresses was a women of dogged calculation and repressed emotions, at once tough and vulnerable, earthy, instinctive, and sarcastic. She covered deep psychic scars with a flinty façade and was not very good at the games of love. People would swear she was, with Garbo, Hollywood's most famous closeted lesbian, that "everybody" knew.

Her close friends Joan Crawford and Dietrich were rumored to have been her lovers, but she would figure in few lesbian memoirs.

The conflict that shaped her life—and made her so interesting to watch on the screen—was the struggle between her wish to give of herself and her need to be in control. She was born in Brooklyn of English-Irish working-class parents, became an orphan at the age of three, and grew up mistrustful, afraid of people finding out she didn't belong to anybody. She hated her childhood and at fifteen started out as a Ziegfeld chorus girl. She landed in Hollywood with the talkies and became a sharp-tongued, wise-cracking woman of allure. Acting—getting up in the morning and, on a soundstage, becoming someone else—was her lifeblood. Stardom taught her how to resort to one-of-the-boys chumminess, to elaborate surfaces and campy disguises. Clifton Webb, the gay actor and wit who played her husband in *Titanic,* called her "my favorite American lesbian." She never mixed her on-screen persona with her off-screen self. In public, she was the poised, husky-voiced, self-mocking pro. When no one was around, she let herself be her butchy self. Her thirty-year friendship with her publicist, Helen Ferguson, was framed within the public bounds of a working relationship that no one could question.

Stanwyck closed doors behind her, even to friends. She choked off subjects she didn't want to talk about and threw out of her house the only journalist who dared to ask if she was gay. Too special to play Everywoman, she saw many prestigious roles slip away, yet she survived the cameras for fifty-five years and in more than eighty films developed a distinctive image as a gusty, self-reliant, and self-assured woman. She endowed her cowgirls and faith leaders, her gold diggers and wives, chiselers and cardsharps, lovers and victims, with a strength of purpose and made the screen sizzle with carnality and cynicism. Right up there with her friend Joan Crawford, she was the incarnation of grace, beauty, and save-your-ass resilience.

She was born Ruby Stevens and stage-named Stanwyck by Broadway producers. Her only school was the backstage, her teachers other performers. Chorus girls stuck together in self-defense against stage-door johnnies and ballroom rakes. As Mae West said, the theater was full of odd men and odd women. It was provocative for an entertainer to admit to a "touch" of lesbianism, but most dancers expected to marry and live as heterosexuals. Stanwyck shared the stage in *Burlesque* with a clergyman's daughter who, to save her family from embarrassment over her lesbianism, ran away from home and changed her name from Mary Tomlinson to Marjorie Main. Chaperoned by Oscar Levant, the pianist who played in the smartest nightclubs and jazz dives, the two chorines sampled the Harlem speakeasies where transvestites performed and lesbians flaunted themselves. Ten years later, Marjorie played the mother-in-law to Barbara's title role in *Stella Dallas.*

Stanwyck was twenty-two when on August 26, 1928, in St. Louis she married a twice-divorced comedian ten years her senior. The Great Faysie, as Frank Fay styled himself, was a cocky, conceited, and outstanding wit of vaudeville who never missed a beat. He was also, according to Harry Hay, a fellow actor who became the founder of the modern gay movement in California, a closet homosexual. A week at New York's Palace Theater was every vaudevillian's dream, two weeks an accomplishment. Fay was the only song-and-dance man to play ten successive weeks at the Palace, at $17,500 a week in 1925 dollars. Hollywood scouts combing stage doors for actors with voices for dialogue brought the newlyweds to California in 1929. After a promising start, Frank sank into alcoholism and spousal abuse while Barbara established herself as an actress with a trademark sneer and alluring, all-business delivery. Heterosexual males found the suggestions of smutty sex in many of her films provocative. Lesbians enjoyed her perversity and control.

Frank and Barbara fought for the same professional turf, each in turn using success to hurt the other. With her money, they bought a mansion in Brentwood that made them the back-fence neighbors of Joan Crawford and *her* alcoholic third husband, Franchot Tone. Joan would recall how Barbara climbed over the fence one night, saying she was leaving Frank and asking if she could spend the night. "Their fights were dreadful," Joan would remember. "He hit her often. Franchot hit me, too."

We do not know whether Joan and Barbara found solace in each other's arms, but they remained lifelong friends. Barbara knew Garbo and Dietrich were lesbians and admired Garbo for not yielding to studio demands that she marry. Rumors circulated that Barbara tried to seduce Bette Davis when they were filming Edna Ferber's *So Big.*

Stanwyck's seesaw marriage became the source material for *A Star Is Born.* Early drafts of the screenplay were so close to Fay and Stanwyck that attorneys specializing in invasion-of-privacy litigation listed twenty pages of similarities in incidents and situations between the script and the Fays. Like Joan, Barbara insisted she and Frank adopt a child. They named their adopted son Dion and quickly lost interest in him.

In 1935, Barbara filed for divorce, bought a ranch in the San Fernando Valley, and for the rest of her life lived by her own rules. Work, not love, was the vital center of her existence. Robert Taylor, her costar in *His Brother's Wife,* was MGM's matinee idol who, at studio-engineered dates, proved to be a polite, if inexperienced, young man. He insisted he was not homosexual but had a hard time pretending he wanted any woman in the flesh. For one year, he had been the fair-haired boy of Gilmor Brown, the Pasadena Playhouse's notorious homosexual director. Harry Hay would remember the two of them attending a soiree at Mercedes de Acosta's.

Rumors of homosexuality dogged Taylor so much he begged Louis B. Mayer to let him play rugged, brawny parts. If we do not know what Louis B. thought of his respectful and wholesome matinee idol's sexual leaning, we know what the studio boss told Peter Lawford in 1942 after Lawford's mother asked Mayer to advise her on her son's chiefly imagined homosexuality. "We have other young men at the studio with your problem, Peter, and we're giving them hormone shots to help them," Mayer told Lawford. "And we can fix you up with some beautiful woman."

Howard Strickling went to work burnishing the Bob Taylor image by planting stories about the actor's affection for firearms and hunting, and "linking" him to several actresses. When Taylor and Stanwyck made a second picture together—*This Is My Affair,* in which he is President McKinley's undercover agent and she a dance-hall belle with shady connections—Fox press releases trumpeted how intense their love scenes were, how each remained on the set during the other's solo work for the camera.

Four years younger than Barbara, Taylor bought a ranch next to hers in 1936 and made a habit of coming over for swims and barbecues, and of taking her on studio functions and to Crawford's house. Barbara had been in charge of herself since she was fourteen; Bob heeded his mother, his teacher, and Louis B.

The January 1939 issue of *Photoplay* targeted them as one of Hollywood's "unmarried husbands and wives." The others were Gable and Lombard, Constance Bennett and Gilbert Roland, Paulette Goddard and Charlie Chaplin, and George Raft and Virginia Pine. Although the points were made entirely through innuendo, "Unmarried Husbands and Wives" was the most outspoken article about the stars' private lives ever published. Mayer was furious. The magazine was told that if it did not publish a retraction, the studio would not only cancel all advertising but choke off access to its stars. *Photoplay* knuckled under and the following month lamely wrote that the quotes attributed to the celebrities mentioned in "Unmarried Husbands and Wives" made "these friendships appear in a light far from our original intention."

Selznick International was in the middle of shooting *Gone With the Wind* (in return for lending Gable to his son-in-law, Mayer won the right to distribute the epic), and the early damage control was centered on Gable. Everybody knew he and divorcée Carole Lombard had been together since 1936. When he permitted the publicity department to tell the press he would ask for a divorce, he robbed his older wife, Rhea, of the one little triumph that had always been hers: when the inevitable happened, *she* would do the announcing and the divorcing. Mayer had to advance $300,000 on Gable's $7,500-a-week salary before the spurned wife agreed to leave for Las Vegas to seek a Nevada quickie divorce. The Stanwyck-Taylor case was easier. Mayer's ultimatum that Taylor marry Stanwyck only had the force of law for Bob. But Barbara, who was filming *Golden Boy* with newcomer William Holden at Columbia, was smart enough to realize that if she wanted to sustain her star stature in the company town, it behooved her not to offend MGM's formidable boss.

On Saturday, May 13, 1939, studio publicists whisked Taylor and Stanwyck to San Diego for a civil wedding before a municipal judge. After a press reception in Beverly Hills later in the day, Stanwyck returned to the ranch while Taylor spent the wedding night calming his possessive mother. The next morning, he reported to the set of *Lady of the Tropics* and filmed a wedding scene with Hedy Lamarr. Barbara went back to the set of *Golden Boy*. Joan Crawford would remember Taylor telling her, "All I had to say was, 'I do.' I didn't know what happened." When he added that something good had come of it and Joan asked if he meant the marriage, he hesitated. "Well, yes, but I was actually referring to the tough roles I'm assigned now . . . boxers, cowboys, gangsters, that kind of thing."

The marriage was not only a deep cover but turned out to be an astute move. Marrying Metro's matinee idol gave Stanwyck radiance, and gravity. For Taylor, wedlock meant social acceptance, moorings, and shelter from marauding females. Stanwyck insisted on Helen Ferguson's becoming Taylor's publicist, and few people glimpsed their intimate lives or saw any reason to look askance at their separate bedrooms. Bob was the first to say he fell asleep the moment his head hit the pillow. Barbara made no bones about her chronic insomnia that had her reading in bed until all hours. It would be decades before anyone wrote that Stanwyck and Taylor were both drawn to same-sex love.

Barbara was in charge in the marriage. She treated Taylor as her son and on occasion humiliated him in front of men like John Wayne, with whom he associated in the hope of having their macho strutting rub off on him.

A few years before Stanwyck lit up the screen with portrayals of young women who didn't surrender the direction of their lives, lesbians found a role model in a book. In *The Well of Loneliness* by the British poet, short-story writer, and novelist Marguerite Radclyffe Hall, Stephen Gordon suffers because of her masculine body. Her mother doesn't love her because she sees no reflection of her own femininity in her daughter. Later in the novel, when Stephen is abandoned by her lover, she tries to console herself by acquiring elaborate men's clothing. The novel caused such a sensation when it was published in 1928 that it was banned in England, but distributed in the United States. For decades, it remained the only widely available lesbian novel, and Radclyffe Hall was so influential she was called "our matron saint." An article in the late 1940s suggested that in her honor "the inelegant word *butch* be replaced by *clyffe*."

Tallulah Bankhead loved the joke about a teenage girl asking another on a Fifth Avenue bus what she was reading.

"The Well of Loneliness."

"What's it about?"

"Lesbians."

"What's lesbians?"

"Oh, you know. People like Billie Holiday, Rosalind Russell, Cary Grant."

It is said that Samuel Goldwyn, the maddeningly self-centered mogul, suggested filming *The Well of Loneliness,* only to be told this could not be done since the leading character was a lesbian. To which the studio mogul retorted, "So what. We'll make her an American!" Apocryphal or not, the Goldwynism captures the essence of Tinseltown's casual dismissals of realities that might puncture the dream machine.

One of the better in-jokes of 1935 was that in spending $50,000 for the rights to Lillian Hellman's *The Children's Hour,* Goldwyn bought an unfilmable play. Everybody knew the Hays Office frowned upon the play—the Production Code was explicit: "sex perversion or any inference of it is forbidden"—and the quip was that Goldwyn had acquired *The Children's Hour* with the understanding that he could use neither Hellman's title nor her plot nor even mention the fact that he had bought it.

The title was changed to *These Three.* When William Wyler came on board to direct, Hellman told him *The Children's Hour* was not about lesbianism, but about slander: what is important is what a lie can do to people, not the nature of the lie. Martha Dobie and Karen Wright are teachers in a boarding school. Between them are evil little Mary and her wealthy grandmother. The drama is about three adults trying to cut through the porous fabric of lies—and one grain of truth—told by Mary, and their defeat in the ever-widening circle of *explanations* of lies. As scripted by Hellman and directed by Wyler, *These Three* turned Miriam Hopkins and Merle Oberon's love for each other into rival infatuation for Joel McCrea. When Wyler remade *The Children's Hour* in 1961 with Audrey Hepburn, Shirley MacLaine, and James Garner, he was allowed to use the original title, but the Production Code still forbade the use of the word *lesbian.*

13

Hollywood and Broadway: Transcontinentals

A hog, it was said, could travel across the United States without switching trains; a person could not. The fastest way from New York to southern California was aboard New York Central's crack Twentieth Century Limited to Chicago, where one transferred to the Santa Fe's no less famous Super Chief to the coast. The 2,985-mile journey took four days. In the spring and fall, the journey could be a restful time-out, but in the summer, in those days before air-conditioning, it was hell. If one didn't want one's clothes blackened by soot, it was seldom safe to open the windows. In winter, it was often too stifling in the cars close to the locomotive, too cold in the rear coaches. Movie stars and studio executives booked "drawing rooms" on both legs of the journey. Nöel Coward would remember an eastbound trip in 1938 where Marlene Dietrich, Katharine Hepburn, and Gertrude Lawrence spent most of the time gossiping in his compartment. They were less sensitive than the New York crowd of sophisticates like Dorothy Parker and S. N. Behrman commuting across the depressed land to pull down $2,000 a week and beginning to hate their own facile wit in the face of the prolonged Depression. While the Twentieth Century Limited and the Super Chief sped across the continent, the performers traveled with the curtains pulled.

Had they looked out, they would have seen the slow progress of the New Deal recovery in the burning eyes of men staring back from freight cars on sidings, and in the tarpaper shacks at the edges of cities where the homeless warmed themselves with coal tossed to them by sympathetic locomotive brakemen.

Barbara Stanwyck was a homebody who only traveled under duress, but she was a lifelong icon of gay women. Tallulah Bankhead practically commuted between Broadway and Hollywood, but had no gay following, perhaps because she made fun of everything, including sex. When she toured as Blanche Dubois in *A Streetcar Named Desire* in 1956, Tennessee Williams asked her if she had ever had a lesbian relationship. "Yes," she answered, "but that was in 1932. With Hope Williams, who had a boy's body." The next time the playwright asked, she said Eva Le Gallienne had seduced her when she was sixteen.

Bankhead's much-quoted tirade against performing oral sex had her tell people that lovemaking was a bore: "What is it after all? If you go down on a woman, you get a crick in the neck. If you go down on a man, you get lockjaw."

Nobody beat her to a punch line. A young student at Yale was enamored of her. He had a friend who managed to get him backstage to meet his idol. When they were introduced, the Yale graduate announced, "Guess what, Miss Bankhead. I am going to fuck you tonight."

To which she volleyed back, "And so you shall, you dear, old-fashioned boy."

Bankhead and her fellow commuters saw little difference between lesbians in the theater and their sisters in the movies. Both were beyond the pale, and both stage and screen presented women who practiced same-sex love as suicidal, self-loathing creatures. The central character in Gale Wilhelm's novel *We Too Are Drifting* tells her woman lover, "Except for the dirty satisfaction we manage to squeeze out of our bodies, I hate it." When the other woman protests love, Jan, the main character, replies, "Sometime I will kill you."

The legitimate theater could afford to be more tolerant than the movies. For one, straight people working in the theater were more aware—and accepting—of alternative lifestyles, whereas movie people, from Louis B. Mayer down, were fearful, and no one in

Hollywood talked about lesbianism. Also, the audiences were different. A Broadway actor was someone to be seen on a stage in midtown Manhattan; a movie actor was seen in Podunk, Iowa, and everywhere else. Nöel Coward and Eva Le Gallienne could be relatively open about their homosexuality because Coward never had to play a believable sex partner to Vivien Leigh. Le Gallienne was fifty-six when she made her first movie appearance, playing Richard Burton's mother in *Prince of Players* (1955), and in her sixties followed up with a pair of supporting parts in *The Devils Disciple* (1959) and *Resurrection* (1980).

If Hollywood had its Production Code, theater owners—and publishers—feared censorship from the newly established National Organization for Decent Literature. The rule of thumb was that if lesbian characters were miserable or convertible to heterosexuality, the occasional play and book might slip by. Threats of injunctions and interference by the New York Police Department nevertheless marred the opening of Lillian Hellman's *The Children's Hour* on Broadway in 1934. In *Odd Girls and Twilight Lovers,* Lillian Faderman would write that 1930s would-be censors seemed to believe that even lesbians who wallowed in tragedy were dangerous, because "to learn of the existence of other lesbians through the media, no matter how unfortunate those characters were, must have been reassuring to women who loved other women and feared by now, in the reticent 1930s, that they were rarities."

Bankhead was notorious for not wearing underwear on the set. Alfred Hitchcock declined, when asked by Fox higher-ups, to tell her to wear panties on *Lifeboat,* saying the matter should be handled by wardrobe. "The whole point about Tallulah," he would reflect, "was that she had no inhibitions." To shock people gaping at her and Dietrich when they had adjoining dressing rooms at Paramount in 1932 and Marlene wore gold dust in her hair, Tallulah got some, put it on her pubic hair, showed herself to people, and asked, "Guess what I've been doing?" Tallulah and Marlene told each other how boring it was to be polite to girls before seducing them, how they had to show them the house before taking them into the bedroom.

With age, booze, and pills, Tallulah became her own caricature. Comedians and gossip columnists quoted and misquoted her, biographer Denis Brian would write in 1972, "and today it would be impossible to separate fact from fiction—especially as she was inclined to accept the better fiction as her own."

Of all the people who came out of Alabama, she was, with Zelda Fitzgerald, the most fascinating, said playwright Lawton Campbell. Like her grandmother, she was named after a waterfall, Tallulah Falls, and her vitality, raspy accent, golden hair, and scorn for conventions conquered everybody. She called herself "pure as driven slush." On the eve of Helen Hayes's marriage to Charles MacArthur, the twenty-seven-year-old bride-to-be sought Bankhead's advice: "When a girl gets married, what can she do to keep from getting pregnant?" To which Tallulah answered, "Just what you've always been doing, darling." When Alfred Kinsey asked her to tell him the facts of her sex life, she told the sex researcher, "Of course, darling, if you'll tell me yours." She said such things as, "I'll come and make love to you at five o'clock. If I'm late, start without me."

In 1933, she dived into the Garden of Allah swimming pool fully clothed and came up naked, croaking, "Everybody's been dying to see my body." Her body was lean, and with her high cheekbones and lacquered, pulled-back hair, her face had a chiseled look reminiscent of Garbo's. No party was in full swing, said her friend Anita Loos, "until Tallulah arrived to put her particular type of zizz into it."

Tallulah was the daughter of the Speaker of the House Representatives William Bankhead and Adelaide Eugenia Sledge, whose name in Alabama was synonymous with beauty. Adelaide died shortly after Tallulah was born, and her father was always the best-loved man in her world. She agreed with his one piece of advice: "If you know your Bible and your Shakespeare and can shoot craps, you have a liberal education." Tallulah always put brakes on her outrageousness if she sensed it could threaten her father.

She was often lighthearted about her affairs with women, and biographer Denis Brian would suggest her lesbianism had to do with her father's warning to beware of men and her failure to find any man who could measure up to him. She made fun of that, too. "Daddy always warned me about men and alcohol, but he never said a thing about women and cocaine."

From her earliest years in Montgomery, Alabama, where she and her elder sister Eugenia began a fierce rivalry for the attention of her congressman father and even more famous senator grandfather, Tallulah sought fame. After winning a local beauty contest when she was fifteen, she made her stage debut in New York and, in 1923, went to London to score in Gerald De Maurier's *Dancers*. The play ran for 344 performances, her longest until her 408 performances on Broadway in Lillian Hellman's *Little Foxes*. For the next seven years she was the toast of London.

Her wild, flossy beauty attracted some of the most interesting lesbians of the theater, and her bed partners included Katharine Cornell, Laurette Taylor, Sybil Thorndyke, Beatrice Lillie, and Harlem's Gladys Bentley, a three-hundred-pound black Mae West who composed and performed dirty songs and, sometime in the 1920s, donned a tuxedo and married a woman in a New Jersey civil ceremony. Bankhead was as tender and loving toward gay men as she was cold and predatory with the heterosexual men she selected, seduced, and dismissed. She hated to be touched, especially by surprise.

"She had that magnificent beauty that is ugly in a funny way," Vincent Price would recall, comparing her with two other lesbian actresses. "Judith Anderson and Laurette Taylor had it, too. They came off as being the most beautiful women in the world through an illumination of their own personality."

Anita Loos, who first met Bankhead when she arrived in New York from Alabama, would write affectionately about her: "Tallulah never believed in the middle-class theory that ambition is praiseworthy. She saw it for what it generally is, a matter of conceit, mixed, more or less, with cupidity. And so Tallulah never allowed ambition to interfere with play. She lived in the grand manner of a free soul with aristocratic disdain for caution. And although many of her impulses were unfortunate, none harmed anybody but herself; the great majority of them came straight from her enormous interest in others."

Tallulah returned to America in 1930 and signed with Paramount to star in a mix-up comedy. *Tarnished Lady* was filmed in New York. The director was George Cukor, who became a lifelong friend. On the train to Los Angeles, she met her former lover, Douglas Fairbanks Jr., with his new wife, Joan Crawford. It was Crawford's introduction to Bankhead and she would never forget

Tallulah telling her, "Darling, you're divine. I've had an affair with your husband. You'll be next."

Tallulah spent a year in Hollywood. She rented the home of William Haines, the MGM matinee idol fired by Louis B. Mayer for refusing to live apart from his boyfriend, and proceeded to give parties. Her coterie soon included Laurence Olivier and Jill Esmond, the Barrymores, Anita Loos, and Cukor's gay crowd. She succeeded in thawing Garbo by clowning around. Not everybody fell for her. At their first meeting, Bankhead and Katharine Hepburn disliked each other. Tallulah called Hepburn a prude, and Kate called Bankhead rude. Tallulah was a favorite, if not a lover, of Cheryl Crawford, Broadway's only independent woman producer in the late 1930s.

Cheryl was twenty-four when she arrived in New York from her native Akron, Ohio, armed with her favorite line from the play *Shakuntana,* which she adopted as her motto: "There are doors to the inevitable everywhere." Within a year she was casting director of the Theater Guild, and the first to sign Katharine Hepburn to $30 a week as an ingenue understudy. In 1931, Harold Clurman, Lee Strasberg, and Cheryl Crawford became directors of the Group Theater, the ensemble formed in emulation of the Moscow Art Theater and dedicated to Stanislavsky's acting method. Over the next years she acted as coproducer and codirector on works of Clifford Odets, William Saroyan, Sidney Kingsley, and Irwin Shaw. In her memoirs, *One Naked Individual,* she would tell of sharing the backseat of a car with Tallulah's baby lion cub, Winston.

Bankhead returned to New York from her first brush with Hollywood with $100,000 in the bank. She thought it undignified for a star to be married, but to please her father married John Emery, her Barrymorish leading man in a whodunit stage production, in 1937. After her father died four years later, she divorced Emery and continued her boozy high-celebrity life. "Tallu was best in a crisis, and she manufactured 'em," said the comedienne Patsy Kelly, who shared her later life.

The Little Foxes opened in February 1939, two weeks after Bankhead's thirty-seventh birthday, and her performance as Hellman's evil, grasping monster enthralled the most discriminating critics. The twenty-five-year-old Tennessee Williams failed to persuade her to star in a play he claimed he had written for her, but the homosexuality, and affection for alcohol and barbiturates they shared made them friends. Six years later she made the mistake of turning down his offer to play Blanche Dubois in *A Streetcar Named Desire*. But she persuaded Williams to cast Laurette Taylor in *The Glass Menagerie*.

Laurette was nineteen years older than Tallulah and living in an alcoholic haze when she triumphed in *The Glass Menagerie*. Tallulah came backstage to congratulate her old lover. "You must play the part on the screen," whispered Laurette. Four years later when Hollywood was ready to film Williams's play, Jack Warner feared Bankhead's alcoholism and instead cast Gertrude Lawrence.

Laurette Taylor, the Manhattan-born Loretta Cooney, was the toast of Broadway in the 1910s. As a teenager, Laurette created a style of acting that was spontaneous and eloquent, a technique that relied on variations in tempo, tentative, unfinished movement halted in midair, quizzical glances, attention to what her partner was saying, and a warm, expressive voice that seemed to be addressed to the individual theatergoer. As she didn't use the mannerisms of the conventional acting of 1910, some people thought she was not acting. Wrote the dean of the American theater, Brooks Atkinson, "After years of obscure and often mortifying experiences as a trouper, she became a star in 1910 in a now-forgotten play called *The Girl in Waiting*. Then everyone understood that her spontaneity behind the footlights was indeed acting, and perhaps the most original and virtuous acting of the time."

Alla Nazimova taught Laurette sapphic love and how to hold out for great roles. Laurette married a gentlemanly English playwright, J. Hartley Manners, who wrote parts especially for her. In 1912, he came up with *Peg 'o My Heart*, a Cinderella story of an Irish girl who inherits a fortune and moves to London, where her artless simplicity proves to be more practical than her London relatives' snobbishness. Laurette played *Peg 'o My Heart* at the Cort Theater for 607 performances—the longest run of any dramatic play on Broadway. Many things went to pieces for her in the 1930s. Her husband died, and she became an alcoholic. In 1938 she played a deeply moving part in Sutton Vane's *Outward Bound*. Of her parts in *Outward Bound* and *The Glass Menagerie,* Brooks Atkinson said, "She looked into the dark corners of two human hearts and flooded them with the light that had always radiated from her acting."

Alcohol ruined the health of both Bankhead and Taylor, but they never bored anyone. Laurette died in December 1946. Tallulah carried on, touring the South with Nöel Coward's *Private Lives,* and interrupting her famous sofa love scene with her leading man, Donald Cook, by pulling a Confederate flag from her bosom and roaring to the audience, "Get this damn Yankee out of here."

Her last words before she died in 1968 at sixty-five were "Codeine, bourbon."

Libby Holman was from Ohio, but her offscreen notoriety was purely southern gothic. Nearsightedness lent intensity to her conventional beauty, and she was in full bloom at twenty-five—"rotten ripe," said Clifton Webb. As a teenager Libby wrote a jingle about herself: "I am tall and very slim / Am I a she or a him ?"

She was born Elspeth Holzman, the daughter of a noted Cincinnati attorney. She had a sister who committed suicide and two brothers, one of whom was close to her, and another estranged from her. She was a precocious child who played the piano and the violin, read her father's legal briefs, and, she once said, "studied Jung and Oscar Wilde before I got the curse." She attended Columbia Law School in New York, but dropped out to become a jazz singer. She made her Broadway debut playing a harlot in *The Fool* in 1924 and, four years later, starred in *Three's a Crowd* with Webb and Fred Allen.

Friends said Libby was a ball breaker with men, and tender, compassionate, and enormously sensual with all her close women friends. She lived with Jeanne Eagels until she met and fell in love with Louisa Carpenter, the slender, blond southern aristocrat and Du Pont heiress. The two of them often dressed in men's suits and bowler hats, going to the Clam House to eat spareribs and coleslaw with Bankhead and Beatrice Lillie.

Libby and Louisa were famous for showing up in Harlem nightclubs to mix with Bankhead, Eagels, and Marilyn Miller, the quintessential Ziegfeld girl. In 1931, Libby and Louisa were carousing in London and Paris with de Acosta and Nöel Coward when twenty-year-old Zachary Smith Reynolds, heir to the Camel cigarette fortune, fell hopelessly in love with Libby. She married him when she turned thirty. Eight months later, they quarreled violently during a party. The following morning Smith was found dead of a gunshot wound. Libby was charged with murder.

Her lawyer father defended her, and when the trial ended on November 15, 1932, she was cleared for lack of evidence. A bitter court battle over the estate followed. Libby moved to Louisa Carpenter's estate near Wilmington, Delaware, and, two months later, gave birth to a sickly boy weighing two pounds. She named the infant Christopher Smith Reynolds. She eventually inherited $7 million, and Christopher $6.6 million, of the Camel cigarette fortune. Hollywood retold the Reynolds tragedy twice, with Jean Harlow and Lauren Bacall as Libby.

For four years, Libby lived in near-seclusion in a house she rented near Louisa's and spent lavishly on the best doctors for her son, who grew up to be a slender, reserved young man. With the help of Clifton Webb, she tried to relaunch her career in 1938. When this failed, she bought a twenty-four-acre estate outside Stamford, Connecticut. Her son was the center of her life. He graduated near the top of his class at Putney School in Vermont. At eighteen, his frozen, broken body was found in a crevasse on Mount Whitney. Libby blamed herself for his death, saying she should have seen to it that he was chaperoned on the mountain outing.

After another estate fight with the Reynolds family, she was awarded her son's millions. People were after her for handouts. In her son's name she established a foundation for civil rights. One of the first Christopher Reynolds grants allowed the young Martin Luther King to travel to India to study Mahatma Gandhi's nonviolent civil disobedience.

Holman was always attracted to young gay men she could dominate. She was a longtime soul mate—and drug supplier—to Montgomery Clift, who she met in 1941 when he was twenty-two. She thought of him as another Garbo, whose pictures filled her house. Both were androgynous and mysterious. "Monty elicited great sympathy by the little-boy way he conducted himself, seeming always on the verge of tears," wrote his *Misfits* and *Freud* director, John Huston. Clift feared Libby and knew she could destroy him. In 1949, she made him turn down Billy Wilder's offer to play the kept young man in *Sunset Boulevard* because she was convinced the film was about her.

Holman and Garbo were friends during the 1950s, but it was Jane Bowles who became Libby's lover. Paul and Jane Bowles were figures in the transatlantic world of the arts. "Although unknown to the general public, the Bowleses were famous among those who were famous," Gore Vidal would write. "They lived in Mexico (the unknown Tennessee Williams made a pilgrimage to their house in Acapulco); they lived in New York, sharing a house with Benjamin Britten." They settled in Morocco and, when they were in America, spent months at Libby's Connecticut estate. Jane was envious of Paul's high-toned, alienated fiction, he was politely uninterested in her lesbian infatuations. Jane made fun of her stiff knee, her Jewishness, and predilection for women by calling herself Crippie, the Kike Dyke. In Libby's care she slowly went mad.

Bankhead, Eva Le Gallienne, Gertrude Lawrence, and Beatrice Lillie commuted not only between Hollywood and Broadway, but east, via transatlantic oceanliners, to London's West End. A frequent shipboard companion was Adele Astaire—Fred's raven-haired sister. She loved the girls but married Lord Charles Cavendish, who drank himself to death.

No one was ever nastier in a nicer way than Lillie. During her half-century theatrical career, Bea earned the title "the funniest woman in the world." Hers was a sustained triumph of manic high spirits. The two most stylish lyricists wrote songs for her—Noël Coward, *Marvelous Party;* and Cole Porter, *Mrs. Lowsbrough-Goodby.* "I love her," said Tallulah when they were both in their sixties.

With her trademark close-cropped hair, fezlike cap, and long cigarette holder to punctuate her barbs, the Canadian-born Lillie worked with some of the best-known names in comedy—Coward, Ziegfeld, and Charlie Chaplin—and her stage activities ranged from sheer high spirits and an almost zany sense of the ridiculous to a sharp, acid wit and a devastating ability to deflate haughtiness and mawkishness. What happened between her and a live audience, she said, was "that they recognized something I'd known for years—I was a natural-born fool." Homosexuality, her own and others, was no exception to her sarcasm.

Revue sketches and songs established Lillie's West End stardom, often in partnership with Lawrence. A popular song of the time ran:

> Lillie and Lawrence,
> Lawrence and Lillie
> If you have not seen them
> You are perfectly silly.

Lillie married Sir Robert Peel, a great-grandson of the British statesman, when she was twenty-four. He died fourteen years later, leaving her a family estate and a son, killed in World War II. She titled her autobiography *Every Other Inch a Lady*, wore her title, in Kenneth Tynan's words, "like a halo on an anarchist," but was still Lady Peel when she died in 1989 at ninety-four.

She was a lover of Le Gallienne, Judith Anderson, and Katharine Cornell. Her passion, when in Hollywood, was directed at Garbo, who found her adorable and endlessly funny. In London one afternoon in October 1928, she and Tallulah watched Aimee Semple McPherson hold a revival meeting at Albert Hall. The evangelist had shown the midwesterners filling the Los Angeles tract homes that worship could be fun, and Tallulah invited her to her home and, with Lillie, tried to shock her by telling her of their sins. As long as they didn't hurt anybody, Aimee said, she didn't mind what they did.

Lillie's career in films began in 1926 with a comic masterpiece called *Exit Laughing*, in which she woos a reluctant suitor while swirling a huge chain of beads, and ended with *Thoroughly Modern Millie* in 1967. She was up for the part of the Good Witch in *The Wizard of Oz* in 1936, but was considered too funny. Her long stage career covered more than forty stage shows. On Broadway, she starred with Mercedes de Acosta's old flame Hope Williams, and in *Too True to Be Good* in 1932.

To be beyond the pale provokes opposite reactions—a wish to conform and be accepted, and an up-yours rebellion. Lillie was ruthless, and unpredictable under any spotlight, and if her classic female clown can prove anything, it is that before the bold new world of end-of-the-century lesbian chic, there was more to women loving women than the "boring loyalty ... earnestness ... and complete lack of humor" that Cecil Beaton and Mercedes de Acosta made fun of. Like young Dietrich and Margo Lion doing "Sisters" on the 1920s Berlin stage, and k. d. lang singing her sultry ballads 1990s style, Lillie was always on the edge of the permissible.

14

Sodom-on-the-Pacific

Minta Durfee Arbuckle was a slim, elegant lady who had survived them all and was usually seated at the head of the table when, in the early 1970s, survivors of the silent era met younger *cinémanes* eager to hear firsthand reports from the Paleolithic age before sound. Her recollection of the William Desmond Taylor murder was no less vivid than the scandal that destroyed her husband's career. The decades, and perhaps the fact that both took place less than six months apart, evened up the two in her mind. Both cases blew sky-high. Arbuckle was heterosexual and the press played up the sensational case. Taylor was not, and stayed buried for sixty years.

Roscoe "Fatty" Arbuckle was a grossly fat man weighing over three hundred pounds. What made him a star of Mack Sennett's Keystone Kops two-reelers was that he was fantastically coordinated and light on his feet, an unlikely combination that served as a basis for much of his comedy. The public adored him. After being successfully teamed with Chaplin, Mabel Normand, and Buster Keaton in movie shorts, he was a $7,000-a-week Paramount player beginning to direct and star in feature-length pictures. Roscoe and Minta Arbuckle bought a Tudor mansion on West Adams Boulevard for $250,000. The garage housed their Cadillac, Renault, and Rolls-Royce, and a $25,000 Pierce-Arrow.

Over the 1921 Labor Day weekend, Arbuckle threw a party at the St. Francis Hotel in San Francisco. Virginia Rappe was a twenty-five-year-old bit player whom Arbuckle's friend Buster Keaton would later describe as being "about as virtuous as most of the untalented other young women knocking around in Hollywood for years." She had one orange blossom too many, fell ill, and began tearing off her clothes—a habit of hers when she had too many cocktails. Partygoers would disagree on what happened next.

Friendly testimony would allege that Arbuckle, in the presence of other women, viewed the prostrate Virginia on his bed, tested to see if she was faking by holding a piece of ice against her thigh, then helped carry the nude girl to a bathtub to try to revive her while somebody called the house physician. Less friendly witnesses would tell of screams from behind the locked door, of Fatty emerging, his pajamas dripping under a dry bathrobe, and the girl on the bed moaning, "I'm dying. He broke me inside. I'm dying." She was taken to the exclusive Pine Street hospital. Her bladder had been ruptured by some form of violence. Four days later she died of peritonitis.

Minta was in New York with her mother when it happened. She rushed to her husband's side, stood by him during the trial for manslaughter, and lost her savings on lawyers. Minta had been Chaplin's costar at Keystone and knew Rappe as a sweet fellow actress, and more recently as the girlfriend of Henry "Pathé" Lehrman.

The Arbuckle case inflamed public opinion. Ever mindful of the healthy effect of scandal on circulation, the press whipped up the sex-orgy-with-murder investigation. The Arbuckle scandal came on the heels of Mary Pickford's Nevada quickie divorce from Owen Moore and her marriage, a month later, to Douglas Fairbanks; Charlie Chaplin's trying to escape charges surrounding his divorce from the teenage Mildred Harris; and the California State Board of Pharmacy revelation that over five hundred film personalities were listed on its rolls as drug addicts.

The evidence against Fatty was considered so unspeakable that it could not be discussed aloud in court but was passed around

silently in typewritten notes. At his first appearance, the head of
the Women's Vigilante Committee of San Francisco was so aroused
by the sight of women applauding the famous comedian's entrance
that she cried, "Women of America, do your duty," and with the
members of her committee covered Fatty with spit. The Hearst
chain whipped the trial into a national scandal. Buster Keaton, who
once overheard William Randolph Hearst say the Arbuckle story
sold more Hearst newspapers than the sinking of the *Lusitania,*
would suggest the press baron never believed Arbuckle guilty.

Two trials resulted in hung juries. Cheers broke out in the court-
room when the jury in a third trial acquitted Arbuckle and, in a remarkable statement, said, "We feel a great injustice has been
done." The trials had cost the State of California $25,000; Roscoe
and Minta $50,000. Under the banner headline "Arbuckle Acquit-
ted in One Minute," Hearst's *Los Angeles Examiner* said, "Comedian
to Come Back If Public Wills." But Paramount canceled Roscoe's
$3-million contract and junked his unreleased films. The
Arbuckles sold the house on West Adams to Joseph Schenck and
Norma Talmadge. To cheer Roscoe up, Keaton suggested he
change his name to Will B. Good. Together, they refined the
moniker to William Goodrich, and it was under that name that
Fatty directed Marion Davies in *The Red Mill* in 1927. In the March
1931 issue of *Photoplay,* Arbuckle pleaded to be allowed back before
the cameras. Broke and broken, he died a year later in New York.
He was forty-six.

William Desmond Taylor was the first British actor-turned-director
of note to work in Hollywood. When the Arbuckle scandal broke,
the handsome bachelor, with a reputation as a ladies' man and a
preference for having himself photographed in his British Army
major's uniform, was elected president of the new Motion Picture
Directors Association. He was liked by Paramount's boss, Adolph
Zukor, because he didn't try to bed every actress he worked with,
and because he knew how to keep his mouth shut. Paramount had
its share of drug addicts, including Wallace Reid, a blue-eyed, six-
foot charmpot who was fast becoming the newest matinee idol and
making $2,000 a week, and Mary Pickford's younger brother Jack.
And Bill Taylor knew how to handle them.

Taylor's friends were fellow directors Mickey Neilan and James

Kirkwood, Latin-lover actor Antonio Moreno, and their girlfriends Colleen Moore, Mabel Normand, and Mary Miles Minter. Neilan was the lover of newly divorced Paramount star Gloria Swanson. Colleen Moore was a fast-rising new face; Mabel Normand, whose adult career owed much to Taylor, was currently Sam Goldwyn's $1,500-a-week leading lady, while Minter was Paramount's newest Mary Pickford look-alike. Kirkwood and teenaged Minter were former lovers, and their deep dark secret was an abortion that Charlotte Shelby, Mary's mother, had forced upon her meal-ticket daughter. Shelby took a third of her daughter's earnings for herself. Mary sued her mother in 1926 for $1,345,000, but curiously settled out of court for $25,000.

When Colleen and Antonio, Mabel and Mary, and their dates didn't sail to Catalina Island on Sundays or go for spins to Lake Arrowhead or Palm Springs in their fabulous roadsters, they sipped bootleg cocktails and one-stepped in nightclubs. After a year at the Hollywood Health Club, the tony residence for moneyed bachelors, Bill Taylor had moved to an apartment court at Alvarado Street. Edna Purviance, Chaplin's leading lady and intimate friend, occupied the other half of the building.

On February 1, 1922, Bill Taylor was shot to death in his bungalow apartment by an unknown assailant. "Mabel Normand Quizzed in Screen Chief's Murder," screamed the *Los Angeles Evening Express* the next day. Mabel was indeed the last person to have seen the director alive, and as the details became known, the murder mystery sold more newspapers than the outbreak of World War I. When police arrived at the scene, they found Edna Purviance watching Paramount executives burning papers in the fireplace. In the bedroom, detectives found love letters and undergarments belonging to the underage Mary Miles Minter. The ladies' underwear, some of it initialed MMM, was of a larger size than the diminutive Mary and was said to have been worn by Bill Taylor during visits to unmentionable drag parties. Homicide detectives quickly established that Mabel Normand, Mary Miles Minter, and Mary's mother had visited Taylor the night of the murder. Within days, rumors had it that Taylor had been having simultaneous affairs with all three. A fourth paramour was added when newspapers insinuated he had been the cause of the suicide of Zelda Crosby, a Paramount screenwriter.

Police—and the press—discovered William Desmond Taylor was in fact William Deane Tanner, who, after the Great War, had gone to New York, tried stage directing, married, fathered a child, and skipped out on mother and daughter to try gold prospecting in the Yukon and Alaska. The director Allan Dwan, who gave the war-veteran-turned-director-turned-gold-rush-prospector his first break as a movie actor, would dismiss the name change as inconsequential.

"Everyone did it," Dwan would say. "I was christened Aloysius Dwan. Mary Pickford was Gladys Smith. It was a matter of setting the right image. And William Desmond Taylor was a brilliant choice. It sounded like someone from an English novel, the kind Hollywood liked making into films. It set him apart from the aspiring actors arriving by the trainload from places like Kansas and Nebraska. Taylor was sharp."

Further sleuthing revealed that Sands, Taylor's butler, who had skipped to Mexico after forging his master's signature on a $5,000 check, was actually his brother. Next, a "dope angle" developed. Because Taylor had been trying to get Mabel Normand off her $500-a-week addiction, the murderer was perhaps her cocaine dealer.

At the funeral, Mary Miles Minter approached the open casket and kissed Taylor's lips. A second later, she announced to the assembled mourners the dead man had whispered to her that he would always love her.

"When everything came out in the papers," Gloria Swanson would recall, "I knew better than to ask." She knew plenty. She knew Mabel was a cocaine addict seeking help in her friendship with Taylor, that Mary's love letters and panties—bandied about by police as evidence—had been planted by the studio to cover Taylor's deep dark secret—his homosexuality.[1]

Press reports were limited to such mentions as that Taylor had

---

1. The Taylor murder inspired mystery novels and screenplays, but was never solved. Former Hearst Hollywood correspondent Adela Rogers St. Johns told a 1979 television interviewer there was never any doubt that Charlotte Shelby was the murderer. After an intense investigation over many years, director King Vidor came to the same conclusion. Feeling spurned by Taylor in favor of her daughter, Charlotte Shelby shot and killed the director on February 1, 1922, and for years paid off successive Los Angeles district attorneys.

recently visited "queer meeting places," dens of iniquity where strange effeminate men and peculiarly masculine women dressed in kimonos, and where morphine and opium were wheeled in on tea carts. The presence of a black teenage boy at Taylor's Alvarado Street home was never mentioned. Modern authors tend to see the six-decade-long hush-up of the Taylor case as proof that homosexuality was a greater scandal than unprosecuted murder.

"Gays served as the perfect scapegoats in crackdowns and arrest sweeps," Harry Hay would say in recalling how, before every mayoral or city-council election, the parks where gay men met for midnight trysts were raided so politicians and police could brag of cleaning them up. "The front page of the [Los Angeles] *Times* in 1930 blared that when the body of a murdered boy was found, the house of 'every known deviant' was searched."

Sex and suicides, dope addiction and murder—both Mabel Normand and Mary Miles Minter were finished—seemed the very warp and woof of Hollywood's loom of life. And the shocks didn't let up. Valentino married Natasha Rambova in Mexico without waiting the full year required by California law for his interlocutory divorce from Jean Acker. While Paramount managed to suppress the fact that both wives were lesbians, the studio was less lucky when its all-time all-American Wallace Reid died a drug addict. If that wasn't enough, his widow, Dorothy Davenport, charged that, in order to maintain the grueling schedule Paramount demanded of its stars, the studio bosses had supplied him with morphine and that in order to finish his last picture underlings had propped him up before the camera. Cecil B. DeMille had visited Reid in a padded cell in a private sanatorium and came away shocked at seeing the strapping actor reduced to a gaunt skeleton weighing just over a hundred pounds.

The fan magazines printed open letters to the stars, pleading with them to abandon their wicked ways. Politicians sensed that being in favor of censorship spelled votes. In self-defense, Paramount's Adolph Zukor and Jesse Lasky, and twelve other studio chiefs, adopted baseball's strategy after the 1919 World Series fix came to light. The baseball bosses had found a $50,000 solution in making Judge Kenesaw Mountain Landis their keep-the-game-clean-boys "czar." The movie moguls doubled the money and hired Will H. Hays, a Presbyterian elder and Indiana politician who, as chairman of the Republican National Committee, and with money from oilman Harry "Teapot Dome" Sinclair, had secured the nomination of easygoing Warren G. Harding as presidential candidate in 1921 and served as postmaster general in the Harding administration.

In March 1922, Hays was given absolute authority to police the morals of the film industry. He began a public relations blitz and made it clear to everybody in the business that personal lives would have to withstand public scrutiny. The studios inserted "morals clauses" permitting contract cancellations if their players were so much as accused of immorality, while those whose behavior was beyond the pale were blacklisted. The Doom Book soon included 117 names deemed "unsafe" because of their no-longer-private lives. To put an end to the influx of eager young actresses lured west by "scouts" from shady talent schools, Hays established a central casting agency through which extras could find employment at the studios and where applications could be screened. To further shelter the Goldilocks, Bess Lasky, the wife of Paramount boss Jesse Lasky, and several other matrons organized the Hollywood Studio Club, where "decent" girls could find lodging, board, and protection, often from the good ladies' own husbands.

A thornier issue for Hays, trickier than anything his fellow czars in baseball and horse racing had to deal with, was what to forbid. How do your protect the public by removing from the screen what people pay to see? Snipping the films to the varying requirements of different state—and sometimes even municipal—censorship boards brought constant headaches. The answer was a code—a codification of existing state, provincial, and municipal censorship edicts that would allow producers to get their movies shown in a maximum of territories with a minimum of costly changes.

In the name of free speech, Hays rallied citizens' committees *against* censorship and, to prevent Congress and state lawmakers from rushing through censorship bills, announced the creation of the Production Code, the film industry's self-censorship. The Production, or Hays, Code was sweeping and explicit. The moguls adopted the Code with the enthusiasm of a tax bill in an election year. With one tightening and several loosenings, it survived until 1968.

15

Talking Pictures

I cannot talk—I cannot sing,
Nor screech nor moan nor anything.
Possessing all these fatal strictures,
What chance have I in motion pictures.
—*Photoplay,* January 1929

The microphone—"King Mike" or "Terrible Mike" to perplexed casts and crews—played havoc with careers and spelled new trouble for performing homosexuals. What had been a pantomime of hints, winks, and allusions in silent movies was shockingly amplified when words matched the action, and the coming of sound gave ammunition to pro-censorship pressure groups. The 1920s series of scandals gave churchmen, clubwomen, schoolteachers, and editorial writers the chance to inveigh against the new Sodom-on-the-Pacific. Direct reference to homosexuality was forbidden. A certain latitude existed, however, in characterization and dress, allowing for three stereotypes—the villainous mannish woman, the predatory, sophisticated bitch, and the neurotic, usually closeted spinster.

Borderline male homosexuals were tolerated if they were pathetic-comic characters. Edmund Goulding started the trend in talkies by letting Jed Prouty play a sassy, nervous-Nellie costume designer flitting around like a butterfly in the 1929 *Broadway Melody.* Edward Everett Horton was a pansy reporter in Lewis Milestone's *Front Page* in 1931 and went on to play a series of jittery, befuddled, mild-mannered sissies. Eric Blore, a London lawyer-turned-actor, was Stanwyck's foil as Herbert Marshall's limp-wristed butler in

Breakfast for Two and made a career of playing haughty and petulant manservants—his discourse on crumpets and scones in *The Gay Divorcée* set a new high for a gentleman's gentleman hilarity. Franklin Pangborn taught Lupe Velez how to be a lady in D. W. Griffith's *Lady of the Pavement* and went on from there to play harassed, flustered sissies in smart-aleck comedies like William Seiter's *Professional Sweetheart* with Ginger Rogers and Mitchell Leisen's *Fast Living* with Jean Arthur.

Lesbians were not fun. The boys could be mocked and parodied as bitchy sissies, but lesbians were grim, twisted creatures whose sick and tormented lives had no place on the screen. To prove it, a *Photoplay* reviewer condemned the use of "disgusting perverts" in Rex Ingram's 1926 film *Mare Nostrum*. The fan magazine charged that the adaptation of the Vicente Blasco Ibáñez romantic tragedy starring Antonio Moreno and Alice Terry featured a vaguely lesbian spy.

Defiance of society's sexual definitions became riskier when the realism of sound and the fierce demands for stricter censorship resulted in the tightening of the Production Code in 1930. The studios fell over backward to comply with the new restrictions. At MGM, the title of a Jean Harlow movie about a chorus girl determined to be virtuous until the right millionaire comes along was changed from *Born to Be Kissed* to *100 Percent Pure* to *Eadie Was a Lady,* then soberly released as *The Girl From Missouri*. Warner Brothers kept the title *Baby Face,* but in postproduction editing toned down Barbara Stanwyck's gold digger. Back in vogue were films based on Dickens, Louisa May Alcott, and J. M. Barrie that brought Victorian life to the screen. When Dietrich, Garbo, and Katharine Hepburn appeared in men's clothes in 1930s movies, the point was to add spice to the war of the sexes and to make the goddesses more appealing to their leading men.

Irving Thalberg and many leading directors weren't sure talking pictures were more than a fad. They felt sound would destroy a unique art form and lessen the commercial value of Hollywood movies in non-English-speaking countries. None of the top directors were anxious to rush into talkies, partly because they were afraid of losing their reputations, partly because they disliked the new technology. Josef von Sternberg thought that unless sound became as pliable as the camera, it was little more than a saccharine, charmless frosting. Directors, like stars and writers, had to prove themselves all over again, and several directors of repute, including Fred Niblo, who had directed Garbo in *The Temptress* and *Mysterious Lady,* had difficulties adjusting.

The free-flowing action and continuity everybody was comfortable with was displaced by a static, stagelike technique, both because the cameras had to be immured in soundproof booths and because the microphone was at first immovable and all action had to be geared to its location. Directors tore their hair when their most cherished dramatic efforts were vetoed by their sound engineers, new despots trained by the telephone companies, whose only concern was that all conversation be conducted at one voice level. Soundmen with earphones plugged into black magic boxes lorded it over the movie sets. They concealed microphones in flowerpots, dictated where actors could stand in order to record, and yelled "Cut!" if any actor turned his or her head away from the mike. Since sound film ran at twenty-four frames per second instead of sixteen, twice as much light was needed to expose the same strip of celluloid. Already nervous actors were soaked to the skin under the heat of the added kilowatts.

On the theory that perhaps only stage players could deliver acceptable accents, studios brought out Broadway actors by the trainloads. The list of stars playing a waiting game before "going sound" included Gloria Swanson, Lillian Gish, and Norma Talmadge. Fearful of fluffing her battle with King Mike, Swanson hired Broadway actress Laura Hope Crews at $1,000 a week to teach her elocution. The opportunities presented by Hollywood stars with uncultured and untrained vocal cords resulted in a second California gold rush. Still, failures outnumbered successes. At Paramount, Thomas Meighan, Richard Dix, and Bebe Daniels were let go; the studio disdained even giving them a voice test. Milton Sills became the first suicide.

MGM was more worried about Garbo's accent than Gilbert's voice. As it turned out, Gilbert was not only the victim of imperfect sound equipment that registered his tenor voice like Donald Duck's, but of Mayer's turf battle with Loews Inc., Metro's parent company in New York. The Loews office had negotiated Gilbert's contract, and Mayer was hell-bent to reassert control of all studio operations. The way to do it was to sabotage Gilbert's career and prove him a has-been. Not that Gilbert didn't try to fight back. His $10,000-a-week contract still had years to go, and he spent two hours a day with each of three speech coaches. When Mayer wouldn't see him, Gilbert broke into Mayer's office, crying, "Listen to me now. I can talk."

Mayer and Thalberg delayed Garbo's sound debut and in choosing Eugene O'Neill's *Anna Christie* found a near-perfect vehicle for her speaking debut.

Garbo's last silent, *The Kiss,* was completed in September 1929, nearly two years after Al Jolson burst into song in *The Jazz Singer.* Few believed she could pass the microphone test, but Mayer and Thalberg were shrewd in picking O'Neill's 1922 theatrical work-horse. For one, her accent as a Swedish sea captain's daughter was appropriate. Thalberg assigned Frances Marion to adapt O'Neill's play, and the script gave Garbo a few antimale zingers: "That's men again! How I hate 'em, every mother's son of them."

The film gave Garbo a new lover.

"I will never forget her warm body, simple love, wisdom, and perceptive, friendly attitude toward me," Garbo would say of Marie Dressler. "She gave me the opportunity to meet other women and displayed great love for all her friends. She taught me not to be ashamed of this kind of love."

The massive, homely Marie Dressler was Metro's unlikeliest star. She had known fame in her youth, and neglect in her middle years. After waiting fourteen years for a comeback, she reached overnight stardom opposite Wallace Beery in *Min and Bill,* winning the Best Actress Oscar over Dietrich, Shearer, Irene Dunne, and Ann Harding. After *Tugboat Annie,* Dressler and Beery held the number one spot on the annual exhibitors' poll of the biggest box-office stars.

Dressler spiced up with humor her brief *Anna Christie* scenes as the dowdy barfly. Offscreen, she knew how to comfort and humor her star, who said, "When I was sad or emotionally exhausted, she would come to see me, sensing my need for her. Standing on my doorway, she would sing 'Heaven Will Protect the Working Girl.' This song would mark the beginning of our evening. And when she was ready to return home the next day, she would sing her goodbye with the same song."

Since Garbo spoke German, MGM decided to shoot a German-language version of the expensive *Anna Christie*. The movie was filmed a second time on the same sets, with Jacques Feyder replacing Clarence Brown as the director and Salka taking over Dressler's role. Salka regaled Garbo with trenchant comments on everybody. "I wish I could be like you," Garbo told her one day. "If I had your vitality and temperament, I'd be world famous. "

For the March 4, 1930, U.S. premiere, MGM blanketed the country with "Garbo talks!" publicity. And Clarence Brown held back the pivotal moment until, in a waterfront dive twenty minutes into the picture, she uttered the memorable words, "Gimme a wyskey. Chinger ale on the side."

16

Hepburn and the Lady Director

Dorothy Arzner was Hollywood's only woman director and, as such, was one of the boys—in her own mind and in the minds of her fellow directors. Writer Zoë Akins was the sewing circle's resuscitator of flagging careers, and Katharine Hepburn was Arzner and Akins's lucky star. This proto-feminist triad came together in 1933 to make *Christopher Strong*, an Amelia Earhart-inspired box-office flop that Hepburn hated and latter-day feminists turned into a cult movie.

The director of the silent era was the original jack-of-all-trades, and, with the cameraman, the original technician. The cameraman had to prove he could thread the camera, but the director didn't have to prove anything. All he had to do was to shout and beguile his actors. He often dressed up for the part, sported puttees, and wielded a riding crop. Nobody could think of letting a woman direct until Arzner, James Cruze's assistant on the epic western *Covered Wagon,* came along. Born with the century, Arzner dressed butch and knew the rules included never discussing her sexual preference.

"She looked more like a man than any actress they ever let work in front of a camera, so it wasn't a big relevation," Marjorie Main would recall. Arzner was a lover of Laurette Taylor and of Zoë Akins, the successful playwright and screenwriter of four of her movies. As Hollywood's only woman director during the 1930s and

1940s, Arzner directed eighteen films between 1927 and 1943 and worked with Crawford, Hepburn, Colbert, Clara Bow, Rosalind Russell, Lucille Ball, Merle Oberon, Frances Dee, Anna Sten, Sylvia Sidney, Ginger Rogers, and Ruth Chatterton, and cast Fredric March in four of her films. Her one regret was she and Dietrich never got to make *Stepdaughters of War,* a story showing how war makes women hard and masculine.

Arzner was something of a rarity in the movie business, a native of Los Angeles. Her father, Louis Arzner, owned a famous restaurant on Hollywood Boulevard, and she grew up seeing Maude Adams, Sarah Bernhardt, David Warfield, and other touring stage actors at the Pantages Theater next to her father's restaurant. D. W. Griffith, Mary Pickford, Douglas Fairbanks, Mack Sennet, and other picture people dined at Louis Arzner's, and for Dorothy they held little interest. She went to University of Southern California (USC) medical school, but abandoned medicine at the first sight of surgery. "I wanted to be like Jesus—heal the sick and raise the dead without surgery and pills."

William DeMille, Cecil's brother, gave her a chance to start at the bottom typing scripts at Paramount. She watched Cecil B. in action and decided that if anyone wanted to be in pictures, he or she should be a director because the director tells everyone else what to do. Within six months, she was a film cutter, editing fifty-two silent pictures, including Fred Niblo's *Blood and Sand* with Valentino, for which she got to shoot some second-unit footage of a bullfight. Then came *The Covered Wagon,* James Cruze's epic western filmed in Utah, eighty-five miles from the nearest railhead. She stayed with Cruze through *The Covered Wagon* and *Old Ironsides,* scripting and editing as the two big pictures were in production, and was the continuity girl on a Nazimova picture.

She felt a woman has to be twice as good as a man to be regarded as comparable and expected to be let go when she told B. P. Schulberg she would leave to direct low-budget pictures at Columbia. Instead, he gave her a French farce called *The Best Dressed Woman in Paris,* and told her to write the script and be ready to start directing Esther Ralston in the title role in two weeks. Herman J. Mankiewicz and Jules Furthman were the heavyweight scripters of the retitled *Fashions for Women.* Her ninth film, *Honor*

Among Lovers with March and Claudette Colbert, was considered the smartest comedy of 1931.

In the early 1930s, Arzner and Zoë Akins were each other's best inspiration, foil, and collaborator. Zoë, who was four years older than Arzner, was also the sewing circle's emergency service for reviving acting careers. This dramatist and screenwriter wrote plays and scripts for lovers, former and present, and best friends' lovers. To boost Laurette Taylor's sagging career, she wrote *The Furies*, a whodunit about a wife accused of killing her millionaire husband that later became a Barbara Stanwyck vehicle. For Tallulah Bankhead and Lilyan Tashman, she wrote *Girls About Town*, a play about a pair of love-struck gold diggers. Tallulah inspired Akins's play *Morning Glory*, which Katharine Hepburn got to do on the screen. To help the sixty-year-old, destitute Alla Nazimova, Zoë and George Cukor created a job for her as technical adviser on *Zaza*.

Akins was the daughter of a rich and strongly Republican St. Louis, Missouri, family. She wrote her first play when she was twelve, but was thirty-three when she made her debut as a playwright with *Déclassée*, a drawing-room drama in which Ethel Barrymore committed the unpardonable sin of becoming involved with a man who cheats at cards. Despite a cool reception by Alexander Woollcott and the Algonquin crowd, the play gained Zoë public acclaim. Unlike Edna Ferber, who went down on her knees to ask for an invitation to lunch with the Algonquin crowd, the grand and aloof Akins refused to beg Woollcott, Franklin Pierce Adams, Heywood Broun, Ruth Hale, Robert Benchley, George and Beatrice Kaufman, and Dorothy Parker.

The Washington Square Players made Akins's *Magical City* a part of its repertory in 1919, and because she knew European society, Edith Wharton had approved of her to adapt *The Age of Innocence* to the silent screen. Since then, Zoë had won a Pulitzer Prize for her dramatization of Wharton's *Old Maid* for the stage, revised *Zaza* to fit Claudette Colbert's talent, and, without credits, rewritten *Keeper of the Flame* to strengthen Katharine Hepburn's great man's widow part.

Zoë Akins had come to California for her health in 1928 and, in less than two years, established herself as a screenwriter. She found movie people vulgar and lived snobbishly in a Pasadena mansion staffed with liveried British servants. In 1932, her search for gentility made her marry the son of a British diplomat, Hugo Rumbold, who, perhaps all too conveniently, died within months of the wedding. As Joseph Mankiewicz would recall, she "wrote all terribly elegant Maugham imitations and adopted the most incredible English accent." At Paramount in 1933, Akins and Mankiewicz had offices next to each other on the fourth floor of the Writers Building. He was working with his writing mentor Grover Jones one afternoon when Zoë stuck her head in: "Do pardon me for interrupting you, but could you tell me what exactly is the *shedule* on *Tom Sawyer?* To which Jones said, "Oh, *skit.*"

Zoë put a lot of Tallulah Bankhead and a bit of herself in *Morning Glory,* a play about a selfish young actress from Kansas who wants to rise to the top and prove she is more than just a "morning glory." RKO producer Pandro Berman thought *Morning Glory* was ideal for Hepburn, and when the play was staged at the Pasadena Playhouse, he got tickets for her and her live-in companion, Laura Harding.

Katharine Hepburn liked to shock with her boyish looks, strident voice, breeding, and, when she met people for the first time, her affection for purposely creating a bad impression. Rigid and repressed, the twenty-four-year-old, freckle-faced Connecticut Yankee always lived with women, mingled with sewing-circle members, and made Garbo and Katharine Cornell her icons. She was swimming naked in director George Cukor's pool when she first met Garbo and, in printed versions of the encounter, grabbed a towel, curtsied, and solemnly said, "Oh, Miss Garbo, how nice to meet you!" Hepburn was seen about town with her agent, the dashing, successful Leland Hayward, but Hayward's third wife, Margaret Sullavan, called Kate "that dikey bitch."

From the ages nine to thirteen, Kit or Kathy had shaved her head and called herself Jimmy. The family of Dr. Thomas Hepburn of West Hartford, Connecticut, summered at Fenwick at the mouth of the Connecticut River, and the eldest daughter wore her elder brother Tom's cast-off clothes to go sailing, clam digging, and fishing. Tom's suicide when she was ten turned her into a bitter, moody, aloof, and suspicious adolescent. Her years at Bryn Mawr College, her mother's alma mater, were painful. Only the chance to appear in college theatricals made her study. Her decision during her sophomore year to become an actress led to the Edwin H. Knopf stock company in Baltimore and the Theater Guild in New York.

Laura Harding, heiress to the American Express fortune, and Hepburn were inseparable, and Berman was not the only executive to realize that the way to persuade Kate to take on a role was to arouse her friend's enthusiasm. Laura was an athletic New Englander who met Hepburn in 1928 and was still a friend when Kate played Coco Chanel on Broadway in 1969. The two had met fresh out of college, and their companionship was framed within the public bounds of feminine friendship. Harding would call their relationship "intense" and tell Hepburn's biographer Charles Higham that she didn't approve of Kate's bohemian ways. "I adored her and I still do," Harding said in 1975.

Hepburn reminded Ethel and John Barrymore—and *Time* magazine—of Maude Adams. Hepburn's gamine manners were in the Adams style, and Kate was flattered when told of her resemblance to the actress who, at seventy, was still playing the strawhat circuit. David O. Selznick, RKO's young boss, and director George Cukor thought themselves heroically bold when they signed her to play Sidney Fairfield in the movie version of Clemence Dane's *Bill of Divorcement*. Katharine Cornell had played the part on Broadway, and Selznick wanted a new face for the picture.

"When she first appeared on the RKO lot, there was consternation," he would remember. "'Ye gods, that horse face!' they cried, and when the first rushes were shown, the gloom around the studio was so heavy you could cut it with a knife." Adela Rogers St. Johns thought the appallingly dressed person she was introduced to was Cukor's new boyfriend.

Arzner wanted to adopt Zoë's stage hit *The Greeks Had a Word for Them* (eventually cinematized by Samuel Goldwyn), but *Sarah and Son*, her second collaboration with Akins, launched the screen careers of Ruth Chatterton and Fredric March and broke Paramount box-office records in New York. When Lowell Sherman got to direct and act in *The Greeks Had a Word for Them*, Arzner and Akins made *Anybody's Woman*, a tedious matrimonial melodrama about an alcoholic lawyer (Clive Brook) who, to his regret, marries a chorus girl (Chatterton), only to see her reform him. After *Working Girls,* the fourth Arzner-Akins collaboration about two beautiful country girls learning city life from a pair of slickers, they came up with *Christopher Strong,* Katharine Hepburn's second film, and first starring role.

Christopher Strong looked promising, and speculation centered on whether Hepburn would repeat her "initial smash impression," as *Variety* put it, in *Bill of Divorcement.* Before *Christopher Strong* got under way, she pitched Eugene O'Neill's *Mourning Becomes Electra* to Louis B. Mayer with Garbo as Christine and herself as Lavinia. The idea originated with Theresa Helburn, a board member of New York's Theater Guild. Alice Brady and Alla Nazimova had played O'Neill's mother and daughter in love with the same man, and Hepburn came west to look for a film deal. O'Neill thought Hepburn was a wonderful choice for Lavinia but feared censorship would ruin his trilogy. Kate went to see Mayer to suggest MGM buy the play and borrow her from RKO. Louis B. hated the idea.

Akins was distracted by personal problems during the writing of *Christopher Strong,* but Kate dutifully motored to Arzner's Grecian home on Los Feliz Terrace every night for dinner and discussions of her role. When Zoë finished the script, she read it to the cast members sitting around her in a circle.

Director and star didn't get along once filming started during the rainy winter of 1932–33. Hepburn would always have a hard time simulating sexual passion, and her romantic scenes would always remain stylized, with a lot of swooning and artful backlighting. She thought Arzner's direction limp and uninspired. Arzner, in turn, was put off by her star's blue-blood superiority complex, which also grated on producer Pandro Berman. What didn't help was that Hepburn found out she was the second choice, that Arzner had wanted Ann Harding to play the aviatrix.

"Her tone was all wrong," Arzner would remember. "I had to soften her constantly. But sometimes she was wonderful; there was a scene in a boat with her married lover, and she said, 'Do you love me, Chris?' and he replied, 'Call it love if you like.' I wanted the scene played without any emotion at all. I canceled a whole morning's work because I couldn't make the scene 'play,' and finally I decided it had to be two people who couldn't express any emotions. At first she played the scene headlong, but when I told her to look blank, she did, and her voice went wonderfully flat and tone-less. She and Colin Clive played it superbly—people said it was the best love story on the screen."

Hepburn's portrayal of the aviatrix prompted Samuel Goldwyn to call *Christopher Strong* the best picture of 1933. Reviewers were less kind, although critic Gerard Peary wrote, "Hepburn demon-strates with the certitude of an Isadora Duncan that a woman's true happiness comes through intense, front-seat participation in an ex-citing profession." Fifty years later, Pauline Kael would call it one of the rare movies told from a woman's sexual point of view.

In her later years, Arzner would remind interviewers that al-though her picture was made at the height of the Amelia Earhart craze, it was based on the life of the British flier Amy Lovell, who made a round-the-world flight and also broke the altitude record in her time. Akins's screenplay gave Christopher Strong (Colin Clive), the distinguished politician the aviatrix falls in love with, an angel of a wife (Billie Burke) and a marriageable daughter (Helen Chandler), who is attracted to a much-divorced friend of the fam-ily's (Ralph Forbes). Rather than hurt his wife, Cynthia Darring-ton, as the aviatrix was renamed, Chris decides to end the liaison. As soon as she goes to bed with Chris, he insists—late on the first night—that she not fly in the round-the-world race she is entered in. In New York, where the race ends with Cynthia winning, the af-fair is on again. But back in London, Strong's daughter catches the lovers at a clandestine rendezvous. Upbraided by the daughter, Cynthia decides to work her own way out. She intimates to Chris that she is pregnant and takes off on a solo altitude record- breaking flight. At thirty thousand feet, she commits suicide by removing her oxygen mask and losing control of the aircraft.

In analyzing the film, Kael calls the lovers' night where the man insists she not enter the race the intelligent woman's primal post-coital scene: "In movies up to the seventies, this primal scene was never played out satisfactorily; the woman always gave in, either in pasteup screwball style that provided fake resolutions of the forties, or, as in this picture, fatally (the heroine commits suicide)."

Arzner thought Chris more interesting than any of the women characters. He was a man completely absorbed in his career. "He loved his wife, and he fell in love with the aviatrix," she would re-call. "He was on the rack. I was really more sympathetic with him, but no one seemed to pick that up. Of course, not too many women are sympathetic about the torture the situation might give to a man of upright character."

Akins was adapting her *Morning Glory* play when her husband died. "He's dead, poor fellow," she told Pandro Berman, who had rushed to her house in Pasadena. Zoë continued writing and Berman showed her finished script to Harding, whose enthusiasm made Hepburn say yes. Lowell Sherman directed *Morning Glory,* in which Hepburn won her first Oscar as the rebellious and ruthless young actress on the make. Arzner got to direct Goldwyn's Russian import, Anna Sten.

The shooting script Goldwyn handed Arzner was the fiftieth draft. At one point, he scrapped $400,000 worth of finished film and had everybody start over again. Goldwyn believed he had found *his* Garbo in the Rubenesque Sten, and he hired speech coaches to help with her impenetrable accent, masseurs to trim her down, and ordered his press chief, Lynn Farnol, to pull out all the stops. For Sten's debut, he had chosen *Nana,* Emile Zola's 1880 tale of a skid-row girl turned demimondaine who humiliates the upper-class men responsible for her former misery. When the revised *Nana* opened at New York's Radio City Music Hall in 1934, it broke all first-day records, thanks to Farnol's publicity. The next day, the reviews killed it.

Fearlessly, Goldwyn gave Sten a Russian story, Rouben Mamoulian as her director, and Fredric March as her costar. *We Live Again* was a rewrite of Tolstoy's *Resurrection,* a drama of sin and regeneration. When the picture flopped, Goldwyn got Arzner back to take Sten through the paces in *The Wedding Night,* and from Paramount he borrowed Gary Cooper to play a novelist who, while staying at a Connecticut farm, becomes involved with a Polish peasant girl. When this drama was laughed off the screen, Goldwyn gave up on Sten.

Cukor and Hepburn had a surprise hit in *Little Women,* Louisa May Alcott's novel of four sisters in pre–Civil War New England. Joan Bennett, Jean Parker, and Frances Dee played the sisters to Hepburn's tomboy, who becomes the story's focus as she yearns to be a writer. The shoot was as happy as the subject with cast and crew picnicking during the filming. Cukor, however, found newcomer Spring Byington too saccharine as the girls' mother, a part he felt demanded gentle sternness. The forty-seven-year-old Byington was an active lesbian who lived with the comic Marjorie Main.

Joan of Arc was again a movie possibility during the summer of 1934, not for Garbo, but for Hepburn. The screenplay was not by de Acosta but by Thornton Wilder, and the studio was RKO, which had hit paydirt with *Little Women*. While Wilder rewrote Joan of Arc, Hepburn and Laura Harding went to Mexico so Kate could obtain a quick divorce from Ludlow Ogden Smith. The December 1928 marriage to the Philadelphia stockbroker had lasted six weeks. "In my relationships, I know that I have qualities that are offensive to people—especially men," she would say in 1975. After four weeks as Mrs. Ogden Smith, she had begged Broadway producer Arthur Hopkins to let her be the understudy for Hope Williams.

Laura Harding's place with Hepburn was usurped by a young film editor in 1935, and with much bitterness Laura returned to her family in New Jersey. "It had become obvious that I did not belong at the center of her life," Harding would remember forty years later. Jane Loring was the film editor of *Alice Adams*, Kate and RKO's smash of 1935, and the film's editor became the new young woman in Hepburn's life. Like Barbara Stanwyck's association with publicist Helen Ferguson, Loring's profession gave their friendship the veneer of a working relationship.

Louis B. Mayer lured Arzner and Akins and, in 1939, Hepburn to MGM.

Arzner was to direct Garbo, and Zoë's first assignment for Irving Thalberg was to write the new version of *The Green Hat*. The moment was not propitious. In signing on to the revised (and tightened) Production Code, the studios pledged not only to refrain from showing "any licentious or suggestive nudity—in fact or in silhouette, white slavery, sex hygiene," but also venereal disease. As cleaned up by Akins, directed by Robert Z. Leonard, and played by Constance Bennett and Herbert Marshall, the third screen rendition of the Michael Arlen novel had the hero commit suicide because his bride finds out he has served a term in a German prison for a crime described as infamous but never named. The picture was filmed under the title *Iris March* but released as *Outcast Lady* after the Hays Office complained audiences with long memories might associate it with Arlen's 1924 bestseller. *Outcast Lady,* said *Variety,* was "the chassis of *The Green Hat* with the motor taken out . . . dull, jumbled, and pointless."

Mayer killed the Arzner-Garbo project and assigned the director to give Crawford a new image, starting with *The Girl From Trieste,* Molnárs intimate case history of a young woman's descent into prostitution. As soon as Arzner reported to work, however, she was told her leading lady would be Luise Rainer, the Vienna-born actress. Arzner was scouting locations when Rainer was fired. The reason: she was marrying Clifford Odets, the playwright identified with the New Deal's more aggressive social agenda, and, to Mayer, a suspected communist. Joseph Mankiewicz rewrote the Molnár story to accommodate Crawford. The heroine was no longer a jaded prostitute who goes straight but a slightly cynical cabaret singer who gets to spend two weeks at a tony Austrian resort with Robert Young and Franchot Tone pursuing her. Arzner had her misgivings: "I knew that it would be synthetic, but Mayer knelt down, with those phony tears in his eyes, and said, 'We'll be eternally grateful to the woman who brings Crawford back.' " Adrian confected a red-beaded gown that Howard Strickling's publicity said cost $10,000. Cedric Gibbons did the sets.

Offscreen, Franchot Tone and Crawford were man and wife at the end of their marriage. To avenge himself from Joan's sexual taunts, he went to bed with a starlet. "It wasn't the cheating that bothered me," Crawford told *Photoplay's* Katharine Alberts. "It was the possibility that the girl could blackmail us."

For publicity photos, star and director dressed in matching men's suits. Renamed *The Bride Wore Red,* the film was a whimsical but less than successful star confection.

The National Theater Distributors of America put Crawford on its 1937 list of stars that its members considered box-office "poison." Dietrich and Hepburn joined her on the list. Franchot Tone reminded his wife of his suggestion that they live part-time in New York and try for more prestigious and gratifying stage work. Joan wailed, "No. We made those plans when I was a *star.* I can't go to New York and be a nobody." She decided to stall on MGM's offer of a straight $300,000 for her next two pictures but settled for $250,000 a year. Director Richard Boleslawski started her next film, *The Last of Mrs. Cheyney,* jewel thieves in a high-society comedy costarring Robert Montgomery and William Powell. When Bole-slawski died during the filming, Arzner took over.

Much later, when Crawford became the president of Pepsi-Cola, she hired the retired Arzner to make sixty commercials for Pepsi. Francine Parker, a 1990s filmmaker, believes Arzner was closeted "even to herself," that if she had been born fifty years later, she would have been openly gay.

We do not know Laura Harding's and Jane Loring's sexual orientation, but Hepburn's lifelong friend and mentor was the playmate of Mercedes de Acosta, Alla Nazimova, and Katharine Cornell. Constance Collier was a British actress twenty years Kate's senior. She had started out as a chorus girl, made her film debut in 1916 in D. W. Griffith's *Intolerance,* and a year later opened the Broadway season with John and Lionel Barrymore in a sensational *Peter Ibbetson.* When John Barrymore took his *Hamlet* to London in 1925, Connie played the queen and since then had appeared in more than one hundred theater productions.

Hepburn and Collier made *Stage Door* together, Kate billed third, Connie sixth. Hepburn wanted so much to be in the screen version of the scintillating Edna Ferber and George S. Kaufman play about the backbiting and camaraderie of young actresses waiting for the big break. Ginger Rogers and Adolphe Menjou were top-billed. Connie was cast as a wonderful old actress and drama coach, hard up but still proud. "With her gypsyish black hair and dark eyes, heavy figure, and delicious extravagant humor, Connie fascinated Kate, and her adoration is visible in their many scenes together in the picture itself," Charles Higham would write, adding delicately that "a now softer, more tender and considerate Kate learned to draw from Constance Collier's vast experience of the British and American stage, giving her in return a sense of understanding of her worth that was not easily found in Hollywood."

Connie was still there to coach Hepburn in Shakespearean drama when Kate played Rosalind in *As You Like It* on Broadway in 1950.

17

Odd Girls Abroad

Actors committed "indiscretions" under penalty of career death. Hollywood's and Broadway's women in love with women did not seem to need to bond like middle-class career lesbians, nor did they dare seek out the bars where lesbians on society's lower rungs acted out their sexuality in often rigid butch and femme demarcations. In the days before airline jet service and frequent-flyer mileage, however, there was one distant refuge—Natalie Barney's sapphic oasis. Paris and Barney's celebrated Friday nights were a destination of choice for traveling members of the sewing circle.

During the 1920s and 1930s, the wealthy, the brilliant, the sensual, and the unbalanced mixed in Barney's salon. Her male friends included the gay Marcel Proust, André Gide, and Max Jacob, the straight writers Gabriele d'Annunzio, Ezra Pound, Sherwood Anderson, the composers Darius Milhaud, Virgil Thomson, and George Antheil. But her house was most famous as a lesbian haven. Eccentric, self-mocking, outside the pale of society, Barney was a woman whose love life was notorious, her lovers beautiful, famous, and often full of violence. In her eighties, she suggested her own epitaph: "She was a friend of men and the lover of women, which for people full of ardor and drive is better than the other way around."

Natalie Clifford Barney was born into wealth in Dayton, Ohio, in 1877. A shapely, alert teenager, Natalie seduced a lady visitor of her mother's, conquered a servant girl and a governess. She completed her emotional education at Les Ruches girls school in Fontaine-bleau, France, and spent the money her parents sent her entertaining available women. She fended off her father's wish that she find a husband by suggesting she marry Lord Alfred Douglas, Oscar Wilde's ex. With an inheritance of $3.5 million in 1909 money, Natalie settled in Paris.

Her first serious love affair was with the notorious courtesan Liane de Pougy—Henri Meilhac, coauthor with Jacques Offenbach of *La Vie parisienne,* paid eighty thousand francs to see Pougy naked.[1] Natalie fell in love with Liane de Pougy merely by seeing her ride in the Bois de Boulogne and, after sending her passionate notes and flowers, seduced her. Liane insisted she rationed herself to men so she could save so much more of herself for Natalie.

Natalie's next conquest was the English poet Renée Vivien. They were both twenty, and although the charming Renée had little of the courtesan's sensational beauty, it took Natalie's serenading under the poet's windows to lure her away from another woman. Natalie and Renée fought and loved and fought again. After one poignant reconciliation, they set off in the splendor of the Orient Express to re-create Lesbos. They did not found a poets colony on the Greek island, but in verse and carnality exalted the love that since antiquity, as they said, had never been fittingly celebrated.

Barney liked the Parisians' indifference toward foreigners. She wrote poetry and prose in French, saying that a bilingual education was rather like having a mistress and a wife: you could never be sure of either. She appeared as Flossie in a Colette novel, as Valerie Seymour in *The Well of Loneliness* (Radclyffe Hall lived in Paris when she wrote the book), and as Moonbeam in a Liane de Pougy story. She treated men like hurt dogs but at times supported the writers Remy de Gourmont and James Joyce, and until her nineties remained the doyenne of the wealthy American women who felt freer in Paris. There was little love lost between Barney and Gertrude Stein. La Stein said of Natalie that she was famous before she was famous, and Barney thought Stein's writing "never really comes to the point."

Gertrude Stein, the "Mother of Us All," as Ernest Hemingway

---

1. Nearly $170,000 in 1995 money.

"The whole point about Tallulah," said Alfred Hitchcock, "was that she had no inhibitions." Tallulah by Beaton. *Photo: Bettmann Archives*

Bankhead being made up for *Tarnished Lady*. After her seven-year
triumph on the London stage, Tallulah returned to America and signed
with Paramount to star in the mix-up comedy, directed by George
Cukor. *Photo: Library of Congress*

Bankhead agreed with her
Congressman father that if
you know your bible and
your Shakespeare and can
shoot craps, you have a liberal education. She
returned to New York from
her first brush with Hollywood with $100,000 in the
bank. *Photo: Library of
Congress*

Libby Holman was "rotten ripe" when she was twenty-five, and acquitted of murdering her millionaire husband when she was thirty. Attracted to young gay men she could dominate—and longtime soul mate and drug supplier to Montgomery Clift, she was the lover of Jane Bowles, who with her *Shimmering Sky* author husband, lived off Libby when they were in America. *Photo: Library of Congress*

Dorothy Arzner. She was Hollywood's only woman director of the studio era, and, as such, one of the boys. *Photo: Library of Congress*

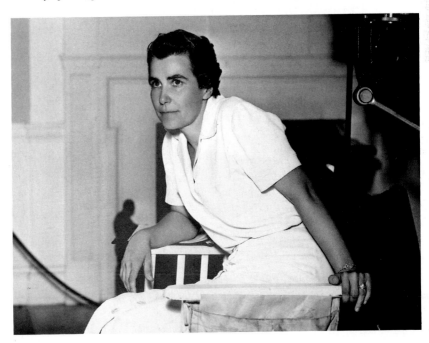

Katharine Hepburn hated herself in *Christopher Strong*. Latter-day feminists have turned Dorothy Arzner's Amelia Earhart-inspired box office flop into a cult movie. *Photo: The Academy of Motion Picture Arts and Sciences*

A June wedding. Vincente Minelli and Judy Garland wed June 15, 1945.

Photo: National Archives

"Some years I could do no wrong, others I could do nothing right." Patsy Kelly made and gave away $4 million doing dead-pan comedy. *Photo: author's collection*

Lizabeth Scott sued *Confidential* for $2.5 million and lost because the magazine was not published in California. Paramount publicity promoted Scott as the new Lauren Bacall or Veronica Lake in 1942. Ten years later, she became the only Hollywood actress to be accused in print of unnatural sex practices. *Photo: author's collection*

The woman you love to hate—
Agnes Moorehead. She was the
soul of discretion, but Paul
Lynne called her "one of the
all-time Hollywood dykes."
*Photo: The Academy of Motion Pic-
ture Arts and Sciences*

"I used to think I
needed a man to de-
fine myself," Capucine
told *Harper's Bazaar* in
September 1982. The
former Paris model
played William
Holden's guerrilla an-
tagonist in *The Seventh
Dawn* (1964).
Photo: author's collection

"They shouldn't have killed me off." Sandy Dennis, shown here, and Anne Heywood were two lesbians living on an isolated farm in *The Fox* (1968), but the plot exigencies demanded Dennis' character be killed off when Keir Dullea arrives. *Photo: author's collection*

called her, and her mousy companion, Alice B. Toklas, were too severe for traveling Hollywoodites, but de Acosta, among others, was always in contact with that other Amazon duet, the petite, hawk-nosed Sylvia Beach, owner of the Shakespeare & Co. bookstore and publisher of James Joyce's *Ulysses,* and her mountain of a lover, Adrienne Monnier.

Elsa Maxwell, the famous socialite-gossip columnist, shared her life with Dorothy (Dickie) Fellowes-Gordon, the scion of a Scottish family. Together, they gave masquerade fetes where everybody was bidden to come like someone everybody else knew—at least by sight. Maxwell, who had brought her considerable talents as a professional hostess to Paris in the late 1920s, dressed as the poet Aristide Briand and Fellowes as the hatcheck girl at the Ritz. Dolly Wilde came as her uncle Oscar, and Barney as a female warrior. Chanel did a roaring business cutting and fitting gowns for young men-about-town who appeared as some of the best-known women. On a trip to Venice, Dickie and Elsa had taken the penniless young actor Noël Coward along, prompting him to note in his diary that "the life of a gigolo, unimpaired by amatory obligations, could undoubtedly be very delightful indeed."

The sewing circle ran deep in the worlds of the avant-garde, fashion, and Parisian nightlife. Frédérique Baulé, alias Frédé, was Dietrich's lover, and owner of a succession of nightclubs where gender, she said, was as mysterious as that of angels. For a while her rival was Jean Cocteau, the arresting homosexual who left his elegant thumbprint on the arts, theater, ballet, and life on the high wire, and whose Boeuf sur le toit boîte was the gathering place of the avant-garde and high society. Cocteau and Christian Bérard, the gay fashion illustrator, concocted plaster masks and wigs for the Maxwell-Fellowes costume parties and counted in their lesbian entourage Princess Alis Dilkusha "Dil" de Rohan and Maria "Poppi" Kirk. Dil was the daughter of an American mother and a British Army officer, who picked his offspring's name while stationed in India. At twenty-three, she had married Carlos de Rohan, the descendant of a line of French princes, generals, and one cardinal. After he died in a car crash in Austria, she worked in haute couture. Kirk, who was also in fashion and in the late 1940s was de Acosta's lover, felt Dil was not interested in sex, while Alice B. Toklas thought her "bawdy."

Madame Poppi, as Maria Kirk was called in Molyneux's couture salon, was the daughter of a Philadelphia diplomat. At twenty-two, she had been pushed into a marriage to an Italian lawyer fifteen years her senior. She left him, worked in Paris as a model, loved Chinese artifacts, read Chinese poetry, converted to Buddhism, and associated with Cocteau, who in his prewar magazine, *Schéhérazade,* published poems by de Rohan and Barney.

Lady Mendl, as Bessie Marbury's old lover styled herself after her 1926 marriage to Sir Mendl, was famous as an international hostess and for the astronomical prices she charged clients along Park Avenue and in such golden ghettos as Palm Beach, Cannes, Nice, and Portofino for telling them how to decorate their homes. Sir Mendl was something of a womanizer, although F. Scott Fitzgerald modeled the homosexual Campion in *Tender Is the Night* after him. As Elsie was by far the richer of the two, she would say he had married her for her money, to which he would retort that she had married him for his title. They were friends of Linda and Cole Porter, who also found marriage a bulwark of social respectability.

A swelling chorus of American twang was to be heard over the Riviera's traditional expatriate British voices. Cole and Linda Porter had rented in Cap d'Antibes since 1921, and Gerald and Sara Murphy, the toniest of the New York expatriates, had bought a villa with a huge garden trailing down to a rocky cliff. They brought in their wake Gertrude Stein, with the indispensable Alice B. Toklas, the Hemingways, the MacLeishes, Picasso, his wife, son, and mother, Fernand Léger and his Russian wife, and F. Scott and Zelda Fitzgerald.

In season, Cocteau and his hangers-on desported themselves at the notorious Hotel du Cap, which also housed Jo Carstairs, a millionairess famous for her wit, blond crew cut, Jack Dempsey shoulders, tattooed body, and gorgeous motorboats. "Toughie" Carstairs was the daughter of a Scottish colonel and an American oil heiress. She had made a pilgrimage to Los Angeles in 1932 when Dietrich, Garbo, and de Acosta launched women-in-slacks chic. Seven years later, Jo lured Marlene away from U.S. ambassador to Britain Joseph P. Kennedy to join her aboard her yacht.

Salka Viertel and Mercedes de Acosta helped with introductions to such eastern meeting points as Eleonora von Mendelssohn's

Austrian aerie. So did the *New York Post's* formidable foreign correspondent Dorothy Thompson. Besides being the wife of Sinclair Lewis, Thompson was the lover of Christa Winsloe, the divorced author of the book on which *Mädchen in Uniform* was based.

Carstairs, Dolly Wilde, Connie Collier, and Beatrice Lillie provided entrees in London. Lady Ottoline Morrell was a duke's sister, a colorful personage, and the Bloomsbury set's most formidable bisexual hostess. Brought up in Victorian rectitude and the wife of a member of Parliament, she was famous for her eccentricities of dress and decor. Stein praised her as a "marvelous feminine version of Disraeli," and the catty Cecil Beaton described her as a scarecrow with "magenta cheeks, beetroot hair, and two protruding teeth."

Her rival was Victoria "Vita" Sackville-West, who loved many women and a few men and had a knack for turning lovers into friends. Her physical liaison with Virginia Woolf was brief, but their friendship lasted for the rest of their lives (Woolf's *Orlando* is said to be a portrait of Sackville-West), although it almost broke up Vita's marriage to the diplomat Harold Nicolson.

Her affair with Virginia's elder sister, the painter Vanessa Bell, was short, but led Vanessa to paint innovative nudes. Everybody remembered Vanessa's 1931 masked party where Vita came as Sappho, Leonard Woolf was in a wig, and the Lady Ottoline Morrell had herself painted. Vita was a writer of bestsellers such as *The Edwardians* and *All Passion Spent*. Her forebears included Thomas Sackville, to whom Queen Elizabeth I had given the ancestral home, Knole Castle in Kent, that was now hers.

If the Bloomsbury circle was a tad too rarefied for traveling Californians, British *Vogue* editor Dorothy Todd's sapphic circle (in a play of words on *The Well of Loneliness,* de Acosta jokingly called Todd "the bucket in the well of loneliness") and Lynn Fontanne's high-keyed West End monde were not. Various sewing-circle members became friends or lovers of Gladys Calthrop, Noël Coward's companion and set designer of all his stage productions until Cecil Beaton usurped her in 1950. Coward was devoutly and exclusively homosexual, and the dark-haired, chain-smoking Gladys was, when in New York, Le Gallienne's lover and art director.

18

Camille:
The All-Gay Production

Hollywood told stories of heiresses and gold diggers, debutantes and adulteresses, of the woman who chases the leading man until he catches her, or the woman who sacrifices *everything* on the altar of love. The only on-screen professions open to females during the 1930s were courtesans and torch singers, spies, and, for Stanwyck and Carole Lombard mostly, that staple of comedy, the smart-ass secretary. In the spring of 1936, *Camille* provided gainful employment for a half dozen members of the sewing circle and the boys' club. Irving Thalberg needed a hit, and with Garbo in the title role, *Camille* seemed a low-risk project.

Thalberg's latest prestige pictures had been costly disappointments. Chiang Kai-shek's Nationalist government was opposed to filming *The Good Earth* and sabotaged a second unit sent to China to shoot background footage. It didn't help when a pair of Jewish actors in makeup, Paul Muni and Luise Rainer, played Pearl S. Buck's eternal Chinese peasants. Casting also ruined Thalberg's other big production, *Romeo and Juliet*. Instead of fresh-scrubbed young actors, Thalberg cast his thirty-five-year-old wife, Norma Shearer, and forty-two-year-old Leslie Howard as the doomed teenagers of Verona. George Cukor had directed, and he impressed Thalberg with his wit and sophistication. Cukor spent his lavish $4,000-a-week salary on his Cordell Drive home above Sunset Boulevard and Doheny Drive, where the elite of gay men and the occasional lesbian celebrity gathered.

The heroine in Alexandre Dumas *fils' La Dame aux camélias* is a woman experienced in sex but innocent of love, who in a guileless young man finds her last chance to love. Marguerite Gautier is a courtesan with a weakness for pleasure and camellias who drifts through the Parisian demimonde with scant regard for her delicate health and in the end sacrifices herself for the penniless Armand Duval. She had been played on the stage by Sarah Bernhardt, Eleonora Duse, Eva Le Gallienne, Ethel Barrymore, and Alla Nazimova. Clara Kimball Young, Pola Negri, Nazimova, and Norma Talmadge had portrayed her in silent-screen versions and Yvonne Printemps in a French talkie. Nazimova's all-gay silent film, with herself as a lizardlike Marguerite and Valentino as a sex-starved Armand, had hurt Nazimova's reputation.

On loan to RKO, Cukor had just directed Katharine Hepburn and Cary Grant in *Sylvia Scarlet,* a drag picaresque that was the greatest fiasco of his career and, to posterity, became a cult movie. The *New York Herald-Tribune* called Hepburn's eroticized Peter Pan "the handsomest boy of the season."

The source material was lesbian author Compton MacKenzie's 1918 novel of a woman rebelling against the woman's role. In the screen version, Sylvia crops her hair, dons men's clothes, and goes by the name of Sylvester so she can join her crooked father (Edmund Gwenn) and team up with a big-time scam artist (Grant) and a chiseling lady's maid (Dennie Moore) to tour the English countryside as a theatrical troupe. The story remains high-gear comedy until the unnecessary death of the father, then never recovers the fun. The transvestism had allowed for a risky scene. The maid finds Hepburn's young boy appealing. "You're very attractive," says the maid, and they kiss. Preview audiences had left the theater at this point, and RKO had Jane Loring reedit the scene to make it less obvious.

In writing, directing, art direction, photography, costumes, and stars, *Camille* was Hollywood's golden-age all-gay production, although Cukor found Garbo too dour and lesbian. The screenplay was by Zoë Akins. Cukor would recall that despite Akins sharing writing credits with James Hilton and Frances Marion, the *Camille* script he filmed was entirely Zoë's. The film, Thalberg decided, was about two people who "say they are going to get married, but we know that it is an impossible dream."

The Production Office raised enough objections for Thalberg to think up an alternative and to secure Garbo's agreement to star in a screen version of Prosper Mérimée's *Carmen*. The Production Office gave its grudging consent, however, after Thalberg took personal charge of haggling over what in the story could stay and what had to go. The result was a Marguerite Gautier so rarefied that her being a whore was unthinkable. As Pauline Kael would say forty-six years later, "No movie has ever presented a more romantic view of a courtesan."

Bill Daniels was, as usual, on camera. Cedric Gibbons designed the sets, and Adrian created the Garbo wardrobe. David Lewis, Thalberg's gay second-in-command, was associate producer. The film was an occasion for Thalberg to forget his feud with Mercedes de Acosta and to hire her to research the original Dumas novel. Alphonsine Plessis was the original lady of the camellias, Mercedes discovered, and Dumas had done his own firsthand research and wasted little time getting her story in print. Two years before Alphonsine died at the age of twenty-three in 1847, Dumas was her lover, and his novel was in the bookstores less than a year after her death. Thalberg asked Mercedes to sit in on the screenings of the dailies.

Cukor didn't like Garbo. In a letter to Hugh Walpole, he said her noble suffering depressed him. He believed, however, they might have something if Garbo could make audiences both understand that the story was of a period when a woman's reputation was everything and *forget* they were seeing a costume picture. Salka Viertel told him what made a Garbo picture: "comedy, tragedy, box office, sex appeal, and nothing bourgeois."

They all knew that a Garbo film demanded a screen lover who was young, clumsy, and irresistible so her disillusioned persona could treat him as a love object to whom she never surrenders her authority. Robert Taylor was Thalberg's and Cukor's choice to play Marguerite Gautier's young, inexperienced Armand Duval.

Cukor sympathized with Taylor's fear of being seen as too handsome. The director would tell Gavin Lambert, "In those days, you had to be very virile or they thought you were degenerate." Members of Thalberg's staff feared Taylor was too unseasoned to match Garbo, but Thalberg and Cukor agreed all the role called for was for Taylor to be decorous and pretend undying love for Garbo.

Lionel Barrymore was cast as Monsieur Duval, Armand's father, who, to save his son from the whore's clutches, makes Marguerite leave the boy she loves and return to her former life of dissipation. Henry Daniell, who had played coolly sadistic men of affluence before, was chosen for Marguerite's former lover who offers to relieve her debts if she becomes his mistress again. Rex O'Malley was set to play the homosexual sidekick, Gaston. Thalberg ran the first dailies in a screening room for Mercedes before she set off for France for additional research. From a village in Normandy, she cabled that she had found a farmer's wife who was a descendant of Marguerite's sister.

Armand was Robert Taylor's most ambitious role. If Garbo had Mercedes in on *Camille,* Taylor had Barbara Stanwyck as his off-screen adviser. Stanwyck told him not to approach Garbo between takes. To maintain the tension she felt she needed between the doomed lovers, Garbo kept her distance from Taylor. There were scenes in which Marguerite pulls him toward her, kisses him all over the face, on the mouth, and pushes him away. Cukor's directions were demanding. Everybody put in ten-hour days on the set.

Cukor's arrest in June 1936 on a morals charge nearly shut down *Camille.* Picking up sailors fresh off tours of duty in Long Beach harbor or Pershing Square in downtown Los Angeles was a Sunday thrill, not only for Cukor but for MGM star William Haines, and his boyfriend, Jimmy Shields. Years earlier when Constance Talmadge had been Thalberg's fiancée, her favorite distraction was to comb gay spots with Haines and help him pick up sailors. Although cocaine and sound had killed her—and her sister Norma's—career, Bill Haines was still MGM's popular breezy college-boy smart aleck. His movie career ended that June afternoon at the beach, when Cukor and Haines propositioned the wrong boy, and they were chased by an angry mob. The story hit the Los Angeles newspapers. At MGM, Howard Strickling worked fast. Within forty-eight hours, charges were dropped.

The members of the sewing circle were more discreet, but the gay men's network was, in many ways, more decisive when such self-provoked dangers flared up. MGM costume designer Walter Plunkett often provided bail money for unfortunates caught by the vice squad.

While homosexuals of both genders were half a century away from defining themselves openly, women who dared characterize themselves as lesbians were more invisible than homosexual men. Victorian parents had taught their daughters to keep their passions in check, never to be "blatant," and women in love with women almost never risked admitting their true orientation, even to women they were all but certain were also lesbians.

In Tinseltown, the rules were not the same for lesbians and gay men. As long as a woman could show she was married or occasionally available to men, lesbian affairs were more acceptable in some circles than avant-garde art. If caught in a sexual situation with a man, a "confirmed bachelor" like Cukor was ruined or, if his studio's investment in him was too important for summary dismissal, subjected to executive arm-twisting and made-up publicity barrages.

Cukor was convinced that the public should never know that anyone in the film business was gay, even though his homosexuality was the reason he was fired from *Gone With the Wind* in 1939. He would direct movies into his eighties and, lavished with honors, die comfortably in the closet in 1983.

He was, like Mamoulian, a man of the theater who made a successful transition from Broadway to Hollywood. Literate, witty, cosmopolitan, and persuasive, he made his directing debut in films with *Tarnished Lady,* starring Tallulah Bankhead. The remarkable performances he coached out of Garbo, Hepburn, Shearer, Crawford, Garland, and Ingrid Bergman earned him the reputation as *the* "woman's director," a label he resented. Temperamental and sensitive actresses, however, were comfortable being guided by him.

With Harpo Marx, the directors Sam Wood and Mervyn LeRoy, and Irving and Norma Thalberg spent the long Labor Day weekend of 1936 at the Del Monte Club in Monterey in northern California. Thalberg caught a head cold playing bridge in the sea breeze. The cold turned into pneumonia when he returned to Los Angeles. On September 14, the thirty-seven-year-old wunderkind with a weak heart was dead.

Hollywood shut down for five minutes of mourning as his funeral began, and MGM suspended operations for the rest of the day. Robert Taylor and Cukor attended the funeral at the synagogue B'nai B'rith with the Barrymore brothers, the Marxes, Charles Chaplin, Walt Disney, Howard Hughes, and MGM's top stars. Mercedes heard of Thalberg's death in a wire from Garbo and realized that with his death died any chance of seeing her Joan of Arc reach the screen.

In the face of speculation that Thalberg's death meant MGM would no longer make classy pictures, Mayer asserted his control. In the time-honored Hollywood ritual of nay-saying the work of the person you're taking over from, Mayer dismantled the well-organized Thalberg unit at the studio. A new, confusing beginning was filmed for *Camille*. In the overview of Garbo's career, however, *Camille* is considered her best.

Dietrich was the highest-paid star at work in 1936, but she was also the most bored. None of her directors after Josef von Sternberg cared, or knew how, to bring out her intoxicating personality. What she didn't want to see was that movies with irresistible foreign femmes fatale were becoming passé. Warner Bros. came up with a homegrown Evil Woman who topped the Garbo-Dietrich allure. With her startling eyes, disdainful mouth, clipped, almost British, speech, Bette Davis became the ultimate bitch in a series of reckless, unsympathetic, but smashing high-powered roles.

Marlene had turned down Hitler's 1934 invitation for a "triumphant" return to Berlin, but said yes when Alexander Korda, her old UFA director who had risen to power, wealth, and fame as Britain's most flamboyant movie tycoon, offered her $350,000 to come to England and star in *Knight Without Armour.* Maria was growing up pudgy and complex and was sent to an exclusive girls' school in Switzerland, while Marlene spent much of 1936 in England. Her new flame was Jo Carstairs. If Marlene would abandon the cinema, Jo promised, they could settle for a life of bliss at her estate in the Bahamas.

Dietrich preferred to soldier on. Ernst Lubitsch asked her to come back to Paramount to star in a film he would direct himself. Mercedes de Acosta hosted several welcoming soirees when Marlene returned to Los Angeles in February 1937, rented a house in Beverly Hills, and applied for U.S. citizenship. Instead of a sparkling comedy, *Angel,* costarring Melvyn Douglas, proved to be a clunky and contrived vehicle that substituted narrative starch for the usual Lubitsch wit. Dietrich gave her stiffest performance to date and complained daily to her cameraman. She was barely on talking terms with Lubitsch when the film wrapped in June. She fell under the spell of Carroll Righter, a cultivated gay astrologer with a large Hollywood clientele. Righter was soon in on her sex life and, with grave references to heavenly charts, scheduling her trysts with Mercedes and her new male lovers, the novelist Erich Maria Remarque and Joan Crawford's former husband, Douglas Fairbanks Jr.

The assignations with de Acosta usually took place at Mercedes's house in Brentwood or, on weekends, in a Santa Barbara hotel. When Fairbanks discovered ardent letters from Mercedes and confronted Marlene, she resented his prying. Remarque found Dietrich endlessly beguiling and, apparently more relaxed about sharing her according to Righter's zodiac charts, called her both "a sailor's daughter" of roaring ardor, and the goddess Diana of the wood, "with a silver bow—invulnerable, cool, fatal."

Dietrich returned to Europe, collected her daughter in Switzerland, and invited Fairbanks to join her in Austria. The actor expected a solitary rendezvous in the Tyrol and was bewildered at finding Maria, Rudi Sieber, and his mistress Tamara there. "The arrangement was indeed knotty even by the most tolerant criteria," Dietrich biographer Donald Spoto would write, "and it suggested that Dietrich's relationship with Sieber could occasionally be at least casually carnal. Even as she shared a room with Fairbanks, she extended herself liberally, leaving their bed and blithely toddling down the corridor to join Rudi and Tamara—and not only for hot chocolate."

19

Screen Style

Cinemas were dream palaces. Soothing music and low-key lighting cast against exotic decors and warm, comforting darkness beckoned the audience until the gleaming curtain swept aside to display the title of another movie where true love conquered all, and goodness triumphed in the end. Even if the moviegoers' lives could never match the imagined existence of the stars, the women in the audience could enhance their appearance and project a new awareness of themselves by acquiring a frock or a hat that mirrored the elegance on the screen.

The camera imposed new types of beauty. If the very rich looked to Paris for fashion trends, most women and the couturiers themselves kept an eye on the movies. Millinery shops sometimes placed cards bearing the name of the current film favorite on each hat, with the result that an extravagant creation might one day be labeled Myrna Loy, the next day Joan Crawford, and on following days Carole Lombard, Greta Garbo, or Rosalind Russell, until if finally sold. "Who did that look first, Hollywood or Paris?" *Vogue* asked in 1933. After giving credit for pageboy hair to Garbo, feather boas to Dietrich, and a sixth sense of fashion future to Adrian and Howard Greer, the magazine admitted fashion ideas arrived "by a sort of spontaneous combustion." The fashion industry adopted such Hollywood innovations as false fingernails and eyelashes. Every important star, said *Vogue,* contributed some new look or fashion:

> Garbo—hollowed eye sockets and plucked eyebrows
> Dietrich—plucked eyebrows and sucked-in cheeks
> Joan Crawford—the bow-tie mouth
> Tallulah Bankhead—a sullen expression
> Mae West—the hourglass figure and an attractive bawdiness
> Constance Bennett—a glazed, bandbox smartness
> Jean Harlow—platinum hair
> Vivien Leigh—gypsy coloring, a glittering combination of white skin, green eyes, and dark red hair

Of *Vogue's* eight, Harlow died at twenty-six in 1937. As far as we know, only three of the remaining seven—Constance Bennett, Mae West, and Vivien Leigh—were heterosexual. Blowzy and buxom, and a hit with gays, Mae West owed her popularity, and gay following, to her mocking of her own sex symbol. She was the highest-paid woman in the United States in 1935, but by the end of the decade was running out of steam, only to metamorphose into showbiz legend. Bennett married five times (her second divorce gave her a million-dollar settlement) and was a member of the fast set. She got her break in 1926 when Eddie Goulding teamed her with Joan Crawford and Sally O'Neil as three flappers in *Sally, Irene and Mary.* O'Neil's later career was undistinguished, but Bennett's gift for self-perfection, her big, liquid eyes, husky voice, and natural delivery of wisecracks established her as a leading RKO actress of the talkies. Leigh, who owed much of her *Gone With the Wind* triumph to George Cukor's early instructions, manipulated and dominated her marriage to Laurence Olivier.

Although Coco Chanel had no use for gay fashion designers and, by the 1950s, blamed women for no longer dressing "to please men but to please the pederast," the feminization of male fashion started with her. Intuitive, aware, and quick to pick up on trends and manners, Chanel had taken a fancy to turtleneck sweaters worn by English sailors in Deauville on the chilly Normandy coast during the summer of 1913. Much of her lasting success was in her notion that a secure woman could afford *not* to accentuate her charms. In 1921, she put women into sweaters, short, pleated skirts with dropped waistlines, cloche hats, and bandeaux for a willowy silhouette that Paris called the *garçonne* look, London and New York the flapper. Chanel typified the rest of the roaring twenties, which made it possible for a woman to earn her own living, choose whom to love, and live (mostly) according to her own precepts.

Sam Goldwyn lured Chanel to Hollywood in 1930 to dress United Artists stars Ina Claire and Gloria Swanson. The French-woman came away riled by what she considered a clumsy business and was not much taken by Beverly Hills and the studio system that turned stars into salaried nonentities. Only Katharine Hepburn pleased her. Chanel was forty-seven and saw her younger self in the bony, freckled-faced twenty-three-year-old.[1]

The influence of lesbians and homosexual men on classical Hollywood was both subtle and pervasive. Beyond the graven images of Garbo, Dietrich, Crawford, and Bankhead, the industry had many positions that suited gay people. With Cukor and Arzner, Mitchell Leisen was the gay director who fashioned Paramount's fizziest romances and smartest musicals. Every star under contract and the studio's best writers wanted to work with this former costume designer and Cecil B. DeMille art director because he had a knack for giving visual luster and pace both to "big films" like *Arise My Love, Lady in the Dark,* and *Frenchman's Creek,* and the archetypal screwball comedy *Easy Living,* and to second-rate jobs.

Film historians psychoanalyzed Leisen's films after he died in 1972 and, without taking into consideration such first-class Leisen screenwriters as Preston Sturges and Billy Wilder, discovered repressed homosexuality in his heroines' yearning for emancipation. Wrote Yann Tobin in *American Directors,* "Whereas Cukor's females in *A Woman's Face, Born Yesterday, A Star Is Born,* and *My Fair Lady* need Pygmalion-like heroes, Leisen movies questioned more clearly men's emotional guardianship of women."

Leisen played it straight, although he shared his life with his cameraman, Ted Tetzlaff. James Whale, who lived with Thalberg's

---

1. Chanel designed a few dresses for Charlotte Greenwood in the hokey comedy-melodrama *Palmy Days* starring Eddie Cantor and the high-kicking Goldwyn Girls and, hurrying back to Paris, clothed Swanson in *Tonight or Never.*

former assistant David Lewis, paid for it with his career when he refused to stay in the closet. Imported from England in 1930 to direct the screen version of his stage success *Journey's End,* he is best remembered for his four stylish horror movies—*Frankenstein, The Old Dark House, The Invisible Man,* and *Bride of Frankenstein.* Committed gay activist Vito Russo would see a parallel between Henry Frankenstein's monster, painfully aware of its unnaturalness, and Whale's out-of-the-closet "aberration" as ruining his career.

"The old baron, Frankenstein's father, continually beseeches his son to 'leave this madness,' to come home and marry the young Elizabeth," Russo would write. "The father, Elizabeth, and Henry's best friend go to the castle and force him, for his health and sanity, to leave his creation, to be free of his 'obsession.'" Later the monster fulfills Mary Shelley's prophecy by joining his creator on his wedding night, carrying off Elizabeth, and in the end being hunted by the townspeople "in the same way that groups of men in silent comedies had once run effeminate men off piers and out of town."

Whale made his last picture in 1941 and, after coming out, "retired to pursue other passions," as Ephraim Katz would put it in *The Film Encyclopedia.* Whale drowned in his swimming pool under mysterious circumstances in 1957. His story was told in Bill Condon's 1998 film *Gods and Monsters.* Ian McKellen played Whale, Brendan Fraser his hunky gardener, and Lynn Redgrave his Hungarian housekeeper.

Most of the *names* of the below-the-line, or fixed expenditure, craftspeople were gay, the designers, decorators, choreographers, directors of photography who contributed much to the sleek look of decorative fantasies, domestic dramas, and drawing-room comedies. "Most of the costume designers were homosexuals," said Edith Head, who in 1939 became the first woman to be named chief of a studio's costume department, but classified herself with the men and corrected journalists who ranked her among the industry's women.

Irene (née Irene Lentz) was Adrian's successor at MGM, a severe bachelor girl from Brookings, South Dakota, who was still in her twenties when she opened a dress shop in Los Angeles and, like Chanel, had the knack for making celebrities her clients. At MGM,

Irene and her staff never came onto a set without wearing immaculate white gloves and suitable hats. The wardrobe she created usually spelled taste, position, and means. As Pandro Berman told Elia Kazan, who in 1946 was unhappy with MGM's "exteriors" for the *Sea of Grass,* "Young man, you have one thing to learn. We are in the business of making beautiful pictures of beautiful people, and anybody who doesn't acknowledge that should not be in the business." Before gritty cinema verité and television realism, moviegoers accepted sets, rear projection, and process-screen photography that allowed characters to sit and stand in front of a screen on a soundstage and appear to be anywhere in the world.

Irene began designing clothes for movies in 1933 and nine years later joined MGM. She dressed Vivien Leigh and Robert Taylor in *Waterloo Bridge,* Dietrich in *Seven Sinners,* Carole Lombard in *To Be or Not to Be,* and stars in thirty-three other movies. She was nominated for an Academy Award for Barbara Stanwyck's clothes in the Victorian melodrama *B. F.'s Daughter* and was famous for her arresting all-white outfits for Lana Turner in *The Postman Always Rings Twice,* and for her wardrobes for Doris Day. Unhappy with herself, she committed suicide in 1961 by jumping from the eleventh floor of the Knickerbocker Hotel on Hollywood Boulevard.

Edith Head, who called her eight Oscars "the men in my life," made it out of the shadow of Paramount's alcoholic chief designer Travis Banton thanks to Stanwyck and *The Lady Eve.* "We hit it off immediately and it was the beginning of a long and important friendship," the designer would remember of Stanwyck. Both Banton and Head had been with Paramount since the 1920s, he coming from haute couture, she from teaching art in Los Angeles high schools. Banton was catapulted to fame with the high-gloss feathers, veils, and chiffon ensembles he created for Dietrich, and only he was entrusted with dressing Clara Bow, Claudette Colbert, Carole Lombard, Pola Negri, and Mae West. Everything changed in 1939, however, when he left Paramount for Fox, and Edith became head designer. A year later, director-writer Preston Sturges, Stanwyck, Henry Fonda, and Head's twenty-five gowns made history with the sparkling screwball comedy *The Lady Eve.*

"*Lady Eve* changed both our lives," Head would remember. "It was Barbara's first high-fashion picture and her biggest transition in costuming. Barbara was quite trim and had a better shape than most of the other actresses around. She possessed what some designers considered to be a figure 'problem'—a long waist and a comparatively low rear end. By widening the waistbands in front of her gowns and narrowing them slightly in the back, I could still put her in straight skirts, something other designers were afraid to do, because they thought she might look too heavy in the seat. I just took advantage of her long waist to create the illusion that her derriere was just as perfectly placed as any other star's." Head was born Edith Claire Posener, in San Bernardino, east of Los Angeles. She had married a sales executive, Charles Head, and, because she was a Catholic, stayed married when she and Stanwyck met on the set of *Interns Can't Take Money* in 1937.

She dressed Elizabeth Taylor, Bette Davis, Grace Kelly, Audrey Hepburn, Paul Newman, and Robert Redford, and her pacifying manners with temperamental stars and directors and her quiet authority made them insist on her being rehired on their next pictures. Her biggest professional regret was not designing for Garbo. She divorced Charles Head in 1938 and married art director Wiard Boppo "Bill" Ihnen. She called him her "best friend," and the two of them led separate lives except for their Coldwater Canyon home, where they gardened and collected art together. The marriage lasted thirty-nine years until his death, at ninety-one.

Like Stanwyck, Edith was secretive and dreaded any talk about sexuality, her own or anyone else's. Her lesbianism was widely known, but she kept her distance from the many actresses she dressed with the exception of Stanwyck and Robert Taylor, who were frequent guests at Edith and Bill's rambling hacienda. Said author Paul Rosenfield, "Edith was a terribly closeted, discreet lesbian who had little use for most women as individuals or associates."

20

Judy Garland in the Land of Oz

Tallulah Bankhead, Anita Loos, and Lady Mendl were at George Cukor's pool up on Cordell Drive in January 1941 when someone brought up *The Captive*, Edouard Bourdet's audacious 1926 drama about a young woman who is so obsessed by another woman that she refuses to be happy in her marriage. Before the New York district attorney hauled producer, director, and cast into court on obscenity charges, the play—and Tallulah—had made the gift of violets the mute sign of affection among women lovers. Tallulah offered a bouquet of violets to Lady Mendl, who feigned not to know what the flowers meant.

"What is a lesbian?" her ladyship asked. "Tell me what they do."

Which allowed Tallulah to retort, "If you don't know what lesbians are, who does?"

The first question a woman deciding she loves women asks is, Who else? Unless a lesbian was lucky enough to belong to an informal "sewing club," making contacts with other lesbians was difficult and problematic. To meet Flos and Freddies, as the femmes and butches were called, a newcomer to Los Angeles in the late 1930s would perhaps try the If Club or Open Door at Alvarado Street or the nearby Lakeshore Bar off nearby Westlake Park. The Lakeshore catered exclusively to the gay trade, while the Golden Bull

173

and the S.S. Friendship on Channel Road allowed curious heterosexuals. William Hearst and Marion Davies sometimes appeared
there, along with producers' wives, who, as Aldous Huxley's biographer, David King Dunaway, would put it, "whispered of film roles to
actresses in slacks and cropped hair." Lili Damita and Errol Flynn
never dared to be seen in Los Angeles clubs, but cruised lesbian
bars in Paris together.

To acknowledge a lesbian relationship is to encounter the fear
that, at some time or another, plays a big part in the life of every
lesbian. "There is a fear of public opinion and resulting ostracism,"
Del Martin and Phyllis Lyon would write in 1972. "Fear of identification as a lesbian leads to fear of ridicule, fear of rejection, fear of
group identification, fear of the homophile community, fear of police, fear of family, fear of forming friendships, fear of loneliness,
fear of losing one's job or career, fear of loss of respect, fear of dis-
playing affection, and, perhaps the greatest and most disastrous,
fear of self-acceptance."

Judy Garland struggled with her sexuality, and, with her mete-
oric rise to stardom, with the fear of discovery and the rejection
and banishment that was sure to follow. To millions, she was
Dorothy, the girl next door who traveled over the rainbow. Yet her
life was a careening roller coaster of emotional turmoil, addiction,
tempestuous marriages, and, for romantic solace, other women.
She was intense, headstrong, and explosive, possessed of an insatiable desire to please. While still a teenager, she claimed her life
was "an absolute chaos."

It all started because Louis B. Mayer was envious of Twentieth
Century–Fox's Shirley Temple. At four, Shirley Temple had done
takeoffs of Marlene Dietrich and other leading ladies in one-reel
films called Baby Burlesks, and at six she performed a song-and-
dance number in *Stand Up and Cheer.* Within months of signing
with Fox in 1934, she sang, danced, and charmed Depression
America and the whole world with her plucky optimism. Mayer
thought he had found MGM's answer in thirteen-year-old Garland
and in 1935 put her under contract.

Garland's movie-manager father with showbiz aspirations was
gay; her mother, who knew and resented his proclivities, was the ar-

chetypical stage mother. She had two daughters by Francis Gumm and tried to abort Frances, the third. Once a star, Garland claimed her pushy mother took "delight in telling rooms full of people" about the botched attempt at aborting her. With her sisters, Frances made her singing debut at two and a half and brought down the house with her powerful voice. When she was four, the family moved to Los Angeles to promote the song-and-dance Gumm Sisters Kiddie Act. At the suggestion of George Jessel, the trio changed the name to Garland. Frances became Judy when she was nine, and grew up spoiled and temperamental.

We do not know whether Howard Strickling commissioned Betty Asher to seduce Judy Garland in order to control the teenager. Five years older than Garland, Asher was the daughter of a producer of B pictures at Universal Pictures, and her job was to oversee the behavior of underage Garland and Lana Turner. Garland biographer David Shipman would write, "An unfortunate legacy of this relationship was that Asher encouraged Garland to drink, which until then she had done without enthusiasm."

Deanna Durbin was the girl who got away. A year into Garland's contract, MGM decided it did not need two young singers, and Durbin was traded to Universal. Her smash success in *Three Smart Girls* had Judy in tears, and Mayer wondered if he shouldn't drop Garland and try to buy back Durbin. Judy singing a snappy, jazzy "Dear Mr. Gable" in a carefully rehearsed, "spontaneous" setside tribute to the star's thirty-sixth birthday was repeated on radio and filmed for *Broadway Melody of 1937* (soon retitled *Broadway Melody of 1938*). Garland was declared "a sensational little hot-singing number," and by seventeen, she was America's favorite kid sister. She was jealous of Lana Turner, who turned men's heads, and was given the "glamour treatment," complete with pinup posters in tight sweaters that emphasized her main qualifications.

Garland knew all the tricks of a child performer. Her revenge for being everybody's kid sister when Turner was treated as a sex symbol was to become engaged to David Rose, a musician freshly divorced from the comedienne Martha Raye, and to invite six hundred guests to her engagement party. Convinced she was insufficiently appreciated by the studio, Judy eloped—with her mother, new stepfather, and Asher in tow—and in Las Vegas married Rose, the first of five husbands. Marriage didn't free her from MGM's authoritarian control. The studio prescribed pills to make sure she slept at night, pills to make sure she got to the set bright and early, and appetite-suppressing amphetamines to make sure she stayed thin. By twenty, she was seriously addicted.

A pregnancy was terminated with the studio's concurrence, and when the Roses divorced a year later, Asher moved into an apartment next to Judy's. Her assignment included telling the Strickling office of any of Garland's activities lending themselves to publicity treatment. In a fit of anger, Garland would later call Asher "another MGM spy," but the two remained friends, if not lovers. Asher, who eventually committed suicide, was Garland's maid of honor when Judy married her gay director Vincente Minnelli.

Minnelli was also the child of showbiz people—his father was the half-owner of the Minnelli Brothers Tent Theater, for which his mother was the leading lady. Vincente began performing at three but "retired" five years later, when the movies killed off such itinerant tent entertainment. He had been a photographer's assistant, a costume designer at Radio City Music Hall, and a director of Broadway musicals before MGM signed him up. His boss was Arthur Freed, the lyricist turned musical-department head whose name was synonymous with the glitter and quality of MGM's musicals. Freed's team harbored such a large contingent of gays that it was known as "the fairy unit."

Minnelli's first job was to stage Judy Garland's musical numbers in Busby Berkeley's *Strike Up the Band*. By the time Vincente got to direct her in *Meet Me in St. Louis*, they were best of friends. Judy didn't mind the rumors about him and his Japanese valet, because Vincente was the first man of flair and elegance in her life. He knew how to flatter her, to give fatherly advice, and she showed him off to the press. By marrying a homosexual, David Shipman would write, she could continue to have bisexual flings without feeling any guilt. Oral sex gave her more satisfaction than traditional intercourse. She was always drawn to homosexual men and enjoyed watching gay men in her employ perform oral and anal sex. In later years she drew a cult audience that was heavily gay.

MGM stage-managed the Garland-Minnelli marriage in 1945. "Almost everyone had doubts about the marriage, but Louis B.

Mayer was not one of them," Garland biographer David Shipman would write. "Minnelli's homosexuality was no obstacle." Their daughter, Liza, was born in 1946. Four years later, Judy and Vincente agreed they had failed each other, and Garland moved to an apartment in West Hollywood that had once belonged to Marlene Dietrich.

21

Fresh Faces

The sewing circle was as transitory—and as permanent—as Hollywood itself. Fifteen million Americans went to the movies every week in 1938. There were more cinemas (15,115) than banks (14,952), and the pressure to create ever more stupendous fantasies culminated in *Gone With the Wind*. In the evening of December 10, 1938, George Cukor shouted, "Action!" and Atlanta burned on the backlot of the Selznick International in Culver City with three white-suited doubles for Clark Gable ready to dash into the flames and rescue three different Scarletts. David O. Selznick's brother, the agent Myron Selznick, showed up late, drunk, and in the company of the young English actress Vivien Leigh.

"I want you to meet your Scarlett O'Hara," Myron told David, who, in a ghostwritten account of the legendary introduction, later declared, "I took one look and knew she was right." Less fabled was Cukor's dismissal nineteen days into filming when, during a difficult scene, Gable exploded, "I can't go on with this picture. I won't be directed by a fairy. I have to work with a *real man!*"

The spin publicist Russell Birdwell put on the firing—and on Gable's favorite director, Victor Fleming, taking over—was that Cukor had paid too much attention to Vivien Leigh and Olivia de

Havilland and not enough to his leading man. A month later, Cukor started shooting *The Women* with Norma Shearer, Joan Crawford, Rosalind Russell, Paulette Goddard, and Joan Fontaine—all castoffs, as Hollywood wags noted, from the Selznick-Birdwell publicity hunt for Scarlett O'Hara.

Anita Loos and Jane Murfin adapted Clare Boothe's bitchy play about a New York socialite who gets a divorce but later thinks better of it. The screen version had 135 speaking roles, all of them women, which allowed publicity to tout *The Women* as a story about "135 women with men on their minds."

"Everything was female," Cukor would recall. "The books in the library were all by female authors. The photographs and art objects were all female. Even the animals—the monkeys, the dogs, the horses—were female. I'm not sure the audience were aware of that, but there wasn't a single male represented in the entire film, although nine-tenths of the dialogue centered around them."

The cast included a recent member of the sewing circle. Marjorie Main had come a long way since she and Barbara Stanwyck shimmied on Broadway in 1927. After years in vaudeville and the legitimate theater, she was becoming a salty, crusty character player in movies, notorious as a devastating scene stealer. After playing Humphrey Bogart's mother in *Dead End* and Stanwyck's mother-in-law in *Stella Dallas* in 1937, she was typecast in dramatic slum-mother roles. She was living with actress Spring Byington on Cordell Drive across from Cukor. Byington specialized in young-in-spirit, pixilated mothers and scored in Frank Capra's 1938 hit *You Can't Take It With You.*

Garbo remained a frequent guest at Cukor's soirees. Her popularity was slipping, and after dropping plans to have her star in the life of Marie Curie (the role was eventually given to Greer Garson), Mayer decided the solution was to have her do a comedy. The vehicle was *Ninotchka*, directed by Ernst Lubitsch, who at his beach house seven years earlier had shouted, "Vhy don't you tell those idiots in your studio to let us do a picture together?"

Ninotchka was a sparkling comedy and Lubitsch was in top form. Garbo played a self-absorbed, humorless Soviet commissar who is seduced by Paris and a playboy named Count Leon d'Algout. William Powell and Robert Montgomery were considered before

Melvyn Douglas was cast as the count, and Ina Claire as the grand duchess. Forty years later, Claire would tell Cecil Beaton's biographer Hugo Vickers how Garbo made a pass at her. When Ina declined, Garbo said, "Now I must go to the little boys' room." The next time Claire went to her bathroom, the toilet seat was up. In Antoni Gronowicz's retelling, the two actresses thoroughly detested each other.

Mercedes de Acosta, meanwhile, returned to Los Angeles from a yearlong spiritual voyage to India in the spring of 1939 and found both her own and American values changed. She found American women hidebound and terribly uninformed. She enlarged her circle of romantic relationships, but, at forty-seven, felt her concentration and health decline. She rented a house on Amalfi Road in Brentwood close by Garbo's residence, and the two revived their relationship. From Paris, Jean Cocteau wrote to Mercedes, asking her to persuade Garbo to star in a screen version of his *L'Aigle à deux têtes (The Two-Headed Eagle)*, a romantic Ruritanian melodrama.

It was a happy time for Mercedes and Garbo. After each day's shooting, they walked in the hills above Brentwood, as they had done when Garbo made *Grand Hotel* and Mercedes fought with Irving Thalberg over *Rasputin and the Empress*. Doing comedy, Mercedes would recall in her memoirs, changed Garbo:

> She laughed constantly and she used to repeat the question "Why?" as she did in the picture. She would imitate Lubitsch's accent and ask over and over again "Vhy, vhy?" She acted out scenes for me from the picture, and some days she would really be Ninotchka.

Mercedes de Acosta caught up with sewing circle members, new and old. Judith Anderson was a butchy newcomer, the tragedienne of larger than life stage performances whose features and manners made her the woman moviegoers loved to hate. "She cannot by temperament play wallflowers," said Eva Le Gallienne of her. Richard Sarafian, who interviewed the Australian-born Anderson for a part in 1971, said she would never find anyone manlier than herself to act with. She never wished for a softer face and dismissed questions of whether she would like to play softer roles by asking who would want to play ordinary types. When she was ninety-two and author Boze Hadleigh asked her if it would bother her to be thought a lesbian, she leered defiantly and said, "Many people already do."

She had begun acting at seventeen in Sidney, came to America in 1920, and twelve years later succeeded Lynn Fontanne as Nina Leeds in O'Neill's *Strange Interlude*. At Katharine Cornell's urging, Guthrie McClintic cast her in the play *Divided by Three*. Anderson made her film debut in *Blood Money* playing a nightclub owner in a smart thriller full of ambiguous sexual tension. The writer-director of *Blood Money* was Rowland Brown, a former fashion illustrator with an exciting visual style who loaded the script with gay double entendres. When she warns her bail-bond racketeer brother (George Bancroft) about the kind of women he has been running around with, he snaps, "Don't worry, Sis, this one's different. She wears a tuxedo." She upbraids him when he warns a timid cabdriver not to betray their destination to police by threatening, "Lissen, fag."

The high period of Anderson's stage career began in 1936 when she played Gertrude in John Gielgud's *Hamlet* on Broadway. "Now that I have begun my classical education, do I dare breathe that I have dreamed of Lady Macbeth and now wish to play her?" she said. In London a year later, she played the part opposite Laurence Olivier. Her big break came when Zoë Akins cast her as the star of Zoë's stage version of Edith Wharton's *Old Maid*. Cheryl Crawford, who had become Broadway's only independent woman producer after leaving the Group Theater, starred Anderson in *Family Portrait*.

Through Maria and Aldous Huxley, de Acosta befriended one new arrival, the German painter Eva Hermann. Well-known in Berlin for her caricatures, Eva occasionally shared a bed with both Maria and Aldous Huxley and, at intimate gatherings at the Huxleys, would lie naked on a mirrored coffee table while onlookers photographed or stroked her. "A lovely and sensitive person, she was a great friend of the Huxleys, who introduced me to her," Mercedes would write. "I saw her often those last years in Hollywood and we have remained warm friends."

There were new defections and a lavender marriage. Dolores Del Rio divorced Cedric Gibbons and returned to her native Mexico, unhappy with being typecast in the exotic roles that her physique made unavoidable. Janet Gaynor and MGM's high-gloss designer Adrian married in Yuma, Arizona. Gaynor was thirty-six, Adrian three years older. They called their marriage a close, private one. The tomboy actress told Frances Goldwyn she married to escape her "particular corridor and know the other side of life." Adrian maintained he was a private person because of the way he looked. "Like a camel," he said.

Gaynor's career had rebounded with A *Star Is Born,* produced by David O. Selznick. She was on his short list for Melanie in *Gone With the Wind,* but a year later decided to give up her movie career.

Gaynor was born Laura Gainor in Philadelphia and grew up in Chicago where her divorced mother remarried. At nineteen she was a Fox Film discovery and, after production chief Winfield Sheehan took a personal interest in her, was cast in several of the studio's top films. She starred in *Sunrise,* F. W. Murnau's extraordinary sensual film that is considered a silent classic. Her role as a Paris waif in Frank Borzage's popular *Seventh Heaven* marked her first appearance opposite Charles Farrell. Her pert, determined character turned her portrayals of sweet, adorable, child-women into stardom and, in 1929, gave her the newly founded Motion Picture Academy's first best-actress award for *Seventh Heaven.* Over the next seven years Gaynor and Farrell were Fox's leading screen lovers.

Gaynor was more butch than Farrell offscreen, and she came to loathe the undistinguished musicals they made. She rebelled against Fox chief Sheehan and, in 1930, dramatically left for Hawaii. From Honolulu, she announced she would return only if Sheehan assured her she would no longer play child-women. Like Garbo, she held out for months and turned down the role of Julie in *Liliom,* which Eva Le Gallienne had made famous on the stage. Her victory was Pyrrhic. When William Fox merged his studio with Darryl Zanuck's Twentieth Century, Sheehan was fired. With his departure she lost her ace in the hole.

Huxley's luminous intellect excited Mercedes, and in her memoirs she would tell of lonely walks with him: "We used to go for walks together just before or after sunset. When I was alone with Aldous, I always felt he knew so much that I shouldn't spend a second with him without digging some rare piece of information out of him."

The author of *Brave New World* and *Point Counter Point* was married to a lesbian, who in return for marital freedom procured ladies for her husband. On occasion, she shared the bed with him and the women he seduced and got rid of the paramour when he had had enough of her.

Maria Nys Huxley was Belgian by birth, a tiny, dark, aristocratic-looking woman with large blue-green eyes. With her family, she had been evacuated to Italy during World War I, where she seduced Constanza Fasola, a professor's daughter. In London after the war, Maria fell under the spell of Lady Ottoline Morrell, the Bloomsbury set's bisexual hostess. Lady Ottoline championed D. H. Lawrence, the coalminer's son, and Maria gained a measure of notoriety for having typed *Lady Chatterley's Lover.* Maria believed in stars, studied palmistry, and consulted fortune-tellers.

The Huxleys came to Hollywood in 1937, driving across America with Maria at the wheel and their teenage son in the backseat, the novelist to try his hand at screenwriting, Maria to become a member of the sewing circle. Peggy Kiskadden, Aldous Huxley's long-time secretary, felt Maria never saw any connection between sex and marriage. During her years with the Huxleys, Peggy studiously kept out of Maria's attachments. Huxley biographer David King Dunaway would write, "In the afternoons, Maria frequently dropped Aldous off at a bookshop or museum while she met Mercedes de Acosta." Eva Hermann, the pale, dignified painter who had been Maria's lover in France, sometimes joined them. Mercedes found Maria fragile and charming looking. Sexually, Mercedes was drawn to "the lovely and sensitive" Eva.

Huxley owed his entrée to MGM to the sewing circle. Anita Loos got him a job at MGM turning Jane Austen's *Pride and Prejudice* into a screenplay for Laurence Olivier and Greer Garson, and it was through Garbo, Salka Viertel, and Maria that he was hired to write *Madame Curie,* and through Salka that he was kept on the payroll. It was Mercedes who presented Maria and Aldous to Garbo. With Salka, Mercedes and Maria attended poetry readings and séances at the Brevoort. Another favorite place was the Villa Carlotta. Ona Munson lived here, as did a pair of nightclub singers, Marguerite d'Alvarez and Kathleen Howard.

* * *

The Huxleys loved picnics, and Loos would remember one outing at the outbreak of the war when visiting Bertrand Russell, Krishnamurti, and several Indian ladies in saris joined them, together with Garbo, disguised as a man, Paulette Goddard in a colorful Mexican outfit, and Charles Chaplin and Christopher Isherwood looking like naughty pixies. Afraid of setting the tinder-dry canyons on fire with the Indians' rice cooking, the party chose the sandy bottom of the dry Los Angeles River. Sandwiches were laid out with Garbo's vegetarian carrots and Goddard's caviar, and Krishnamurti's rice was simmering when a sheriff appeared and asked Huxley if he couldn't read. Aldous allowed that he could, but no one got the sheriff's implication until he pointed to a No Trespassing sign. Huxley assured the lawman that they would not desecrate the riverbed, that as soon as their lunch was over, they would clean up and leave. When this failed, Loos would recall:

> Aldous played his trump card. He indicated the presence of Miss Garbo, Miss Goddard, and Mr. Chaplin. The sheriff's measly little eyes squinted only briefly at the group. "Is that so?" he asked. "Well, I've seen every movie they ever made," he said, "and none of them stars belong in this outfit. So you get out of here, you tramps, or I'll arrest the whole slew of you."
>
> We folded our tents like the Arabs and guiltily stole away. It was not until we were in the garden at the Huxley house where the picnic was resumed that we began to think about the titillating head-lines ... "Mass Arrest in Hollywood. Greta Garbo, Paulette Goddard, Charlie Chaplin, Aldous Huxley, Lord Bertrand Russell, Krishnamurti, and Christopher Isherwood Taken Into Custody."

War broke out in Europe in September 1939. There was no enthusiasm in America for the war. Opinion polls showed a majority against any involvement. Germany overran Poland in less than a fortnight, but on the western front French and German soldiers glowered at each other across the Rhine, and the conflict was quickly dubbed "the phony war."

Salka's Maberry Road home drew ever more refugees. Fred and Renée Zimmerman, formerly of Berlin, bought a house on Maberry as did Christopher Isherwood and Donald Ogden Stewart and his wife, Ella Winter. Salka took in Bertolt Brecht when, sponsored by Lion and Marta Feuchtwanger, he arrived, via Denmark and Russia, with wife and mistress. With no reputation in America, Brecht didn't fit easily in the émigré world. Because her friendship with Garbo gave Salka some influence at MGM, Brecht tried to write a script with her.

Guilt permeated the sizable English film colony, including Huxley, who felt ashamed of sitting out the war in California while the Luftwaffe bombed London. Gradually, he became aloof and would view human follies with sorrow and sometimes wry humor. The fall of France in June 1940 turned a pair of sewing circle members, Lili Damita and Marlene Dietrich, into a rallying point and support group of exiled French, starting with Jean Renoir.

22

The Sisterhood and the War

The war in Europe moved into another phase in the spring of 1940 when Germany invaded Denmark and Norway and began a lightning offensive that by June had led to the fall of France. Masters of Europe from Norway to Italy and beyond to North Africa, Germany and its Axis allies barred American films. At home, a slippage of the box office was attributed to moviegoers staying home to listen to world events on the radio. After December 7, 1941, everything changed—for Hollywood and for the sewing circle.

The stars enlisted. A *Chicago Tribune* poll of 20 million moviegoers had crowned Clark Gable "King of Hollywood" (the Queen was Myrna Loy), and Louis B. Mayer feared his premier male star would be swept up in the patriotic fever. As it was, the forty-one-year-old Gable was not eager to join, but agreed to be president of a Victory Committee. Howard Strickling turned the first meeting into a media event. The King's new wife, Carole Lombard, came in a dark fur coat and black silk dress and told everyone she was disguised as a blackout. She beamed with pride when Clark addressed the assembled actors and urged everyone to volunteer for war-bond selling tours. A subcommittee headed by Gable and including Myrna Loy, Claudette Colbert, Charles Boyer, Bob Hope,

Ginger Rogers, and nine others was chosen to coordinate talent for war-bond rallies, camp shows, and hospital tours.

Each celebrity's call to colors was a major event in his studio's publicity department. Henry Fonda, who was thirty-seven and the father of three children, joined as a sailor, only to be ordered back to Hollywood because Twentieth Century–Fox wanted him in a war movie. Jimmy Stewart enlisted as a private, eventually to become a bomber pilot and a colonel; Robert Montgomery joined the navy; Tyrone Power abandoned both wife and male lover to join the marines. Robert Taylor couldn't wait to prove his manhood in the navy and, behind Barbara Stanwyck's back, volunteered for active duty.

The war and the questions it ultimately raised about the postwar social order turned Taylor and Stanwyck into ultraconservatives. With Clark Gable, Gary Cooper, John Wayne, and columnist Hedda Hopper among others, they became founding members of Motion Picture Alliance for the Preservation of American Ideals, a virulently right-wing organization that was as much a backlash against the guilds that had unionized Hollywood as a reaction to the robust leftism of intellectuals and artists of the New Deal. Living ever deeper in the closet, Stanwyck opened her purse and her door to the Alliance and hosted meetings in her living room while her husband flew off for basic training as a navy flying instructor.

With its needs for a female workforce, the war made Hollywood retool and offer not only tough, blue-collar "Rosie the Riveter" types but also Stanwyck-Colbert-Crawford-Hepburn flicks about assertive women surviving on the home front without men. When G.I. Joe came home, society again agreed that a woman's place was in the home, and movie screens filled once more with cool, graceful wives as perfectly complementary to the leading men. Rebellious dames were confined to the new *film noir* genre.

The demand for home-front womanpower threw young women together in all-female worlds. In factories and military units, the pattern followed that of female institutions such as women's colleges and women's prisons. Young women who, perhaps for the first time, came in contact with sexuality among women in the close confines of military life often developed a modicum of tolerance. The war, its purpose and issues, was so much bigger than who kissed whom in barracks.

The life and soul of wartime L.A.'s lesbian sisterhood was Dorothy Binney Putnam. She was the daughter of the wealthy Connecticut industrialist who headed the Binney & Smith Crayola crayon company. An athletic, strong-minded young socialite with an outgoing personality and a sense of humor, she married G. P. (George Palmer) Putnam in 1911 and bore the publisher two sons. After they divorced and Putnam married Amelia Earhart, Dotty, as everybody called her, taught her former husband's new wife to drive. Dotty helped Amelia's campaign to get women into the air by becoming the first woman passenger using Transcontinental Air Transport on a round-trip to Los Angeles. With pioneer flyers Ruth Nichols and Thea Rasche, Dotty formed an association of women pilots. After Earhart disappeared in the Pacific on her attempted round-the-world flight in 1937, and a year later G.P. got her declared legally dead so he could marry Beverly Hills divorcée Jean-Marie Cosigny James, Dotty set up household with Lois Mercer in Hollywood and worked in the film industry as a stuntwoman specializing in doubling leading ladies on horseback.

Dotty came into her own when the army created the Women's Army Auxiliary Corps (WAAC—the word *auxiliary* was soon dropped) in the spring of 1942, and she immediately became an officer. Lois organized the WAC's ambulance corps, and together they gave New Year's Day parties, where, between the pre–Rose Bowl brunch and late-night revelries, an "amazing" throng of women in films made an appearance. Door Legg, the founder of *One, Inc.,* the first aboveground homosexual magazine, would remember being the only male at one of Dotty's parties. However, even after Dotty and Lois died in their nineties, Legg would never say who came to their parties.

Nancy Kulp was one of them. This twenty-two-year-old navy reserve WAVE would become famous as secretary Jane Hathaway hopelessly in love with the dopey Jethro Bodine in television's *Beverly Hillbillies*. Kulp was attracted to the all-female atmosphere of the women's corps.

In *Odd Girls and Twilight Lovers,* Lillian Faderman would quote

Women Army Corps (WAC) sergeant Johnnie Phelps, answering General Eisenhower's request that she ferret out lesbians in her battalion, as follows:

> Yessir. If the general pleases, I will be happy to do this investigation. . . . But, sir, it would be unfair of me not to tell you, my name is going to head the list. . . . You should also be aware that you're going to have to replace all the file clerks, the section heads, most of the commanders, and the motor pool. I think you should also take into consideration that there have been no illegal pregnancies, no cases of venereal disease, and the general himself has been the one to award good-conduct commendations and service commendations to these members of the WAC detachment.

With that, Eisenhower canceled the order.

The war was fought with movies—obsessively. On the home fronts of both sides, audiences flocked to the only existing distraction. Movies were shown not only in cinemas, but in factories, schools, and union halls. Millions of men in uniform saw movies endlessly, aboard ships, in barracks and mess halls. In American boom towns, movie houses remained open around the clock to accommodate swing and graveyard shifts. Attendance reached 80 million a week. Hollywood became an assembly line—a total of 488 features were made in 1942, a number never to be surpassed.

Changing attitudes, easy camaraderie, and new arrivals loosened and enlarged the sewing circle. Agnes Moorehead was one newcomer who had no trouble finding intimate women friends. She was the soul of discretion, her friend Elsa Lanchester would say, but as Paul Lynde put it, "The whole world knows Agnes was a lesbian—I mean classy, but one of the all-time Hollywood dykes."

Moorehead was thirty-four when she joined Orson Welles's Mercury Theater in 1940, and the following year she made her film debut playing his mother in *Citizen Kane*. In 1942, she was nominated for best supporting actress for her portrayal of a spinster in Welles's *Magnificent Ambersons*, followed by *Journey Into Fear*. She became famous for the one-woman radio play *Sorry, Wrong Number* (when it came to do the movie version, Barbara Stanwyck played the bedridden neurotic who gets crossed wires when she calls her husband, hears a couple of men arranging a murder, and comes to realize she is to be the victim).

"There's the actress who works mostly before forty, and the one who works mostly after forty," Moorehead said when she was in her sixties. Like Judith Anderson, she was typecast in flashy supporting parts as neurotic, possessive, or puritanical. She played a nun like a witch in *The Singing Nun,* and for eight years on television played Endora, the witch, in the series *Bewitched.*

The war brought other members of the sewing circle together. Mercedes de Acosta spent the early war years with Garbo and came to believe her friend's increasingly neurotic wish for solitude was the result of deep-rooted disappointment in herself—for not fighting harder for worthwhile films. Garbo brought her mother, brother, and sister-in-law to Los Angeles and found a house for them. Garbo's mother, Anna Gustafsson, was all nagging and petty criticism, slowly slipping into physical and mental collapse.

As Louis B. Mayer pressed Garbo to star in *Two-Faced Woman,* she sought advice from the dead Mauritz Stiller. In a repeat of the exorcism in the New York hotel room where Mercedes had lit candles and made Garbo kneel naked next to her, Garbo locked herself in her bedroom, put Stiller's picture between lighted candles, and waited for him to speak *d'outre tombe.* When nothing came of it, she visited mediums and fortune-tellers. Mercedes would write, "She has what I consider a very striking quality, a deep purity of intention in all that she does. I believe her own greatest problem and one that causes her untold unhappiness is an underlying suspicion toward people and life itself."

George Cukor was set to direct *Two-Faced Woman.* To bury the fact that Sweden was neutral in the war, the picture was, as Mayer pointed out to her, designed to Americanize Garbo. Patriotism demanded all-American heroines, and in *Two-Faced Woman* she would play a ski instructor who, fearing she may lose her husband to another woman, poses as her own more vivacious twin sister. (Never mind the source material was Ludwig Fulda's 1901 play, *Die Zwillingsschwester.*) When she still expressed reservations, the studio ordered George Oppenheimer to join Salka Viertel and S. N.

Behrman for another rewrite. Everybody reassured Garbo, and she would claim she said yes so Salka wouldn't lose her writing fee. Melvyn Douglas was cast as her foil, Constance Bennett as the other woman. Before filming started, Adrian resigned. When no one would take the responsibility of okaying his half-finished wardrobe for Garbo, he walked out of MGM.

Two-Faced Woman was a disaster, earning the famous line in a *Time* review: "It is almost as shocking as seeing your mother drunk." Garbo would claim that Louis B. Mayer told her he wouldn't have anything for her until after the war. Projects continued, however, and she was reported to be mulling over de Acosta's old suggestions that she play Teresa of Avila, Dorian Gray, or Eleonora Duse. Salka tailored a George Sand script for her.

Salka had devoured George Sand's novels as a young woman, and both she and Garbo were convinced that Garbo would be sensational as Aurore Dupin, baroness of Dudevant, who was twenty-seven when she left her husband to be a writer and, besides adopting the nom de plume George Sand, began dressing like a man. It had been exhilarating, the baroness wrote, "to go unnoticed, unremarked, uninhibited, feet solid on the slippery ice, shoulders covered with snow, hands in pockets, stomach a bit empty at times but the head all the more filled with songs and melodies, neither *dame,* nor *monsieur.*"

Garbo had only been off the screen for a year when *Mourning Becomes Electra* resurfaced as a Garbo–Katharine Hepburn possibility. Louis B. Mayer vetoed the idea, declaring Eugene O'Neill's mother and daughter in love with the same man too provocative. Hepburn was furious and lashed out at the Production Code. She had great respect for O'Neill, she told the *Los Angeles Times,* and once the war was over and American films would once more be seen on European screens, "I feel that his plays might prove a good means of carrying a message about our creative achievements to foreign countries. If censorship stands in the way, then perhaps there is some need for modification and change."

Lady Mendl, Bessie Marbury's old companion Elsie de Wolfe, took refuge in Los Angeles with her companion Hilda West, and her aging husband. Although she no longer gave parties of Gatsby-esque proportions for seven hundred guests, she still decorated the homes of Hollywood's nouveaux riches of insecure taste. Hugo

Vickers would write that Lady Mendl encountered hostility because she employed a German housekeeper. In 1943, however, she was offered an editorial position on a propaganda magazine called *Victory* and moved herself and her loved ones to New York. Garbo followed and rented an apartment in the Ritz Towers on Manhattan's Park Avenue. Her plans for the future were vague, and in Los Angeles, Salka didn't give up. In 1944, she tried to have Garbo do Joan of Arc, not Mercedes's Joan, but George Bernard Shaw's *Saint Joan.*

Writer-director Preston Sturges, whose mother, Mary Desti, was a friend of Mercedes de Acosta, gave Stanwyck—and Edith Head—a sparkling comedy in the 1941 slapstick comedy *The Lady Eve.* The saucy satire had Stanwyck as a lady cardsharp and Henry Fonda as a befuddled millionaire. Two years later, Billy Wilder turned *Double Indemnity* into Stanwyck's most famous picture. Her steely, rotten-to-the-heart blonde who helps insurance man Fred MacMurray bump off her husband turned the thirty-seven-year-old Stanwyck into the quintessential *film noir* actress and prolonged her career by forty years.

Nazimova was in contention for evil parts. David O. Selznick was interested in having her play the chilling and ultimately incinerated Mrs. Danvers in *Rebecca,* although he and Alfred Hitchcock eventually settled on Judith Anderson. In the early 1940s, Nazimova played mothers to a pair of gay actors—Robert Taylor in Mervyn LeRoy's anti-Nazi *Escape,* and Tyrone Power in Rouben Mamoulian's remake of *Blood and Sand.* By then she had sold the Garden of Allah with the stipulation she be allowed to stay rent-free as long as she lived. She saw the new owners replace her semitropical gardens with twenty-five guest cottages. The Garden of Allah hotel and cottages became a raffish if pricey haven for people in transition. F. Scott Fitzgerald paid $400 a month to live in one of the units in 1937. At one time or another, Orson Welles, Errol Flynn, Dorothy Parker, and Robert Benchley were tenants. Nazimova died in 1945, destitute and forgotten.

Patsy Kelly was a lesbian who, like her friend Tallulah Bankhead, made jokes about her sexuality. A reporter from *Motion Picture* asked the "queen of wisecracks" if, as a little girl, she had wanted to be a boy. Not a boy with a penis, she answered.

When author Boze Hadleigh interviewed furtive Hollywood lesbians in the 1970s, Kelly was the only one to tell him she was gay. No lavender marriage was ever imposed on her, but had it been, wouldn't she have preferred a gay husband?

"Yeah . . . Cole Porter, but he was taken."

Would she have married a heterosexual?

"Yeah, I wouldn't. I mean no. Yeah, wait a minute, I'm a dyke. So what? Big deal."

She was born Bridget Sarah Veronica Kelly in Brooklyn and grew up wanting to be a fireman. To keep her off the streets, her mother sent her to Jack Blue's dance school. A tap dancer at twelve, she met and became a lifelong friend of Ruby Keeler's. In Hollywood, Patsy was a star of Hal Roach comedies, specializing in being someone's salty sidekick or the frightened maid. Her inseparable friend was Thelma Todd, another Hal Roach comedienne, who in 1935 was found dead in her car in a never-solved mystery.

Patsy was busy during the war, making eight films between 1941 and 1945, but fell on hard times in the late 1940s. She became a paid companion to Tallulah Bankhead—"guest resident" was the discreet term when they lived together. Tallulah gave Patsy a part in her *Dear Charles* touring company. Together they toured in Tennessee Williams's *Streetcar Named Desire* in 1956.

Patsy helped Tallulah through more than one night of boozing. Patsy threw herself on the floor one night to soften Bankhead's landing when Tallulah tore off her clothes, announced she could fly, got up on a dresser, and jumped. Patsy played the saucy maid in the 1971 revival of *No, No, Nanette* and, as a witch, made *Rosemary's Baby* her seventieth film. "I got paid just as much for the crummy movies as the good ones," she told Boze Hadleigh. She said she made and gave away $4 million. "Some years I could do no wrong, others I could do nothing right."

The war was Dietrich's second coming. She was not the only waning star to entertain the troops on endless USO tours, but better than old troupers such as Al Jolson, Nöel Coward, Bob Hope, and Maurice Chevalier, she remade her legend. Tirelessly and good-humoredly, she sang her movie songs, the international wartime ballad "Lili Marlene," and played a musical saw, a skill she had mastered for the Berlin stage, for half a million Allied troops and war prisoners across North Africa and Europe. She had started right after Pearl Harbor with Orson Welles performing for GIs passing through Los Angeles and emerged in 1945 with a one-woman show that gave her a worldwide audience she would draw on for the next thirty years.

Dietrich and Garbo met for the only time at war's end when Dietrich returned from her final USO tour in Europe and was the houseguest of Welles and his wife, Rita Hayworth, on Carmelina Drive in Brentwood. "According to him, Dietrich simply adored Garbo," Dietrich biographer Donald Spoto would write. "Others had the impression that she wanted to see how Garbo looked after several years' absence from the screen, and that she also wanted to meet the woman whom Mercedes de Acosta had once loved, perhaps because Dietrich's affair with de Acosta was also history by this time." A get-together was arranged at the home of Clifton Webb in Beverly Hills. Marlene gushed over Garbo, who managed only a curt acknowledgment.

Garbo was criticized for doing nothing for the Allied cause. Thirty years after the war, however, a book entitled *A Man Called Intrepid: The Secret War* by William Stevenson told of her helping British counterintelligence identify Nazi sympathizers in neutral Sweden.

Discomfort with what was different pervaded the postwar psyche. The optimism of VJ-day gave way to a vague defensiveness, to xenophobia and anticommunist hostility. Communism was a big issue in the 1946 congressional elections. In California, the Republican Committee of One Hundred asked demobilized navy lieutenant commander Richard M. Nixon to run, all campaign expenses paid, against Democratic incumbent Jerry Voorhis, who had been an effective member of Congress and was the sponsor of the National School Lunch Act. With never proven charges that Voorhis was "the candidate of the Kremlin," Nixon won.

After communists, homosexuals became a specific target. It was said that an adherent of the Communist Party would admit membership before a Hollywood lesbian would come out of the celebrity closet.

23

The Dark Age

Lizabeth Scott's sexy voice and icy looks put her in instant orbit in 1945. The launching pad was a Paramount romance called *You Came Along,* about a girl from the Treasury Department who takes three GIs on a war-bond tour and falls in love with the officer, who dies of leukemia. Robert Cummings was the air force officer, Don DeFore and Charles Drake his buddies. The director was John Farrow, who, with wife, Maureen O'Sullivan, had named their newborn daughter Mia. Paramount publicity promoted Lizabeth Scott as a new Lauren Bacall or Veronica Lake and described her as "beautiful, blonde, aloof, and alluring." Anticipating her assault on the other tough-girl screen sirens, the publicity department dubbed her "The Threat."

The studio bio described her as a former fashion model and stage actress who, after serving as Tallulah Bankhead's understudy in the Broadway production of *The Skin of Our Teeth* in 1942, was given a screen test, signed, and shipped to Hollywood. Critics liked *You Came Along* and hailed her "sonorous speaking voice," "intriguing manners," and "fragile and appealingly candid face." Ten years later, she became the only Hollywood actress to be accused in print of unnatural sex practices.

Her real name was Emma Matzo. She was born in Scranton, Pennsylvania, and had just turned twenty when she joined the cast of Thornton Wilder's *Skin of Our Teeth*. Elia Kazan was the director of the unconventional comedy. Frederic March played the paterfamilias, Florence Eldridge his wife, Montgomery Clift their son, and Tallulah the maid Sabrina, who manages to survive the world upheavals from the Stone Age to 1942. She is a French-farcical maid in the first act, a mincing bathing beauty in the second, the camp follower in the third, and all through the perennial "other woman."

Bankhead proved too healthy, and Scott left the show after seven months of sitting backstage. Months later she was frantically summoned when Bankhead was taken ill. Producer Hal Wallis was in the audience one of the nights she played Sabrina. A screen test ensued. Wallis, who produced independently for Paramount, signed her and, two months after her arrival in Los Angeles in November 1944, gave her the female lead in *You Came Along*.

Double Indemnity made Barbara Stanwyck the icy spider woman everybody wanted for *film noirs*. Billed after Stanwyck and Van Heflin, Scott caught the updraft of the new genre with *The Strange Love of Martha Ivers*. Wallis got Lewis Milestone to direct, Stanwyck to play the hard-boiled, ruthlessly wealthy Martha Ivers, who has one murder in her past and another on her mind. Kirk Douglas was cast as her sappy district attorney husband, Van Heflin was a rekindled passion from the past, Scott a girl on parole, and Judith Anderson as Martha's aunt. If Lizabeth had some pretty silly lines and her performance lacked conviction, the *New York Times* said, the reason was that her character was poorly written.

With her bedroom eyes, husky voice, and sultry manners, Scott was perfect for the *film noir* genre, with its predilection for ambiguity, entrapment, sexual obsession, and a vortex of crime. She costarred with Humphrey Bogart in *Dead Reckoning* and over the next ten years made nineteen other movies.

She was in *Loving You* with Elvis Presley when she sued *Confidential* magazine for $2.5 million. An article in the September 1955 issue, she complained, "was under a title and descriptive language that would have a natural tendency to hold plaintiff up to contempt and ridicule and implied improperly relationships in the eyes of every reader and would imply indecent, unnatural and illegal conduct." The story insinuated she "was prone to indecent, illegal and highly offensive acts in her private and public life."

The Cold War demanded sexual correctness along with political conformity, and *Confidential* took its cue from the House Un-American Activities witch-hunt when it published innuendos of homosexuality and misogyny. To augment its night-court reportage of celebrity drunks and brawls, the magazine copied the *Police Gazette* vernacular (example: "Vic Mature, Remember That Cute Trick You Dated? She Was a He"). What scared Hollywood's gays was that the reports in the sleaze tabloids like *Confidential* were more often than not deadly accurate. Lizabeth Scott lost her suit before Los Angeles Superior Court judge Leon T. David because *Confidential* magazine had no California representatives.[1]

"You can hardly separate homosexuals from subversives," U.S. senator and Republican floor leader Kenneth Wherry from Nebraska told the *New York Post*. "Mind you, I don't say every homosexual is subversive, and I don't say every subversive is a homosexual, but [people] of low morality are a menace to the government." The United States Senate decided gays must be fired from government jobs because they lacked "emotional stability, which is not found in most sex perverts."[2]

There were no lesbian political organizations, and no "alternative press." Seventy-five percent of women who sought support and advice from one lesbian support group said they had had sex with men more than once and enjoyed it. Heterosexual intercourse had come while dating, in a marriage, out of curiosity, or as a test of sexual identity. What was lacking was the kind of emotional involvement the women experienced in lesbian relationships.

1. At a March 7, 1956, hearing, Judge David granted *Confidential* attorney H. F. Birnbaum's motion to squash service of summons, after Birnbaum argued that the magazine was not published in California and that, when published, each issue was turned over to a distribution firm that purchased it for circulation. Jerry Giesler, Scott's attorney, talked of refiling the action in New York federal court, but the case was not pursued.
2. Echoing Senator Wherry, *Human Events,* a weekly Washington newsletter that claimed a readership of forty thousand "business and professional leaders," said homosexuals must be tracked down and purged because "by the very nature of their vice they belong to a sinister, mysterious, and efficient International, [and] members of one conspiracy are prone to join another conspiracy." (Source: Rose G. Waldeck, "Homosexual International," *Human Events,* in New York Lesbian Herstory, file: 1950s.)

Ambivalence about the sexes came early to many young women and, in the case of Emma Goldman, would plague her throughout her life. After a first, brutal deflowering by a young clerk, "I always felt between two fires in the presence of men," the radical socialist would write. "Their lure remained strong, but it always mingled with violent revulsion. I could not bear to have them touch me." However, at thirty-nine she would discover heterosexual passion in the arms of Ben L. Reitman and write intense erotic letters to her young lover. When in 1954 Door Legg's *One* magazine published a short story about a woman choosing to become a lesbian, the Los Angeles postmaster general confiscated all copies in the mail and demanded that the publisher prove the story was not obscene. A federal district court upheld the postmaster's decision. There were few irregular special-interest groups, and only a few, often working-class, bars where lesbians could meet with no fear of being raided by vice squads. Professional women had the most to fear as the FBI infiltrated the Daughters of Bilitis, a private organization of lesbians dedicated to improving the image of same-sex love. The organization began as a secret club in San Francisco in 1955 only to split along economic lines a year later. Working-class members wanted a secret, exclusive lesbian club, and white-collar women wanted to interact with the Mattachine Society and One Inc., two nascent gay male organizations in Los Angeles.

Policewomen were used as decoys, and after raids on bars the charges were generally "visiting a house of ill repute," "disorderly conduct," or "conduct contrary to the public welfare and morals." Many frightened lesbians were badgered into pleading guilty because they were made to feel ashamed of being homosexual. In *Lesbian/Woman,* Del Martin and Phyllis Lyon would detail a 1956 raid at Kelly's, a San Francisco bar catering to lesbians, that resulted in thirty-six arrests on charges of "visiting a disorderly house." All except four pleaded guilty and received suspended sentences. The four young women who pleaded not guilty had their cases dismissed.

Harry Hay, the founder of the Mattachine Society, was an actor who since 1945 had tried to promote tolerance toward homosexuals by invoking the United Nations charter of civil rights. Hay organized the Circle of Loving Companions, a gay collective that included Stella Rush and Sandy Sandoz, a pair of lesbians who, under the name of Sten Russell and Sandy Saunders, edited *The Ladder.* The magazine stressed that lesbians had nothing to fear in joining the Daughters of Bilitis. "Your name is safe," they assured the readers about the mailing list. If the Constitution of the United States guaranteeing freedom of the press wasn't enough, the Supreme Court ruled in 1953 that a publisher did not have to reveal the names of people buying reading material, even to a congressional investigating committee. Which didn't prevent the FBI from infiltrating the Daughters of Bilitis.

Lesbians felt compelled to live covertly, to marry gay men and make sure everybody addressed them as Mrs. Pressured by home and community, many acceded to family pleas to submit to psychoanalysis, which promised to cure lesbianism on the couch. Barbara Stanwyck felt exposed to pity and ridicule when Taylor divorced her in 1950. Katharine Cornell judiciously cultivated her "beard" marriage to Guthrie McClintic and, despite her shrewd appreciation of Hollywood, stayed away from the movies. Libby Holman married Ralph Holmes, a handsome homosexual actor twenty years her junior, who seven years later committed suicide. Agnes Moorehead married Robert Gist, also twenty years her junior. The marriage lasted less than a year. Sandy Dennis, who made her film bow in Elia Kazan's *Splendor in the Grass* in 1961, made sure everybody believed she was married to jazz musician Gerry Mulligan.[3]

The methods used by psychologists and others to talk or shock homosexuals into sexual and social conformity included the aversion therapy of electroshocks to repress a man's enjoyment of a naked male body. A Jungian therapist assured a woman that while her love for another woman was "not any worse than alcoholism," he would have her cured in six months. Lesbianism was reversible, many therapists maintained, if doctors went about it in the right way and insisted on unmasking the neurotic motivations behind lesbianism.

Homosexuality was considered a case of "arrested development," as the Freudians put it, even though Sigmund Freud's daughter, Anna, was a lesbian.[4] To show how sick lesbians were, one

3. *People* magazine was unable to unearth a marriage certificate when Dennis died in 1992.
4. Not until 1972 did the American Psychological Association take homosexuality off the "sick" list.

doctor lifted "case histories" from *Life Romances* and *My Confession* magazines; another suggested that cunnilingus was a manifestation of cannibalistic fantasies. Many lesbians did hope to be cured. In *Odd Girls and Twilight Lovers,* Lillian Faderman quotes one woman undergoing therapy with three different Los Angeles psychiatrists in the 1950s as saying, "Many of us were loaded with self-hate and wanted to change. How could it be otherwise? All we heard and read about homosexuality was that crap about how we were inverts, perverts, queers—a menace to children, poisoner to everyone else, doomed never to be happy."

In October 1947, Robert Taylor became the only actor to name names before the House Un-American Activities Committee (HUAC). In 1951, Screen Actors Guild president Ronald Reagan announced the guild would not defend members who defied HUAC. At the Directors Guild, a refusal by Joseph Mankiewicz to insist on loyalty oaths for every member nearly cost him his career.

Salka Viertel was blacklisted. John Huston, who would make her son Peter the screenwriter of *The African Queen,* told columnist George Sokolsky and anonymous members of the FBI that Salka was the most generous and civilized person he knew, and that her "left-wing" activities consisted mainly of making her home on Maberry Road a haven for intellectuals. The McCarthy era disillusioned Salka about America, and she moved to Klosters, Switzerland, where de Acosta, Garbo, and other old lovers visited. Her friend Eleonora von Mendelssohn committed suicide in New York. Dorothy Arzner became a recluse.

The sewing circle actresses closed ranks to make sure their private lives remained deep secrets. Rumors nevertheless surfaced. Claudette Colbert and Dietrich allegedly were lovers. An outraged Frank Sinatra purportedly broke up Lana Turner and Ava Gardner during an intimate slumber party.

The anticommunist hunt did nothing to improve the quality of Hollywood films. Few directors or producers dared target political controversies, and the industry dished out safe, light entertainment. Barbara Stanwyck and Joan Crawford played domineering shrews in limp thrillers and westerns. Both grew increasingly butch in appearance and manners. When movies got fewer and shabbier, Stanwyck spent twenty years in television playing nearly genderless matriarchs and kept her life the best-kept secret in Hollywood. To stave off bankruptcy and keep up appearances, Crawford married Pepsi-Cola chairman Alfred Steele in 1956 and, after he died three years later, hired Dorothy Arzner to direct Pepsi commercials. Crawford returned to the screen every time she was offered a part. She and Bette Davis scored as a pair of crazy hags in *What Ever Happened to Baby Jane?*

MGM dumped Judy Garland in 1950, and the rest of her short life was a series of comebacks, sometimes on film, mostly on stage, from nervous breakdowns, drug addiction, bad luck, and marriages. She looked better in a tuxedo than in chiffon and lamé, and her concert tours kept her famous. Libby Holman reappeared on Broadway after sixteen years, Dietrich performed in Las Vegas, and together with Constance Collier, Katharine Hepburn went to London to star in George Bernard Shaw's *Millionairess* on the stage. Hepburn, too, dared to be butch-gamine and, in slacks, turtlenecks, and casual jackets, told chat-show audiences in clipped humorous and disdainful pronouncements what she thought of women's lib, marriage, her need for privacy and increasing fear of everything.

In 1956, the film version of William Bradford Huie's novel *The Revolt of Mamie Stover,* about a sleazy prostitute and her lesbian madam, turned Jane Russell's hooker into a dance-hall girl, and Agnes Moorehead's madam into an older friend. Six years later, Stanwyck was considered brave when she accepted the role of a lesbian madam in the watered-down screen adaptation of the Nelson Algren novel *Walk on the Wild Side.* Her character's love for her best bordello worker was diluted to the point of unintended implications. Instead of insinuating that she lusted after Capucine, their interaction came across as an employer's admiration for a productive employee.

As a lesbian, the twenty-eight-year-old Capucine (née Germaine Lefebvre) later admitted she wouldn't have minded a fling with Stanwyck, but that she sensed Stanwyck had a lady friend and was not looking for someone else. Said Capucine, "And being such a big star, so known to everybody in Hollywood, she would have to be very careful. In her place, I also would not take chances."

Capucine was a Paris runway model of classical features who

began her acting career in the Franz Liszt biopic *Song Without End* opposite the gay Dirk Bogarde, and partially directed by George Cukor, ended it playing a lesbian in Vicente Aranda's *Las Crueles* in 1971. She was married for three months when she was eighteen and subsequently "linked" with William Holden (who "remembered" her substantially in his will) and producer Charles Feldman. "I used to think I needed a man to define myself," she told *Harpers Bazaar* in September 1982. "No more. Certainly, I'd like to meet my soul mate, but I'm not making an obsession of it." Suffering from profound depression, the fifty-seven-year-old actress jumped to her death from her eighth-floor penthouse apartment in Lausanne, Switzerland, in 1990.

24

Seeking to Belong

Mercedes de Acosta spent the 1950s mostly in Paris, living successively with Maria "Poppi" Kirk and another escapee from Hollywood—Ona Munson. After her parting with Ernst Lubitsch, Ona's screen career had gone nowhere despite her high-profile part as Rhett Butler's pal Belle Watling in *Gone With the Wind*. De Acosta and Munson became lovers in 1939 when Ona was under contract to Republic Studios. Munson was a sensation as the depraved whorehouse madam in Josef von Sternberg's *Shanghai Gesture,* but the bowdlerized, much-censored adaptation of John Colton's theatrical shocker was a dud.

Ona's letters to Mercedes were passionate. "I long to hold you in my arms and pour my love into you," she wrote in 1940. Six years later, she felt they had shared "the deepest spiritual moment that life brings to human beings," and that together they had created "an entity as surely as though [we] had conceived and borne a child."

Together, they mourned the suicide of Eleonora von Mendelssohn. She had come through the war unscathed and in Salzburg had saved her Rembrandts, Titians, Corots, van Goghs, and Goyas, but she was restless and uprooted in her New York exile and jumped out of a window.

Garbo called herself "the wanderer" and traveled aimlessly, forever the guest of the beau monde from Cecil Beaton to Aristotle Onassis to Cecile de Rothchild. In Paris, Mercedes stayed with her at the Hôtel Crillon. When the recluse star was inaccessible to either Mercedes or Cecil Beaton, the two consoled themselves by exchanging letters about her health, mind, and moods. On October 5, 1953, when Garbo was forty-eight, and de Acosta sixty, Mercedes wrote:

Greta is back but I haven't seen her. The night before she left for Europe in July she made a remark about you which I defended (too complicated to tell you about in a letter). We got into a row and I told her one or two truths. She was angry and left without calling me the next morning or saying goodbye. So, now, on her return, she has not called me.

Cecil replied October 11:

Very pleased to hear from you though sad to think you have had a falling out with Greta especially as it was on my account. It is very sad when people who love one another should see less of each other than those on more casual terms, & I feel very sad for Greta, who is far from happy, & making her life all the time more difficult. I don't know why she should turn against either of us as we have always been honest & have wanted to do the right thing for her. I trust she will have got in touch with you, as I'm sure she needs you—& I've always thought that the two of you should end your days together.

Garbo kept Mercedes at a distance because of de Acosta's and Beaton's gossip. To her face, they swore their lips were sealed; behind her back they prattled endlessly about her. Garbo claimed Mercedes had done her great harm by talking about her. "She's always trying to scheme and find out things and you can't shut her up," Garbo told Beaton in 1947. Not that he was any better. Garbo had never really forgiven him for writing in *Cecil Beaton's Scrapbook:*

She is not interested in anything or anybody in particular and she has become as difficult as an invalid and as selfish, quite unprepared to put herself out for anyone: she would be a trying companion, continuously sighing and full of tragic regrets; she is superstitious, suspicious, and does not know the meaning of friendship; she's incapable of love.

Mercedes was working hard on successive drafts of her memoirs, which promised to tell of her and Garbo's long and intimate "friendship." Mercedes was known among gays as "the dyke at the top of the stairs," a play on words on William Inge's 1958 play *The Dark at the Top of the Stairs* about the darkness into which both the child of a family and its parents dare not—whatever they pretend—ascend to.

Freud and Kinsey turned homosexuality into a topic of polite conversations, but nothing changed much in the public attitude toward people who loved members of their own sex. When de Acosta published her autobiography, *Here Lies the Heart,* in 1960, she was careful with the truth. In describing her guests at an early 1930s Hollywood luncheon, she never said that two-thirds, if not all, were women she had loved; "Fearlessly I invited the guests I wanted and the place cards read like the all-star cast of a benefit performance: Mrs. Patrick Campbell, Doris Keane, Jeanne Eagels, Alla Nazimova, Elsie Ferguson, Constance Collier, Laurette Taylor, Helen Hayes, Helen Menken, and Katharine Cornell."

The title, she explained in the foreword, was a quote from the painter Ignacio Zuloaga. "All great people function with the heart," he had told her when she was young. "Always remember to think with it, to feel with it, and above all, to judge with it." The author played ingeniously with the "half tones of life" and wrote that she could not understand people who believe a man should love only a woman, and a woman only a man. But while everybody, from Isadora Duncan and Nazimova to Garbo and Dietrich, was intimately and revealingly depicted, all portraits were shorn of sapphic implications.

Garbo never forgave the book and, when Mercedes called shortly after publication, hung up on her.

De Acosta's later years were sad and physically painful. She lived in a two-room apartment on Manhattan's East Sixty-eighth Street and had to sell her jewelry to pay for brain surgery. Other operations followed. She turned down a dealer's $10,000 offer for her Garbo letters, but obtained some money by consigning her collection of papers to the Rosenbach Museum in Philadelphia with the stipulation that the Garbo letters be sealed until ten years after Garbo's death. The sculptor Malvina Hoffman was a loyal friend, but she died in 1966. Mercedes died two years later at the age of seventy-five.

Garbo and Dietrich lived more than twenty-two and twenty-four years longer, respectively, each in increasing oblivion and both making sure they somehow didn't totally disappear, Garbo by being caught by paparazzi, Marlene by giving occasional but capricious interviews. Except in drag clubs, neither inspired any real imitators. Garbo lived on Manhattan's East Fifty-second Street overlooking the East River and traveled aimlessly as a guest of the famously rich. In 1933, Janet Flanner had told her *New Yorker* readers, "Fräulein Dietrich is the first foreign female personality Paris society has fallen in love with in years." It was in Paris that Marlene spent her twilight years, in an apartment she could no longer afford on Avenue Montaigne, and became a recluse, to be heard but never seen at the end.

As Flanner said about Natalie Barney, who was evicted from her rue Jacob aerie at ninety-three and lived another two years at the Hôtel Meurice, lesbians lived healthier lives because, among other things, they were spared childbirth. Garbo was eighty-four when she died in 1990. Dietrich was ninety when she died two years later even though she gave birth to a daughter.

Many in the sewing circle lived into their eighties and nineties. Dorothy (Dickie) Fellowes-Gordon lived to be a hundred.

Judy Garland and Tallulah Bankhead were the two exceptions. The tough and damaged Judy, who knew everything about show business, told an interviewer in 1964 that she had had so many comebacks that every time she returned from the bathroom it was a comeback. Five years later, at the age of forty-seven, she locked herself in a bathroom and died of an overdose.

Like Garland, Bankhead lived on a diet of alcohol, barbiturates, amphetamines, cigarettes, and crash diets, a gaunt little woman whose life, her biographer Denis Brian would write, "seemed almost like one long suicide attempt." She made sporadic TV appearances, playing the dastardly Black Widow in a 1967 episode of *Batman*. She attended Marlene Dietrich's one-woman show on Broadway in October 1967 and a year later was dead at sixty-five.

* * *

The early 1960s still gave the world lesbians you love to hate. Stanwyck's lesbianism in *Walk on the Wild Side* was thrown in for the effect in 1962, and in *Lilith, The Haunting, The Night of the Iguana,* and *Seven Women,* lesbians survived in a twilight world of neurotic repression. In the 1963 James Bond movie *From Russia With Love,* Lotte Lenya played Rosa Klebb, a Soviet agent who caresses lissome Daniela Bianchi's knee, her shoulder, and face and, in a lisp, says, "I have selected you for a most important assignment."

Offscreen it was Nancy Kulp who was vilified as a Rosa Klebb by fellow actor Buddy Ebsen. After a decade as Jane Hathaway on *The Beverly Hillbillies,* and small roles in a dozen movies, Kulp went back to Pennsylvania to run for Congress as a Democrat in 1962. During the campaign, Ebsen called Kulp a Hollywood pinko. In radio ads for her Republican opponent, he claimed she was too liberal for Pennsylvania, contributing to her defeat.

The resort towns of Santa Barbara and Palm Springs, both less than two hours' drive from Los Angeles on California's new freeways, became oases for graying members of the sewing circle. Santa Barbara and the exclusive Montecito hills overlooking the Pacific sheltered many of the semiretired members of the sisterhood.

Judith Anderson was the ranking, semicloseted matriarch, who had herself driven down to Los Angeles when directors beckoned. She was eighty-six in 1984 when she appeared in *Star Trek III,* and for the next three years she played Minx on the soap opera *Santa Barbara.* She died in 1992 aged ninety-three.

Virginia Valli led a weekend and holiday exodus of industry lesbians to Palm Springs. Valli was, with Charlie Farrell, the other half of the first known "twilight tandem." She started in movies in her native Chicago when she was seventeen and became one of the most beautiful silent stars. She starred with William Powell in one of Howard Hawks's last silents, *Paid to Love,* crossed the sound barrier with Ronald Colman in *Clothes Make the Man,* married Charlie Farrell, and retired. Farrell and Valli shared bedrooms when William Randolph Hearst invited them to San Simeon. Joel McCrea was put up in the same bungalow and Farrell was never there.

Developing Palm Springs made Valli and Farrell millionaires. Although Dinah Shore was no member of the sapphic sisterhood, her golf tournament became the biggest lesbian event of the year, bringing ten thousand lesbians to Palm Springs every year. Janet Gaynor, Farrell's costar in all those romantic 1930s movies, survived Adrian by twenty-five years, occasionally acting in television and presenting Oscars. Five years after Adrian died in 1959, she married producer Paul Gregory, a Charles Laughton associate fifteen years her junior. Seriously injured in an automobile accident in 1982, she died two years later.

Katharine Hepburn lived in Connecticut between films. In 1969, she returned to Broadway as Coco Chanel in *Coco*, then won a fourth Oscar for her performance in *On Golden Pond* in 1981. Despite ill health she continued to appear in the occasional film and, in 1992, saw her discreet autobiography, *Me*, become an international bestseller.

Agnes Moorehead stayed in Beverly Hills. Paul Lynde, the cynical comic of stage, screen, and television, would say of her, "She had a succession of intimate lady friends she'd often go out with, and there were rumors, but it was all kept in the family. . . . When one of her husbands was caught cheating, so the story goes, Agnes screamed at him that if he could have a mistress, so could she!" After burying her two husbands in 1952 and 1958, she found work in ten movies. When Robert Aldrich's gamble that audiences would love to see aging stars debase themselves paid off with *What Ever Happened to Baby Jane?* in 1964, Moorehead played a ratty maid to Bette Davis's crazy Cousin Charlotte in the follow-up *Hush . . . Hush, Sweet Charlotte.* Stanwyck was supposed to join the cast, but instead played Elvis Presley's boss in *Roustabout.* Her friend Edith Head did her wardrobe and told the press Barbara looked terrific in a pair of blue denims. Moorehead died in 1974. Head and Stanwyck trooped on, Head to win an Academy Award for the natty suits she designed for Paul Newman and Robert Redford in *The Sting.* Her last picture, *Dead Men Don't Wear Plaid,* came out a year after she died in 1981.

Stanwyck and Crawford took each other to lunch, in New York at the 21 Club, in Los Angeles at the Beverly Wilshire hotel's Don the Beachcomber. They reminisced about the good old days when the studios, however brutally, built careers and stars were stars, disparaging actresses who, after one season on television, thought of themselves as stars. Crawford eventually stopped coming to California. "All my friends are out of work, it's so sad," she said.

Her adopted daughter, Christina Crawford, portrayed her as a cruel, manipulative bisexual in a bestselling biography, *Mommie Dearest.* Joan Crawford died in 1977. Four years later, Faye Dunaway played her in the film version of *Mommie Dearest.*

Bad health plagued Stanwyck's old age, but she refused to let the public see her fall apart. She felt restless without a role to pour herself into and, to keep busy, accepted any part. She tried for a reunion with Henry Fonda when *On Golden Pond* was cast, but lost out to Katharine Hepburn. At seventy-five, however, she played a woman assailed by sexual urges in *The Thorn Birds.* She disapproved of scrutiny, and even after her death at eighty-two in 1990, friends felt that talking about her violated her will.

Strictures and taboos drowned in the sexual permissiveness and fractured spontaneity of the Aquarian age, and the conquering nascent feminism of the 1970s made young women demand rights that their mothers had thought unthinkable. In the movies, the shift in public sensibilities and awareness brought about inflation, zap, and intuitive approach and tell-it-like-it-is directness. In 1964, Gore Vidal used the word *homosexual* in his screen adaptation of his own play, *The Best Man,* and a year later John Schlesinger's *Darling* introduced bisexuality. In Mark Rydell's 1968 screen version of D. H. Lawrence's *Fox,* Sandy Dennis and Anne Heywood are two lesbians living on an isolated farm only to be disturbed by the arrival of a wandering seaman (Keir Dullea).

The decade closed with Robert Aldrich's heavy-handed *Killing of Sister George,* the story of the firing of an aging lesbian (Beryl Reid) from a TV serial and the collapse of her life. The film was given an "X" rating because of a scene in which Reid seduces Susannah York. After the scene was clipped in Connecticut and Massachusetts, Aldrich offered to cut the film in exchange for an "R" rating. "The 'killing' in the film," Vito Russo would write in *The Celluloid Closet,* "was not the death of homosexuality but the death of its visibility; the closet was at war with the flamboyance of Sister George herself. Homosexuality had become a fact of life, and Hollywood ballyhooed it as though the movies had invented it."

Tinseltown's anything-goes myth encouraged prurient speculation, but since it was not in any studio's interest if word got out that
its screen heroine was faking it when she kissed the leading man,
same-sex love continued to exist behind a wall of silence. And if we
heard little of Hollywood actresses in love relationships with other
women, it was not only because stars set up emotional barriers that
almost no one was allowed to overrun, but because the wanna-bes
who slept with anybody to get ahead, but didn't make it, often felt
ashamed in old age and refused to tell.

The need for approval is inherent in show business, and an actor
would be suicidal to willingly make himself or herself an object of
scorn and rebuke. Keeping the guard up remained second nature
and resulted in a legacy of distrust. The lesbian subculture stayed
underground for another generation

25

Lesbian chic

It is a story that won't go away. We may be in the twenty-first century and find gay lifestyles served up in mainstream entertainment from novels and sitcoms, but to declare oneself a lesbian in today's star-crazy Hollywood is as much of a career-killer as it was during the halcyon days of Louis B. Mayer and Greta Garbo. Lesbianism may be in the street, and in your face, and serried ranks of women may chant, "Two, four, six, eight, how do you know your grandma's straight," in Washington demonstrations. Any hint of vulnerability is out. Gone are the days when in the final pages of *The Well of Loneliness,* Radclyffe-Hall had her butch heroine pray to God for forgiveness for her deviance. As the mass media pondered the power and the pride of the once invisible homosexuals, *New York* magazine proclaimed lesbian chic with singer k. d. lang on the cover. *Newsweek* estimated that 2 to 3 million American women are lesbians and quoted activists that most women who love women have not yet come out. The Gay Games and Cultural Festival, an Olympic-style competition and celebration, is now a quadrennial event, and companies like AT&T, Anheuser-Busch, Apple, Bennetton and Sony aim sales pitches at gay men and lesbians.

The sharper view came into focus when corporate America tried to get a handle on the dollars-and-cents value of the gay and lesbian market. It wasn't fear of a backlash from conservatives that made Madison Avenue reluctant to go after gay consumers, but the absence of reliable demographics. Mainstream advertisers didn't trust less than pristine samples in gay magazines or nose counts in gay-pride parades. The research company Yankelovich Partners stepped into the breach and, with sexuality only one of fifty-two questions, found that almost 6 percent of American consumers identified themselves as homosexual. The survey showed that, contrary to conventional wisdom, homosexuals do not earn incomes much above the average, but that they are concentrated in top markets, that they are "more accommodating to technology," are more likely to be self-employed, are concerned with physical fitness, well-being, and self-improvement, but also that they report more stress in their lives than heterosexuals. Pridelines Lesbian Statistics report that lesbian and gay youths are up to three times more likely to attempt suicide than their heterosexual peers, and that they make up 30 percent of all teens who actually succeed in killing themselves.

Straight society usually thinks of a bisexual as a homosexual while gays think of a bisexual as a homosexual who, for some reason, hasn't been able to admit the fact. In kitsch and patter, show-biz icons like Madonna joined the parade as sexual outlaws, followed by Chloë Sevigny and Michelle Williams playing out sexual conflicts between lesbians and feminists on HBO. Lily Tomlin and her longtime companion, writer Jane Wagner, created lesbian heroines in skits Tomlin performed in her one-woman shows. In 1991, activists began outing celebrities, not, they claimed, to disgrace them but to free them and their comrades in love from fear and self-loathing. When *Entertainment Weekly* published its first issue on gay Hollywood in 1995, it had a hard time finding a dozen people in the industry willing to be profiled. By the "Gay Hollywood 2000" issue more than a hundred executives, directors, actors, musicians, writers and editors were willing to talk. Still, the magazine was careful not to out anyone. "There's the director of one of this year's blockbuster movies who, having taken a couple of tentative steps out of the closet in interviews earlier in his career, has now decided he's going back in," wrote assistant managing editor Mark Harris (*EW* Sept 29, 2000). "His representative was 'shocked and offended'—two feelings, by the way, of which most agents are technically incapable—when we asked if those earlier interviews were accurate . . . I'm now convinced that the biggest threat to openly gay people in the industry is closeted gay people. You know who they are: the gay agent who won't send his client out for gay roles because it might 'stigmatize' him (You know, the way it 'stigmatized' Tom Hanks when he starred in *Philadelphia*). The gay network executive who's afraid to speak up about homophobic jokes or slurs on his own shows. The gay publicist who trots out that tired old canard about how being openly gay will 'limit' an actor's ability to play romantic roles."

No wonder Hollywood's gay and bisexual stars are less than eager to embrace lesbian chic. While it is no longer acceptable in polite society to *forcefully* condemn, it is all right to admit to not understanding homosexuality. More women are out today, but most are out to friends and family. Admitting to being a lesbian to women coworkers is at best awkward. For most people the workplace is still sacred territory. The media might be quick to name actresses *playing* lesbians, but it is less forthcoming in naming anybody. OutPost, the New York organization outing gay celebrities, put Jodie Foster on an "Absolutely Queer" flier in 1991. Seven years later, Tom Cruise and Nicole Kidman threatened to sue anyone saying theirs was a "lavender" marriage of two gays. David Ehrenstein's *Open Secrets: Gay Hollywood 1929-1998* (William Morrow, 1999) includes a "Tom Cruise" chapter, but the only thing a reader learns is that gay men find Cruise attractive.

Outing Jodie Foster caused a backlash among many women, both gay and straight, and three years later *Mirabella* was calling Foster "a female role model to beat the band," an echo of golden-age double entendres: "Marlene Dietrich and Greta Garbo are gentlemen at heart," in 1932, under the headline "Both Members of the Same Club." Hedda Hopper and Louella Parsons may be gone, but their influence is with us in the tabloid press and on talk shows, from the *National Inquirer* to TV's *Inside Edition*. From its neutral (defanged?) remove, Associated Press reports dutifully on *Daily Variety* examining Hollywood homosexuality. "We've come a long way," the AP quotes the trade paper's senior editor Ramin Zahed as saying. "Yet, we can't lose sight of the fact that we still have a long way to go as well."

It is ironic that fear of lawsuits are keeping the closet doors as closed as they were sixty years ago. Howard Strickling and the other golden-age spin doctors never revealed anything truly "secret." Today, the stars themselves discuss their drug and alcohol problems and their failed relationships on talk shows, and their relatives sell prurient tidbits. Details of substance abuse, wife cheating, and marriage failures are so common that their revelation brings diminishing returns. Intimacy—especially same-sex intimacy—equals risk, and people shy away from revealing truly intimate matters. Despite contemporary society's much-vaunted honesty and openness, no star has gone on late-night chat shows to tell Jay Leno or David Letterman, "You know, I'm gayer than New Year's Eve. I admit it scared me to death. I'm afraid people won't relate to me anymore, afraid they won't find me believable in a sex scene, but, hey, there it is." Character actors like outspoken Ian McKellen have an easier time admitting to being gay. Why? To put it crudely because they don't have to perform erotic scenes with a film's leading lady.

The Anne Heche-Ellen De Generes story should be a warning to any two actresses wanting to shout their love for each other from the rooftops. Cheered on by the lesbian community but stunned by their own audacity, Heche and DeGeneres blamed the media and the entertainment industry for not greeting their pairing with enough enthusiasm. "What did we think?" DeGeneres told the *New York Times* in a February 20, 2000 interview. "That people would wrap their arms around us and say, 'Good for you'?" The industry's response was enough already. "Chill out, I would advise," *Daily Variety* editor Peter Bart told them in an open letter published December 7, 1998. "The 'victim' bit is getting tired. Neither of you is good casting for a victim, anyway. You're both vibrantly intelligent and attractive. According to your CAA agents, whom you fired last week, there are plenty of offers lined up that would pay you vast amounts of money. The biggest obstacle in your life is your own self-destructiveness." With the President Clinton-Monica Lewinsky scandal on every news program and front page, Bart added that as long as Americans weren't told who was sleeping with whom and in what position every day, they were pretty nonjudgmental. "My suspicion is that no one gives a damn about your sexual proclivities,

Anne and Ellen. They want you to be happy and stay true to your-
selves. No more *Time* magazine covers ("Yep, I'm gay"). No more
teary Diane Sawyer interviews. No more smooching at premieres
or White House parties." Six months later, Heche and DeGeneres
split up and their careers seemed to go nowhere.

To many in the industry the whole subject has become a non-
event. By adding sexual orientation to antidiscrimination policies,
the major entertainment conglomerates allowed gay employees to
be more open without fear of reprisal. The Christian Right criticized the Walt Disney Company for extending health benefits to
parts of its gay and lesbian employees, but failed to provoke a popular outcry.

As late as the early 1970s, sapphic activists deemed their liberation
to be little more than an ideal or a goal. For all the upheavals of the
feminist movement, lesbians stepping out of the closet found the
price to be martyrdom. Staying in the closet was, for some, a matter
of decorum. Nancy Kulp was one older actress who refused to
come out because people would say either they had known for
years or that she was coming out because she hadn't worked and
needed the publicity. What did not change was the proportion of
gay men to lesbians willing to identify themselves as gay. The industry's gay men featured in the magazine outnumbered its lesbians
three to one (the women included *Married . . . With Children's* Amanda
Bearse, producer Leslie Belzberg, and casting director Tammy
Billik). The proportion is believed to be the same today. Statistics
are hard to come by. No government data is collected on sexual
orientation. And the Gay and Lesbian Demographics/Sexual Orientation Statistics website *(www.gdsourcing.com/works/faqgay)* advises
researchers to visit British and Canadian sites. Indirect numbers do
surface on occasion. FBI statistics of year 2000 hate crimes show
that of 7,876 bias-motivated criminal incidents, 1,317 were crimes
motivated by a perception that the victim was lesbian or gay, a figure that lesbian activists find preposterously low.

However liberated modern women feel and try to do away with
traditional roles, most shy away from identification as lesbians. The
leadership of the women's movement is sympathetic to the problems of lesbians, yet for fear of alienating, the majority hesitates to
form close alliances with avowed lesbians. Wrote Del Martin and

Phyllis Lyon, "For those of us who recognize ourselves as women as well as lesbians, the emotional furor our presence has wrought in the women's movement has been both comic and tragic. It has been much like an obstacle course to see who feared whom the most."

While biologists admit they should listen to lesbians and not just look at their genes, they also believe sexuality is elastic in humans and that homosexuality is by no means "hard-wired." The subject is being explored by psychotherapists, sex educators, and opinion pools. In *Women and Love,* Shere Hite found that in love relationships between women, the overwhelming enjoyment was a combination of talking and being physically together. The second most frequently mentioned pleasure was sex and sexuality with another woman. A third of women in love with women had been married, and 24 percent fell in love with another woman for the first time after they were forty.

Committed lesbian sexologist JoAnn Loulan conducted a renowned survey in the United States and Canada from 1985 to 1987 and found lesbians not so much tied to sex as to the emotional impact of a relationship. Same-sex love held little attraction for young women. Only 10 percent of the 1,566 lesbians responding to Loulan's written questionnaire were under twenty-five while two-thirds were in their thirties and forties. Only 6 percent identified themselves as being working class, while 70 percent were college graduates or held advanced degrees. Nearly two-thirds said religious upbringing had little to do with their sexual preference, but over a third said they had been sexually abused as children, over half of them between the ages of five and ten, most by their fathers—a figure comparable to that of heterosexual women.

"Now for the good part," Loulan wrote in *Lesbian Passion: Loving Ourselves and Each Other* about current sexual activities. Ninety-six percent reported that they and their partner hugged, 91 percent kissed, 90 percent held each other body to body, 89 percent masturbated, 87 percent were naked together, 72 percent held hands, French-kissed, petted, or necked. Just over half said they kissed each other all over the body, a little less than a third took baths together, while almost a third fantasized during sex. When asked what they did in bed, 63 percent said they had oral sex or stimulated their partner while only 12 percent used a vibrator or a dildo.

Most thought they did more, sexually, to their partner than their partner did to them, which led Loulan to ask, "Do lesbians perceive their sex practices as giving more than they get? Is receiving more difficult than giving? Do we feel shy about reporting exactly what we do with each other?"

In response to Hite's exhaustive questionnaire, 14 percent of lesbians thought there was too *much* talk in a woman-to-woman relationship, that all the introspection was more traumatizing than in a relationship with a man. Ninety-six percent said they felt loved by their partner, but nearly three-quarters also admitted they had their share of emotional insecurities. Fifty-four percent answered that being gay was biological, while 46 percent felt it was a preference—and half of those said that lesbianism as a woman-to-woman culture was a chosen way of life.

A 1994 study of American sexual practices sought to answer the politicized question, How common is homosexuality? Since the 1948 Kinsey report, conventional wisdom has been that one in ten American men was homosexual, and, less well known, that 12 percent of the women in Alfred Kinsey's sample had had lesbian contacts leading to orgasm, and 28 percent of American women had "homosexual tendencies," defined as homoerotic interests in other women at some point in their adult lives. The Kinsey reports, and subsequent *Playboy,* Hite, and *Redbook* magazine surveys, were statistically suspect because they relied on volunteers, that is, people who are interested in sex. When the National Opinion Research Center at the University of Chicago gathered data from 3,432 randomly selected men and women, it found that 2.8 percent of the men identified themselves as homosexual or bisexual while only 1.4 percent of the women did so. When the question was asked differently however, 9 percent of the men and 5 percent of the women reported having had at least one homosexual experience since puberty. Asked if having sex with someone of the same sex seemed appealing, 5.5 percent of the women versus 6 percent of the men said the idea was somewhat or very appealing.

The researchers guessed the overall gay population was smaller than generally accepted by gay advocates because homosexuals tended to migrate to larger cities where tolerance was higher. In the country's dozen largest cities, 10.2 percent of the men and 2.1 percent of the women reported having had a sexual partner of their own sex in the last year, whereas the figures for rural areas were 1 percent and 0.6, respectively. Forty percent of the men who had had a same-sex experience sometime in their life did so before they were eighteen, and not since. Echoing both the Hite and Loulan surveys, most women said they were eighteen or older when they had had their first same-sex experience.

The world of music was the last in the arts to fling open the closet doors, but here, too, the difference between the boys and the girls proved remarkable. While gay composers, from Aaron Copland and Cole Porter to John Corigliano and Ned Rorem were acknowledged as such, lesbian composers stayed invisible because, wrote K. Robert Schwartz, they "don't want to exacerbate the sex-based discrimination they already feel."

The movies' special suggestivity resides in our identifying with the screen characters' emotions. We, the audience, must both project ourselves and identify with the characters we watch. Any break of what Gilbert Cohen-Séat has called the projection-identification, such as actors suddenly talking directly to the camera, has the effect of a power failure. The magic is destroyed. Rock Hudson was smart enough to know his career would be finished the day the whole wide world knew he was faking it when he kissed Doris Day. Gay activists hate this and blame "the power structures" for keeping homosexuals invisible.

Lizabeth Scott's husky voice helped her get dubbing and voice-over work in television. She got back on the screen in *Pulp* in 1972, playing an aging movie star opposite Michael Caine and Mickey Rooney. Lesbian and gay actors live a life of denied attachments, emotions, and infatuations. To the chagrin of many gay activists, closeted lesbians and gay men at the very top of the entertainment industry perpetuate the sexual closet.

"The closeted individuals go to great lengths to keep their closet doors tight shut, hiring lawyers to protect them and squelching any stories about their gay lives," wrote Michelangelo Signorile in *Queer in America*. "Often they marry and have children so as to appear straight and protect their secret. Some hire publicists to actively promote them as heterosexuals. If their homosexuality is inquired about, they deny it outright or offer vague, sometimes ridiculous answers. They also enlist the protection of their straight bosses and friends."

But then again, acting is a matter of becoming someone else. And who are more apt at living invented lives than gays?

Today, cross-dressing by men is considered sick by some, harmless by most people. *The Crying Game, Mrs. Doubtfire,* and *The Adventures of Priscilla, Queen of the Desert* are recent examples of pop-culture acceptability, and, in current psychobabble, of men being allowed to explore their softer sides and new cultural freedoms. Female cross-dressing is different. Although fashion designers have feminized the masculine wardrobe since Coco Chanel put women in jackets in the early 1920s, women in drag are often seen not so much as a challenge to male fashion as to male power. Wrote Kathi Maio in reviewing the feminist western *The Ballad of Little Jo,* "There is no better antihero than a hero who is actually a heroine."

To become a star means to enter a Faustian pact with society. In return for fame, an actor's invented existence becomes public domain. A star's life becomes a kind of work of art, a sculptured artifice, and only that. Stars like to think the mark of actors is to be able to make fools of themselves, to be prepared to examine the self in public, to make mistakes and confess things. For gay actors, however, celebrity demands that they hide part of themselves—not so much from the people they work with as from their admirers.

"I know a fifty-year-old actress who has been out doing benefits, saying, 'I'm proud to be a dyke in public,'" says Ian McKellen. "Now she's gone to Hollywood and is trying to have a career there and she's being told suddenly to be straight." McKellen hasn't stopped playing straight characters in the movies since he came out in 1988, but he's not playing romantic parts. "Will you believe a gay actor playing Romeo, who in his private life fancies Mercutio and not Juliet?" he asked in 1994.

The entertainment industry has never been willing to project what lesbians consider realistic images of their lives. Realities that might puncture the dream machine are still dismissed.

A handful of producers, directors, and agents are out of the closet in today's Hollywood, but little has changed when it comes to putting gay subjects on the screen. Lesbian producers Lauren Lloyd and Leslie Belzberg say that to be successful, a lesbian-themed film must be provocative to mainstream audiences, and, as in Garbo's time, it must star a woman men want to see. "Here's the big issue for me: How do you make a movie where people realize that gay men and lesbians have real lives, too?" Belzberg said in 1994. And writer Fran Lebowitz mused, "If you removed all gay influence from Hollywood, all you'd have left is *Lets Make a Deal.*"

Few modern lesbian moviegoers find anything to identify with in mainstream movies. By default, they are attracted to 1930s and 1940s movies portraying independent and sensitive females who define themselves on their own terms. Garbo's acting in *Queen Christina,* and the stance and presence of Dietrich's incarnations, are as stimulating as late 1940s hard-as-nails swindlers, gun molls, dupes, and sentimental masochists. These films hold greater appeal to gay women than more explicit lesbian characters, such as Beryl Redi in Robert Aldrich's *The Killing of Sister George;* Cher in *Silkwood* falling in love with a woman she can never have; Mariel Hemingway and Patrice Donnelly in *Personal Best,* which presented the same-sex love between two women training for the Olympics as a rite of passage; Julie Andrews in *Victor/Victoria;* Whoopi Goldberg and Margaret Avery's sanitized relationship in Steven Spielberg's *The Color Purple;* or Tilda Swinton's androgyny in the film of Virginia Woolf's 1928 novel, *Orlando.*

Nora Ephron voiced the mainstream misgivings after she wrote *Silkwood:* "Karen was very sexual and pretty much up for grabs. She certainly had a couple of experiences with women. The question was, Did we want to do that film? The real question is, If the politically correct Karen Silkwood had actually been a lesbian, would we have done that on film? I don't know. If she weren't only a slightly unbalanced woman who'd given up her children, but a slightly unbalanced lesbian mother who'd given up her children, who knows how the audience might have reacted?" *Philadelphia* was, despite mixed reviews, a breakthrough, grossing $75 million and proving that an audience will turn out if story and stars are appealing.

Sigourney Weaver could play a happy New Age lesbian, and *Star Trek: The Next Generation's* Patrick Stewart a flamboyant interior designer in gay-themed *Jeffrey* in 1995, but no post-*Philadelphia* boom in gay and lesbian filmmaking was under way. When *Out* magazine devoted its November 1994 issue to Hollywood, it found a quiet revolution in attitudes toward gay and lesbian projects and employees was taking place. Openly lesbian producers with access to studio heads admitted, however, it was an exercise in futility to push projects that, in theme and characters, were not appealing to the community at large. Still, at the height of their notoriety in 2000, Anne Heche and Ellen DeGeneres had the clout to push through "If These Walls Could Talk 2," a three-part drama about lesbians for HBO. The first story, set in the 1950s, had Vanessa Redgrave play a retired teacher who loses the house she had lived in with her longtime companion. The second story, with Chloë Sevigny and Michelle Williams, centered on conflicts between lesbians and feminists in 1970s academia. The third starred DeGeneres and Sharon Stone as a lesbian couple planning to have a baby. Mainstream television came up with *Will & Grace*. To lesbian rock singer Melissa Etheridge, *Will & Grace* was a "big leap" forward from DeGeneres's canceled *Ellen* sitcom.

On the big screen, lesbianism remains an art house "special attraction." Released by Fine Line Features and Lions Gate Films, Jamie Babbit's satire *But I'm a Cheerleader* was an almost "crossover" (to main audiences) in 2000. In this spoof, parents who fear their teenagers are straying toward homosexuality send their kids to a camp called True Directions designed to curb alternate lifestyles. The parents of Megan (Natasha Lyonne) were convinced their cheerleading daughter's faint enthusiasm for her boyfriend is a disturbing sign and ship her off to be deprogrammed. Megan doesn't believe she's a lesbian—or at least she didn't think so before she met her new friend Graham (Clea DuVall), who seems quite sure she likes girls. Noted female impersonator RuPaul appears as a camp guide and Julie Delpy has a cameo as a lipstick lesbian.[1]

The plot is nothing new, but then again 21ˢᵗ century Hollywood is having a hard time inventing new narratives. Eighty years ago when Vita Sackville-West fell in love with Violet Trefusis, there was a trembling blush in writing down her emotions that today's straightforward candor cannot echo. Sackville-West, on whom Virginia Woolf based her title character in *Orlando,* wanted to be sure that if her husband, Harold Nicolson, read her account of her first night with Violet he would understand that she was a different person in that bed. If she wrote honestly of the night, it was:

---

1 *www.qcinema.com.ifilms* lists 58 lesbian films of various nationalities and vintages.

Because I know of no truthful record of such a connection—one that is written, I mean, with no desire to appeal to the vicious taste in any possible readers; and because I hold the conviction that as the centuries go on, and the sexes become more nearly merged on account of the increasing resemblances, I hold the conviction that such connections will to a very large extent cease to be regarded as merely unnatural, and will be understood far better, at least in their intellectual if not their physical aspect. I believe that then the psychology of people like myself will be a matter of interest, and I believe it will be recognized that many more people of my type do exist than under the present-day system of hypocrisy is commonly admitted.

The subject of this book is not so much a case study of lesbians in the movies as the story of how we, society at a certain time, saw them. Have we come a long way? The optimist will say progress is constant. And indeed, when Jane Austin published *Sense and Sensibility* the title page described its author as A Lady because it was unbecoming for women to write novels ("I have an aversion, a pity and a contempt for all female scribblers," a contemporary said. "The needle, not the pen, is the instrument they should handle").

Lesbianism is another way of life, as a vessel for strength, beauty, and new ways of seeing things, wrote Shere Hite in *Women and Love.* "Most women remark on how they feel emotionally closer to other women and how they wish they could talk to the men they love in the same way they can talk to their best friends. Women also "feel that they are basically 'heterosexual'—i.e., they do not feel 'attracted' to women physically, sexually, but see them as basically psychologically accessible, or possible soul mates."

Movie stars who love other women do so at their risk and peril. Pessimists wonder if we have learned anything since each generation, it seems, repeats the same mistakes. Of course Heche doesn't face the same opprobrium as Garbo would have had she dared tell the world she loved women. But as of this writing there are troubling similarities. Garbo and Dorothy Arzner, say, knew how to shut up. DeGeneres and Heche announced to the world they were a couple and suffered consequences—prejudice, ostracism, and, in the end, indifference—that we can easily imagine would have befallen the sewing circle members had any of them dared do the same. Among movie and television stars, making a circle of lesbians friends is as risky today as when Garbo and Mercedes fell in love. The sewing circle gave its members a sense of community and support, if not of family that, seen in retrospect, was lasting, far-reaching, and effective. The lives of Hollywood's lesbians and bi-sexual women were diverse, intense, sometimes contradictory, sometimes moving. Learning their story should not only shape our view of the cinema's all-too-brief golden age, but also help fashion our evolving awareness and attitudes toward issues of mores and comportment yet to come.

Moreover, we might come to see Garbo, Dietrich, Bankhead, Stanwyck, Cornell, Fontanne, Moorhead, and Cukor, Gibbons, Minnelli and Arzner and Head and others as people who, with their presence and gifts, illuminated the youthful silver screen. Their contemporaries treated them appallingly, but that is no reason why we should see them as yet another set of victims on the all-too-long casualty list of intolerance. The greatest compliment we can offer their memory is to see them as people of talent who gave the best of themselves.

Notes on Sources

In researching *The Sewing Circle,* I believe I talked to every major living figure who knew sapphic Hollywood. The entertainment-industry fishbowl forced homosexuals to be imaginative, to resort to sumptuous surfaces, campy disguises, and witty conspiracies. A short-lived lesbian paper, *Vice-Versa,* was published in the 1940s.

Actors talk a lot even if they don't generally leave much in the way of a paper trail—Garbo's letter-writing might most charitably be called minimalist. Sources that I nurtured for this book are survivors of the 1930s and 1940s Hollywood. They include Samson De Brier, legendary lover of André Gide; gossip and background provocateur of Kenneth Anger's two *Hollywood Babylon* books, Ruth Morgenroth, who as Ruth Albu danced with Dietrich before *The Blue Angel;* and Dorr Legg, the founder of One Magazine, the first widely distributed gap publication and forebear of the modern gay press; Forman Brown, founder of the Turnabout Theater; Harry Hay, the founder of the Mattachine Society, who remembers going to a gay soiree at de Acosta's in 1935; James Kepner, curator of the as yet only partially cataloged National Gay Archives in West Hollywood; Joseph J. Cohn, former MGM executive; Talli Wyler, the widow of director William Wyler; actress-dancer Iris Adrian;

1930s Warners publicist Maggy Maskel Ferguson; and Margaret Sherry, the Princeton University reference librarian and archivist.

De Acosta sold the majority of her papers to the Rosenbach Museum in Philadelphia, with the stipulation that Garbo's letters to her be sealed until ten years after Garbo's death, i.e., 2000.

Over a period of nearly three decades, I interviewed Harry Brand, George Cukor, Shirley Eder, Dana Henninger, Rouben Mamoulian, Nolan Miller, Ruth Morgenroth, Anaïs Nin, Milla Recsei, Otto Reischow, David Shipman, Adela Rogers St. Johns, Barbara Stanwyck, Josef von Sternberg, Gloria Swanson, Stuart Thomas, Viege Traub, Gertrude Walker, Billy Wilder, William Wyler, and Paul Zimmerman. Librarian Elizabeth Fuller of the Rosenbach Museum in Philadelphia provided access to the unpublished versions of Mercedes de Acosta's autobiography.

Source citations are given in the bibliography. Documentation supporting certain portions of the narrative is cited below.

Author to Reader

How lavender may have become associated with lesbianism: Diana Fredricks, *A Strange Autobiography* (1933).

Goldman's sexual inclinations: Candice Falk, *Love, Anarchy, and Emma Goldman*, pp. 174-75.

British *Vogue* reviewed Hugo Vickers, *Loving Garbo*, May 1994.

Edmund Goulding, "The thing she balks at": Ezra Goodman, *The Fifty-Year Decline and Fall of Hollywood*, p. 293.

1. The Odd Couple: Mercedes and Thalberg

Mercedes de Acosta's meeting Thalberg on *Desperate:* de Acosta, *Here Lies the Heart*, pp. 231–32.

Irving Thalberg, "Do you want to put all America": de Acosta, *Here Lies the Heart*, p. 233.

Thalberg, "She must never create situations": Bob Thomas, *Thalberg*, p. 308.

Joel McCrea told of Garbo's notorious "I'll go home" response to screenplays she didn't like: John Kobal, *People Will Talk*, p. 403.

Joan Crawford, "She doesn't love him": Roland Flamini, *Thalberg*, p. 103.

Thalberg's office: *Fortune*, December 1932.

Joseph Mankiewicz, "George [Cukor] was really queen": Patrick McGilligan, *George Cukor*, p. 72.

Isadora Duncan's poem to de Acosta: Hugo Vickers, *Loving Garbo,* pp. 13–14.

2. Tangled Lives: Women Who Loved Women

Greta Garbo obituary: *New York Times,* April 16, 1900.

Photoplay, "Where others scrabble": January 1930 issue.

Joseph Cohn, "We tried a lot": to author, 1993.

Clarence Brown, "If she had to look at one person": Kevin Brownlow, *The Parade's Gone By,* p. 146.

Constance Lawrence, "Poor Richard": Richard Stoddard Aldrich, *Gertrude Lawrence as Mrs. A.,* p. 4.

Details of Howard Strickling's career: *Los Angeles Herald-Examiner* and *Variety* obituaries, July 16, 1982.

David Selznick, "I don't want press agentry": to author, 1964.

Harry Brand, "You put them under contract": to author, 1970.

The impact of actors' lives on standards of morality and shotgun weddings: Anita Loos, *Fate Keeps on Happening,* p. 155.

Laszlo Willinger, "He ran MGM": John Kobal, *People Will Talk,* p. 378.

Howard Strickling, "We told stars": Strickling to author, 1970.

Nöel Coward on Nelson Eddy marriage; Boze Hadleigh, *Hollywood Babble On,* p. 164.

Elsa Lanchester, "There was no element": *Herself,* 1972.

Janet Gaynor, "It has become more or less a habit": *Denver Post,* March 29, 1936.

Harry Hay, "We're always in costume": to author, 1933.

De Acosta on John Barrymore's androgyny: Margot Peters, *The House of Barrymores,* p. 132.

3. In Love: Garbo and Mercedes

Salka Viertel on Garbo's observations: Viertel, *The Kindness of Strangers,* p. 143.

F. W. Murnau's homosexuality and death: Kenneth Anger, *Hollywood Babylon,* p. 246.

De Acosta, "To have Garbo" and "She was dressed": de Acosta, *Here Lies the Heart,* pp. 213–14.

Anita Loos on Garbo's beauty creating "a disadvantage": Loos, *Fate Keeps on Happening,* p. 198.

Leonore Coffee, "She makes them all look": Coffee, *Storyline,* p. 129.

Antoni Gronowicz on Garbo-de Acosta first night together: Gronowicz, *Garbo,* pp. 311–17.

4. *"In America, Men Don't Like Fat Women"*

Garbo's childhood: Antoni Gronowicz, *Garbo,* and Raymond Baum, *Walking With Garbo.*

Garbo, "If I were to analyze": Gronowicz, *Garbo,* p. 63.

Stiller's homosexual and chaotic private life: Bengt Forslund, *Victor Sjöström.*

Stiller career evaluation: Georges Sadoul, *Histoire du Cinéma mondial,* and Jean Tulard, ed., *Dictionnaire du Cinéma.*

Cecil Beaton, "An intimated inner": Beaton, unpublished diary, winter 1948–49.

5. *Lover to the Stars*

Mercedes de Acosta's shock at discovering she was a girl: de Acosta, first manuscript, *Here Lies the Heart,* pp. 29–30.

De Acosta, "My mother and father": *Here Lies the Heart,* p. 1

De Acosta, "Every child": *Here Lies the Heart,* p. 17.

De Acosta, "Rita was my first": *Here Lies the Heart,* p. 5.

De Acosta, "I knew this gesture": first manuscript, p. 46.

De Acosta, "It has made me understand": first manuscript, pp. 33–34.

Descriptions of Maude Adams and Katharine Cornell based on obituaries: Adams, *Hollywood Citizen-News,* July 17, 1953; Cornell, *London Times,* June 11, 1974.

Brooke Atkinson, "Only a few people": Atkinson, *Broadway,* p. 27.

Elisabeth Marbury and Elsie de Wolfe biographies: *Notable American Women,* pp. 494–95 and pp. 469–79, respectively.

De Acosta, "Bessie used to refer": *Here Lies the Heart,* p. 71.

De Acosta, "She had thick black hair": de Acosta, *Here Lies the Heart,* p. 74.

Robert A. Shanke, "They began their arranged lunch": Schanke, *Shattered Applause,* p. 54.

Dorothy Fellowes-Gordon on de Acosta and Le Gallienne in love: Hugo Vickers, *Loving Garbo,* p. 18.

Colette's description of Mata Hari: Stephen Longstreet, *We All Went to Paris,* p. 332.

Sam Lyons, "You gotta get a fella": Schanke, *Shattered Applause,* p. 60.

Nöel Coward on traveling with Fellowes-Gordon and Elsa Maxwell: Coward, *The Nöel Coward Diaries,* p. 174.

Cecil Beaton diary notes on gossiping with de Acosta in Palm Beach: Beaton, unpublished diary, January 6, 1930.

6. The Perfect Sapphic Liaison

De Acosta, "One feels in her": *Desperate* script, p. 16.

De Acosta, "To know Greta": de Acosta, *Here Lies the Heart*, p. 319.

Thalberg and MGM beating RKO to Mata Hari story: Pola Negri, *Memoirs of a Star*, p. 355.

Mix-up of de Acosta and Viertel meeting Garbo's train: *Hollywood Reporter*, January 2, 1932.

De Acosta on Eleonora von Mendelssohn's "violent fixation": de Acosta, *Here Lies the Heart*, p. 268.

7. Enter Joan Crawford and Katharine Cornell

Cecil Beaton detailed his meeting Garbo at the Gouldings in *The Wandering Years* and quoted her in his March 1932 diary.

Joan Crawford on meeting Garbo on stairs, and Garbo's "What a pity": Bob Thomas, *Joan Crawford*, p. 84.

Crawford, "If there was ever a time": Thomas, *Joan Crawford*, p. 84.

Christina Crawford, "I knew about my mother's lesbian proclivities": Christina Crawford, *Mommie Dearest*, p. 157.

Louise Brooks on Crawford: David Shipman, *Judy Garland*, p. 180.

De Acosta on Garbo loss in bank failure, and "If MGM knew the position": de Acosta, *Here Lies the Heart*, pp. 228–29.

Ernst Lubitsch, "Mein Gott, mein Gott": Herman G. Weinberg, *The Lubitsch Touch*, p. 139.

Ona Munson, "I long to hold you": Hugo Vickers, *Loving Garbo*, p. 76.

Anita Loos's September 29, 1932, letter to Cecil Beaton: Vickers, *Loving Garbo*, p. 4.

Garbo and de Acosta in New York and quotes of their quarrel: Antoni Gronowicz, *Garbo*, pp. 317–21.

8. Dietrich on the Rebound

De Acosta described her meeting Dietrich in *Here Lies the Heart*, quoting Dietrich on the white roses in the second draft, p. 389.

Dietrich, "Thalberg had one": letter to Sieber: Maria Riva, *Marlene Dietrich by Her Daughter*, p. 265.

Dietrich, "Unconventional as it may seem": de Acosta, *Here Lies the Heart*, p. 242.

Ruth Albu, "The way Marlene looked": to author, 1994.

Dietrich's letters to her husband: Riva, *Marlene Dietrich by Her Daughter*, pp. 265–66.

De Acosta's letters to Dietrich: Riva, *Marlene Dietrich by Her Daughter*, p. 154.

Truman Capote, "You could get": Hugo Vickers, *Loving Garbo,* p. 12.

Josef von Sternberg on Dietrich and their films: to author, 1966.

Descriptions Roxbury interior: Richard Lamparski, *Lamparski's Hidden Hollywood,* p. 44, and *Architectural Digest,* April 1990.

Irving Thalberg, "It must be a very violent" and subsequent quotes of de Acosta-Thalberg clash over Rasputin script: de Acosta, *Here Lies the Heart,* p. 245.

Maria Riva, Rouben Mamoulian on Garbo: Dietrich to author, 1967.

Thalberg and Mayer's pro-Hoover and anti-Sinclair electioneering: Bob Thomas, *Thalberg,* p. 268–69.

9. Queen Christina

Mercedes de Acosta, "To try to explain": Maria Riva, *Marlene Dietrich by Her Daughter,* p. 294.

Writers' "buzz sessions": Axel Madsen, *William Wyler,* p. 127.

S. N. Behrman quotes Garbo on Gilbert: Behrman, *People in a Diary,* pp. 149–51.

Thalberg's illness and impact on *Queen Christina:* Bob Thomas, *Thalberg,* p. 271, and Roland Flamini, *Thalberg,* p. 190.

Adela Rogers St. Johns on Gilbert wanting to kill Louis B. Mayer: to author, 1969.

10. The Flaming Twenties

Marlene Dietrich, "Really": Maria Riva, *Marlene Dietrich by Her Daughter,* p. 207.

Marlene Dietrich, "In fact, I used to dress up in boys'": *Screen Book,* November 1934.

Katharine Hepburn's fight with RKO over her trousers: Gary Carey, *Katharine Hepburn,* p. 48.

"Though a person may": Martin S. Weinberg, Colin J. Williams, Douglas W. Pryor, *Dual Attraction,* reviewed in *Mirabella,* February 1994.

Pat Califia, "It used to be taken for granted": Califia, *Sapphistry,* p. 58.

Anita Loos, "The love affairs": Loos, *Fate Keeps on Happening,* p. 97.

Lillian Faderman, "no one would want to be considered" lesbian: Faderman, *Odd Girls and Twilight Lovers,* p. 105.

Djuna Barnes, on lesbianism being "as daring as a Crusade": *Ladies Almanack,* 1928.

Iris Adrian, "The bars were about": Adrian to author, 1993.

New York World on Los Angeles's lack of culture, 1923: Andrew Rolle, *California: A History,* p. 119.

H. L. Mencken, "And no wonder, for they are worked": *Photoplay*, April 1927.

Diane Vreeland on King Alfonso XIII: Vreeland, *D.V.*, p. 40.

Errol Flynn, "Everything about her was arrogant": Flynn, *My Wicked, Wicked Ways*, p. 187.

11. Stanwyck: The Best-Kept Secret

The Barbara Stanwyck story based on author's *Stanwyck.*

Clifton Webb: "my favorite American lesbian": Boze Hadleigh, *Hollywood Babble On*, p. 147.

Joan Crawford, "Their fights were dreadful": Jane Ellen Wayne, *Crawford's Men*, p. 6.

Louis B. Mayer, "We have other young men": Davis Shipman, *Judy Garland*, p. 186.

Taylor to Crawford, "All I had to say": Wayne, *Crawford's Men*, p. 154.

Lillian Faderman reports on honoring Radclyffe Hall with *clyffe* in *Odd Girls and Twilight Lovers*, p. 173.

12. Hollywood and Broadway: Transcontinentals

Bankhead to Tennessee Wiliams on her lesbianism: Sandy Campbell, *Bankhead: Letters From the Coconut Grove*, p. 15.

The anecdote of the Yale student and Bankhead's reply: Cheryl Crawford, *One Naked Individual*, p. 115.

Lillian Faderman details would-be censors of images of lesbians in *Odd Girls and Twilight Lovers*, pp. 102–3.

Alfred Hitchcock, "The whole point": Donald Spoto, *The Dark Side of Genius*, p. 269.

Bankhead's reply to Alfred Kinsey: Denis Brian, *Tallulah, Darling*, p. 13.

Bankhead, "I'll come and make love": Ted Morgan, *Maugham*, p. 281.

Gladys Bentley discussed her life in *Ebony*, August 1952.

Vincent Price, "She had that magnificent beauty": Denis Brian, *Tallulah, Darling*, p. 90.

Anita Loos, "Tallulah never believed": Loos, *Fate Keeps on Happening*, p. 132.

Brooks Atkinson, "After years of obscure": Atkinson, *Broadway*, p. 37.

Gore Vidal on Jane and Paul Bowles: Vidal, *United States*, pp. 432–34.

Beatrice Lillie on audience rapport: *Los Angeles Herald-Examiner*, January 21, 1989.

"Lillie and Lawrence" ditty: Lillie's obituary in *The* (London) *Times*, January 21, 1989.

13. Sodom-on-the-Pacific

Minta Durfee Arbuckle detailed the Taylor murder to author, 1971.

Buster Keaton's defense of Arbuckle: Kevin Brownlow, *The Parade's Gone By,* p. 486.

Allan Dwan, "Everyone did it": Sidney D. Kirkpatrick, *A Cast of Killers,* p. 50.

14. Talking Pictures

The repercussions of the changeover to sound on studios and directors: to author by William Wyler, 1973.

The tolerance of male homosexuals in comical roles: Vito Russo, *The Celluloid Closet,* pp. 35–36.

Greta Garbo, "I will never forget" and "When I was sad": Antonio Gronowicz, *Garbo,* p. 311.

15. Hepburn and the Lady Director

Details of Dorothy Arzner's life and career: Directors Guild of America tribute to Arzner, October 1975.

Marjorie Main on Arzner, "She looked more like a man": Boze Hadleigh, *Hollywood Lesbians,* p. 49.

Dorothy Arzner, "I wanted to be like Jesus": Arzner interview by Gerard Peary and Karyn Kay in *Film World,* October 1977.

Joseph Mankiewicz reminiscences about Zoë Akins: Kenneth L. Geist, *Pictures Will Talk,* pp. 35–36.

Hepburn, "Oh, Miss Garbo": Anne Edwards, *A Remarkable Woman,* p. 99.

Margaret Sullivan, "The dikey bitch": quoted in Boze Hadleigh, *Hollywood Babble On,* p. 154.

Katharine Hepburn dressing as a boy and calling herself Jimmy: Christopher Andersen, *Young Kate,* p. 140.

Laura Harding, "I adored her": Charles Higham, *Kate,* p. 65.

David Selznick, "When she first appeared": Behlmer, *Memo From David O. Selznick,* p. 43.

Adela Rogers St. Johns on Hepburn: to author, 1969.

Speculation on Hepburn repeating her *Bill of Divorcement* impression: *Variety,* March 14,1933.

Michael Freedland interviewed Pandro Berman on Katharine Hepburn's superiority complex in *Katharine Hepburn,* p. 31.

Dorothy Arzner, "Her tone was all wrong": Charles Higham, *Kate,* p. 41.

Pauline Kael, "In movies up to the seventies": in Kael, *5001 Nights at the Movies,* p. 108.

Notes on Sources

Dorothy Arzner, "I knew that it would be": *New York Times*, February 10, 1976.

16. Odd Girls Abroad

Arlen J. Hansen, *Expatriate Paris*, and Dell Richards, *Superstars: Twelve Lesbians Who Changed the World*, delineate Barney's life and reputation.
Barney comment on Gertrude Stein's writing: Longstreet, *We All Went to Paris*, p. 330.
Victoria "Vita" Sackville-West's life: Dell Richards, *Superstars*, pp. 261–85.

17. Camille: The All-Gay Production

Sylvia Scarlett review capsules: *Hollywood Reporter*, January 15, 1936.
George Cukor on finding Garbo too lesbian: Patrick McGilligan, *George Cukor*, p. 108.
Pauline Kael, "No movie has ever presented": Kael, *5001 Nights at the Movies*, p. 90.
Salka Viertel on what makes a Garbo movie: Manuel Levy, *George Cukor*, p. 144.
Cukor, "In those days": Gavin Lambert, *On Cukor*, p. 115.
Cukor arrest: McGilligan, *George Cukor*, p. 133.
Thalberg's death and consequences for MGM and *Camille*: Roland Flamini, *Thalberg*, p. 271, and McGilligan, *George Cukor*, p. 130.
Erich Maria Remarque on Dietrich: Donald Spoto, *Blue Angel*, p. 156.
Donald Spoto, "The arrangement was indeed knotty": Spoto, *Blue Angel*, p. 141.

18. Screen Style

Vogue descriptions of stars: Georgina Howell, *In Vogue*, p. 109.
Yann Tobin on Leisen: Jean-Pierre Coursodon and Pierre Sauvage, *American Directors*, vol. 1, p. 206.
Vito Russo on James Whale and Frankenstein: Russo, *The Celluloid Closet*, pp. 50-51.
Edith Head, "Most of the costume designers": Boze Hadleigh, *Hollywood Lesbians*, p. 133.
Pandro Berman, "Young man, you have": Howard Mandelbaum and Eric Myers, *Forties Screen Style*, p. 26.
Head, "We hit it off immediately" and *"Lady Eve* changed": Edith Head and Paddy Calistro, *Edith Head's Hollywood*, pp. 33, 45.
Paul Rosenfield quotes: Hadleigh, *Hollywood Lesbians*, p. 122.

235

19. *Judy Garland in the Land of Oz*

Tallulah Bankhead—Lady Mendl swimming-pool exchange: George Cukor to author, 1972. Story also reported in Anita Loos, *Kiss Hollywood Goodbye*, pp. 55-56.

David King Dunaway on lesbian bars: Dunaway, *Huxley in Hollywood*, p. 70.

Del Martin and Phyllis Lyon, "There is a fear": Martin and Lyon, *Lesbian/ Woman*, p. 189.

Judy Garland's youth: David Shipman, *Judy Garland*, pp. 138–40.

20. *Fresh Faces*

David Selznick, "I took one look": Gavin Lambert, *GWTW*, p. 51.

Clark Gable, "I can't go on": Patrick McGilligan, *George Cukor*, p. 150.

Ina Claire's memories of Garbo during the *Ninotchka* shoot: Hugo Vickers, *Loving Garbo*, p. 74.

Mercedes de Acosta's return to Los Angeles: de Acosta, *Here Lies the Heart*, pp. 300-304.

Judith Anderson, "Many people already do": Boze Hadleigh, *Hollywood Lesbians*, p. 176.

Judith Anderson, "Now that I have begun": Anderson obituary, *The* (London) *Times*, January 6, 1992.

De Acosta, "We used to go for walks": de Acosta, *Here Lies the Heart*, p. 304.

David King Dunaway, "In the afternoons": Dunaway, *Huxley in Hollywood*, p. 70.

Anita Loos, "Aldous played his trump card": Loos, *Fate Keeps on Happening*, p. 169.

Bertolt Brecht's Hollywood beginnings: Marta Feuchtwanger to author, 1973.

21. *The Sisterhood and the War*

History of females in the U.S. armed forces during World War II: Martin Binkin and Shirley T. Bach, *Women and the Military*.

The July 9, 1947, issue of *Newsweek* noted changes in military policy toward homosexuals.

Lives of Dorothy Binney Putnam and Lois Mercer: Door Legg to author, 1994.

Sgt. Johnnie Phelps, "Yessir. If the general pleases": Lillian Faderman, *Odd Girls and Twilight Lovers*, p. 118.

Paul Lynde, "The whole world knows": Boze Hadleigh, *Hollywood Babble On*, p. 154.

Agnes Moorehead, "There's the actress": Boze Hadleigh, *Hollywood Lesbians*, p. 188.

Mercedes de Acosta, "She has what I consider": de Acosta, *Here Lies the Heart*, p. 318.

Hepburn on *Mourning Becomes Electra:* Anne Edwards, *A Remarkable Woman*, p. 235.

Patsy Kelly, "Yeah . . . Cole Porter": Boze Hadleigh, *Hollywood Lesbians*, p. 62.

Donald Spoto, "According to him, Dietrich": Spoto, *Blue Angel*, p. 205.

Garbo's contribution to Allied World War II intelligence: William Stevenson, *A Man Called Intrepid*, mentioned in *New York Times* Garbo obituary, April 16, 1990.

22. The Dark Age

Lizabeth Scott's career: *Hollywood Studio*, July 1973.

The Strange Love of Martha Ivers: New York Times, July 25, 1946.

Scott v. Confidential libel suit: *Variety*, July 26, 1955, and court hearing, *Los Angeles Times*, March 8, 1956.

Senator Wherry, "You can hardly separate": *New York Post*, July 11, 1950.

The hunt for homosexuals in government and Hollywood: Michelangelo Signorile, *Queer in America*, and Larry Ceplar and Steven Englund, *The Inquisition in Hollywood*.

Circle of Loving Companions and *The Ladder:* Stuart Timmons, *The Trouble With Harry Hay*, p. 214.

Anna Freud's life as a closet lesbian: Dell Richards, *Superstars*, pp. 243–60.

Capucine, "And being such a big star": Hadleigh, *Hollywood Lesbians*, p. 236.

23. Seeking to Belong

De Acosta-Cecil Beaton correspondence on Garbo: Hugo Vickers, *Loving Garbo*, pp. 209–10.

De Acosta known as "the dyke at the top of the stairs": Cynthia Lindsay to author, 1994.

De Acosta, "Fearlessly, I invited": quoted in *New York Times* review of *Here Lies the Heart*, May 29, 1960.

Janet Flanner, "Fräulein Dietrich": Flanner, *Paris Was Yesterday*, p. 97.

Denis Brian on Tallulah Bankhead: Brian, *Tallulah, Darling*, p. 274.

Paul Lynde on Agnes Moorehead: Boze Hadleigh, *Lesbian Hollywood*, p. 179.

Joan Crawford, "All my friends": Shaun Considine, *Bette & Joan*, p. 402.

Vito Russo, "The 'killing' in the film": Russo, *The Celluloid Closet*, p. 173.

24. Fifty Years Later: Today's Showbiz Lesbians

New York lesbian-chic cover, May 10, 1993.

Newsweek lesbian cover story, June 21, 1993.

The Yankelovich Partners survey of gay consumers: *New York Times,* June 9, 1994.

Village Voice reported OutPost outing Jodie Foster, June 16, 1991.

Mirabella on Foster, June 1994.

Kevin Koffler, "Four years ago": *Los Angeles Times,* October 1, 1994.

"For those of us": Del Martin and Phyllis Lyon, *Lesbian/Woman,* p. 275.

Love relationships between women: Shere Hite, *Women and Love,* part 4, "Women Loving Women," pp. 411–645.

JoAnn Loulan, "Now for the good part" and "Do lesbians perceive" and statistics: Loulan, *Lesbian Passion: Loving Ourselves and Each Other,* p. 192-211.

The University of Chicago study "Sex in America": *New York Times,* October 7, 1994.

K. Robert Schwartz on homosexual and lesbian composers, *New York Times,* June 19, 1994.

Michelangelo Signorile, "The closeted individuals": Signorile, *Queer in America,* p. xv.

Kathi Maio, "There is no better antihero": *Sojourner* magazine, October 1993.

Ian McKellen on coming out as an actor: *Los Angeles Times,* June 26, 1994.

Nora Ephron, "Karen was very sexual": Vito Russo, *The Celluloid Closet,* p. 275.

Vita Sackville-West diary entry for September 27, 1920: Nigel Nicolson, *Portrait of a Marriage,* p. 114.

Bibliography

ACKER, ALLY. *Real Women: Pioneers of the Cinema*. New York: Continuum. 1991.

ACOSTA, MERCEDES DE. *Here Lies the Heart*. New York: Reynal, 1960.

ALDRICH, RICHARD STODDARD. *Gertrude Lawrence as Mrs. A*. New York: Greystone Press, 1954.

ANDERSEN, CHRISTOPHER. *Young Kate: The Remarkable Hepburns and the Childhood That Shaped an American Legend*. New York: Henry Holt, 1988.

ANGER, KENNETH. *Hollywood Babylon*. New York: Dell, 1975.

————. *Hollywood Babylon II*. New York: New American Library, 1985.

ARCE, HECTOR. *The Secret Life of Tyronne Power*. New York: Morrow, 1979.

ATKINSON, BROOKS. *Broadway*. New York: Macmillan, 1970.

BAINBRIDGE, JOHN. *Garbo*. New York: Holt, Rinehart & Winston, 1955.

BAXTER, JOHN. *Hollywood in the Thirties*. New York: Paperback Library, 1970.

BEATON, CECIL. *Cecil Beaton's Diaries: The Wandering Years (1922–1939)*. Boston: Little, Brown, 1961.

BEHLMER, RUDY, ED. *Memo From David O. Selznick*. New York: Viking Press, 1972.

BERUBE, ALLAN, AND JOHN D'EMILIO. *Coming Out Under Fire: The History of Gay Men and Women in World War II*. Chicago: University of Chicago Press, 1985.

BINKIN, MARTIN, AND SHIRLEY T. BACH. *Women and the Military*. Washington, D.C: Brookings Institute, 1977.

BLAIR, FREDERIKA. *Isadora*. Wellingborough, Northamptonshire: Equation, 1987.

BOSWORTH, PATRICIA. *Montgomery Clift: A Biography*. New York: Harcourt Brace Jonavich, 1978.

BRADSHAW, JON. *Dreams That Money Can Buy: The Tragic Life of Libby Holman*. New York: William Morrow, 1985.

BRIAN, DENIS. *Tallulah, Darling*. New York: Macmillan, 1972.

BROWNFLOW, KEVIN. *The Parade's Gone By*. New York: Alfred A. Knopf, 1968.

BURKHART, CHARLES. *I. Compion-Burnett*. London: Victor Gollancz, 1965.

CALIFIA, PAT. *Sapphistry: The Book of Lesbian Sexuality.* Tallahassee, Fla.: Naiad Press, 1988.

CAMPBELL, SANDY. *B: Letters From the Coconut Grove.* Verona: private printing, 1974.

CAREY, GARY. *Katharine Hepburn: A Hollywood Yankee.* New York: St. Martin's Press, 1983.

CEPLAR, LARRY, AND STEVEN ENGLUND. *The Inquisition in Hollywood.* Garden City, N.Y.: Anchor Press/Doubleday, 1980.

COFFEE, LEONORE. *Storyline.* London: Cassell, 1973.

CONSIDINE, SHAUN. *Bette & Joan: The Divine Feud.* New York: E. P. Dutton, 1989.

CORNELL, KATHARINE. *I Wanted to Be an Actress.* New York: Random House, 1938.

COURSODON, JEAN PIERRE, WITH PIERRE SAUVAGE. *American Director.* New York: McGraw-Hill, 1983.

CRAWFORD, CHERYL. *One Naked Individual.* Indianapolis: Bobbs-Merrill, 1977.

CRAWFORD, CHRISTINA. *Mommie Dearest.* New York: William Morrow, 1978.

DAUM, RAYMOND (EDITED BY VANCE MUSE). *Walking With Garbo: Conversations and Recollections.* New York: HarperCollins, 1991.

DAVIS, KATHARINE BEMENT. *Factors in the Sex Life of Twenty-two Hundred Women.* New York: Harper and Row, 1929.

DUNAWAY, DAVID KING. *Huxley in Hollywood.* New York: Harper & Row, 1989.

EDWARDS, ANNE. *A Remarkable Woman: A Biography of Katharine Hepburn.* New York: William Morrow, 1985.

EISLER, BENITA. *Class Act: America's Last Dirty Secret.* New York: Franklin Watts, 1977.

FADERMAN, LILLIAN. *Odd Girls and Twilight Lovers: A History of Lesbian Life in Twentieth Century America.* New York: Columbia University Press, 1991.

FAIRBANKS, DOUGLAS, JR. *A Hell of a War.* New York: St. Martins Press, 1993.

————. *Salad Days: An Autobiography.* New York: Doubleday, 1988.

FLAMINI, ROLAND. *Thalberg: The Last Tycoon With the World of MGM.* New York: Crown, 1994.

FLANNER, JANET. *Darlinghissima: Letters to a Friend.* New York: Random House, 1985.

————. *Paris Was Yesterday: 1925-1939.* New York: Popular Library, 1972.

FLYNN, ERROL. *My Wicked, Wicked Ways.* New York: G. P. Putnam's Sons, 1959.

FORSLUND, BENGT. *Victor Sjöström.* New York: Zoetrope, 1988.

FOWLER, GENE., *Good Night, Sweet Prince.* New York: Viking Press, 1944.

FREEDLAND, MICHAEL. *Katherine Hepburn.* London: W. H. Allen, 1984.

GARDNER, GORDON. *The Censorship Papers: Movie Censorship Letters From the Hays Office, 1934-1968.* New York: Dodd, Mead, 1987.

GEIST, KENNETH L. *Pictures Will Talk: The Life and Films of Joseph L. Mankiewicz.* New York: Charles Scribner's Sons, 1978.

GOLDMAN, EMMA. *Living My Life.* Published 1931; Reprint edition, New York: New American Library, 1977.

GOODMAN, EZRA. *The Fifty-Year Decline and Fall of Hollywood.* New York: Simon and Schuster, 1961.

GORDON, SUZANNE. *Prisoners of Men's Dreams.* Boston: Little, Brown, 1991.

GRONOWICZ, ANTONI. *Garbo, Her Story.* New York: Simon and Schuster, 1990.

GULLES, FRED LAWRENCE. *Marion Davies.* New York: McGraw-Hill, 1972.

HADLEIGH, BOZE. *Conversations With My Elders.* New York: St. Martin's Press, 1986.

————. *Hollywood Babble On.* New York: Birch Lane Press, 1994.

————. *Hollywood Lesbians.* New York: Barricade Books, 1994.

————. *The Lavender Screen: The Gay and Lesbian Films; Their Stars, Makers, Characters and Critics.* New York: Citadel Press, 1993.

HANSEN, ARLEN J. *Expatriate Paris: A Cultural and Literary Guide to Paris of the 1920s.* New York: Arcade Publishing, 1990.

HEAD, EDITH, AND PADDY CALISTRO. *Edith Head's Hollywood.* New York: E. P. Dutton, 1983.

HIGHAM, CHARLES. *Errol Flynn: The Untold Story.* Garden City, N.Y.: Doubleday, 1980.

————. *Kate: The Life of Katharine Hepburn.* New York: W. W. Norton, 1975.

————. *Merchant of Dreams: Louis B. Mayer.* New York: Donald I. Fine, 1993.

HITE, SHERE. *Women and Love: A Cultural Revolution in Progress.* New York: Alfred A. Knopf, 1987.

HOWELL, GEORGINA. *In Vogue.* New York: Schocken, 1976.

HUSTON, JOHN. *An Open Book.* New York: Alfred A. Knopf, 1980.

ISRAEL, LEE. *Miss Tallulah Bankhead.* New York: G. P. Putnam, 1972.

KAEL, PAULINE. *5001 Nights at the Movies.* New York: Holt, Rinehart & Winston, 1985.

KATZ, EPHRAIM. *The Film Encyclopedia.* New York: HarperCollins, 1994.

KENDALL, ELIZABETH. *The Runaway Bride: Hollywood Romantic Comedy of the 1930s.* New York: Anchor Books/Doubleday, 1990.

KIRKPATRICK, SIDNEY D. *A Cast of Killers.* New York: E. P. Dutton, 1986.

KOBAL, JOHN. *People Will Talk.* New York: Alfred A. Knopf, 1985.

KOHLER, JOHN. *Damned in Paradise: The Life of John Barrymore.* New York: Atheneum, 1977.

KUHN, RICHARD. *Greta Garbo.* Dresden: Carl Reissner, 1935.

KURTH, PETER. *American Cassandra: The Life of Dorothy Thompson.* Boston: Little, Brown, 1990.

LAFFEY, BRUCE. *Beatrice Lillie: The Funniest Woman in the World.* New York: Wynwood Press, 1989.

LAMBERT, GAVIN. *GWTW: The Making of Gone With the Wind.* Boston: Little, Brown, 1974.

————. *On Cukor.* New York: G. P. Putman, 1972.

LAMPARSKI, RICHARD. *Lamparski's Hidden Hollywood.* New York: Simon and Schuster, 1981.

LEVY, MANUEL. *George Cukor: Master of Elegance.* New York: William Morrow, 1994.

LEWTON, LUCY OLGA. *Alla Nazimova: My Aunt.* Ventura, Calif.: Minuteman Press, 1988.

LONGSTREET, STEPHEN. *We All Went to Paris: Americans in the City of Light, 1776-1971.* New York: Macmillan, 1972.

LOOS, ANITA. *Fate Keeps on Happening.* London: Harrap, 1985.

————. *Kiss Hollywood Goodbye.* New York: Viking, 1974.

LOULAN, JOANN. *Lesbian Passion.* San Francisco: Spinster Books, 1987.

LOVELL, Mary S. *The Sound of Wings: The Life of Amelia Earhart.* New York: St. Martin's Press, 1989.

MADSEN, AXEL. *Gloria and Joe: The Star-Crossed Love Affair of Gloria Swanson and Joe Kennedy.* New York: William Morrow, 1988.

————. *Stanwyck.* New York: HarperCollins, 1994.

MANDELBAUM, HOWARD, AND ERIC MYERS. *Forties Screen Style.* New York: St. Martin's Press, 1989.

MARTIN, DEL, AND PHYLLIS LYON. *Lesbian/Woman.* San Francisco: Glide Publications, 1972.

MAYER, MICHAEL. *Strindberg: A Biography.* New York: Random House, 1985.

MAYNE, JUDITH. *Women at the Keyhold: Femininity and Women's Cinema.* Bloomington: Indiana University Press, 1990.

McGILLIGAN, PATRICK. *George Cukor: A Double Life.* New York: St. Martin's Press, 1991.

MILNE, TOM. *Mamoulian.* London: Thames & Hudson, 1969.

MORGAN, TED. *Maugham.* New York: Simon and Schuster, 1980.

NEGRI, POLA. *Memoirs of a Star.* Garden City, N.Y.: Doubleday, 1970.

NICHOLSON, NIGEL. *Portrait of a Marriage: V. Sackville-West and Harold Nicolson.* New York: Atheneum, 1973.

PETERS, MARGO. *The House of Barrymore.* New York: Alfred A. Knopf, 1960.

RICHARDS, DELL. *Superstars: Twleve Lesbians Who Changed the World.* New York: Carroll & Graf, 1993.

RIVA, MARIA. *Marlene Dietrich By Her Daughter.* New York: Alfred A. Knopf, 1993.

ROBBINS, JOHN. *Front Page Marriage: Helen Hayes and Charles MacArthur.* New York: G. P. Putnam's Sons, 1982.

ROGERS, W. G. *Ladies Bountiful: A Colorful Gallery of Patrons of the Arts.* New York: Harcourt, Brace & World, 1968.

ROLLE, ANDREW F. *California: A History.* New York: Thomas Y. Crowell, 1969.

RUSSO, VITO. *The Celluloid Closet.* New York: Harper & Row, 1981.

SADOUL, GEORGES. *Histoire du Cinéma Mondial.* Paris: Flammarion, 1949.

SCHANKE, ROBERT A. *Shattered Applause: The Lives of Eva Le Gallienne.* Carbondale, Ill.: Southern Illinois University Press, 1992.

SCHWARTZ, CHARLES. *Cole Porter: A Biography.* New York: Dial Press, 1977.

SHIPMAN, DAVID. *Judy Garland.* New York: Hyperion, 1993.

SIGNORILE, MICHELANGELO. *Queer in America.* New York: Random House, 1993.

SJÖLANDER, TUNE. *Garbo.* Stockholm: Askild & Kärrekull, 1971.

SPOTO, DONALD. *Blue Angel: The Life of Marlene Dietrich.* New York: Doubleday, 1992.

———. *The Dark Side of Genius; The Life of Alfred Hitchcock.* Boston: Little, Brown, 1983.

———. *Lenya, A Life.* Boston: Little, Brown, 1989.

STEARN, JESS. *The Grapevine.* New York: Doubleday, 1964.

TAYLOR, JOHN RUSSELL. *Strangers in Paradise: The Hollywood Emigrés, 1933-1950.* New York: Rinehart & Winston, 1983.

THOMAS, BOB. *Thalberg: Life and Legend.* Garden City, N.Y.: Doubleday, 1969.

———. *Joan Crawford: A Biography.* New York: Simon and Schuster, 1978.

TIMMONS, STUART. *The Trouble With Harry Hay: Founder of the Modern Gay Movement.* Boston: Alyson Publications, 1990.

TUELARD, JEAN, ED. *Dictionnaire de Cinéma.* Paris: Robert Laffout, 1985.

TUNNEY, KIERAN. *Tallulah, Darling of the Gods.* New York: E. P. Dutton, 1973.

VICKERS, HUGO. *Cecil Beaton.* Boston: Little, Brown, 1985.

———. *Loving Garbo.* New York: Random House, 1994.

VIDAL, GORE. *United States: Essays 1952-1992.* New York: Random House, 1993.

VREELAND, DIANE. *D.V.* New York: Alfred A. Knopf, 1984.

WAYNE, JANE ELLEN. *Crawford's Men.* New York: Prentice-Hall, 1988.

WEINBERG, HERMAN G. *The Lubitsch Touch: A Critical Study.* New York: E. P. Dutton, 1968.

WILLIAMS, TENNESSEE. *Memoirs.* Garden City, N.Y.: Doubleday, 1975.

ZIEROLD, NORMAN. *Garbo.* New York: Stein & Day, 1969.

Index

Index